CARVING CLOWNS

WITH TOM WOLFE

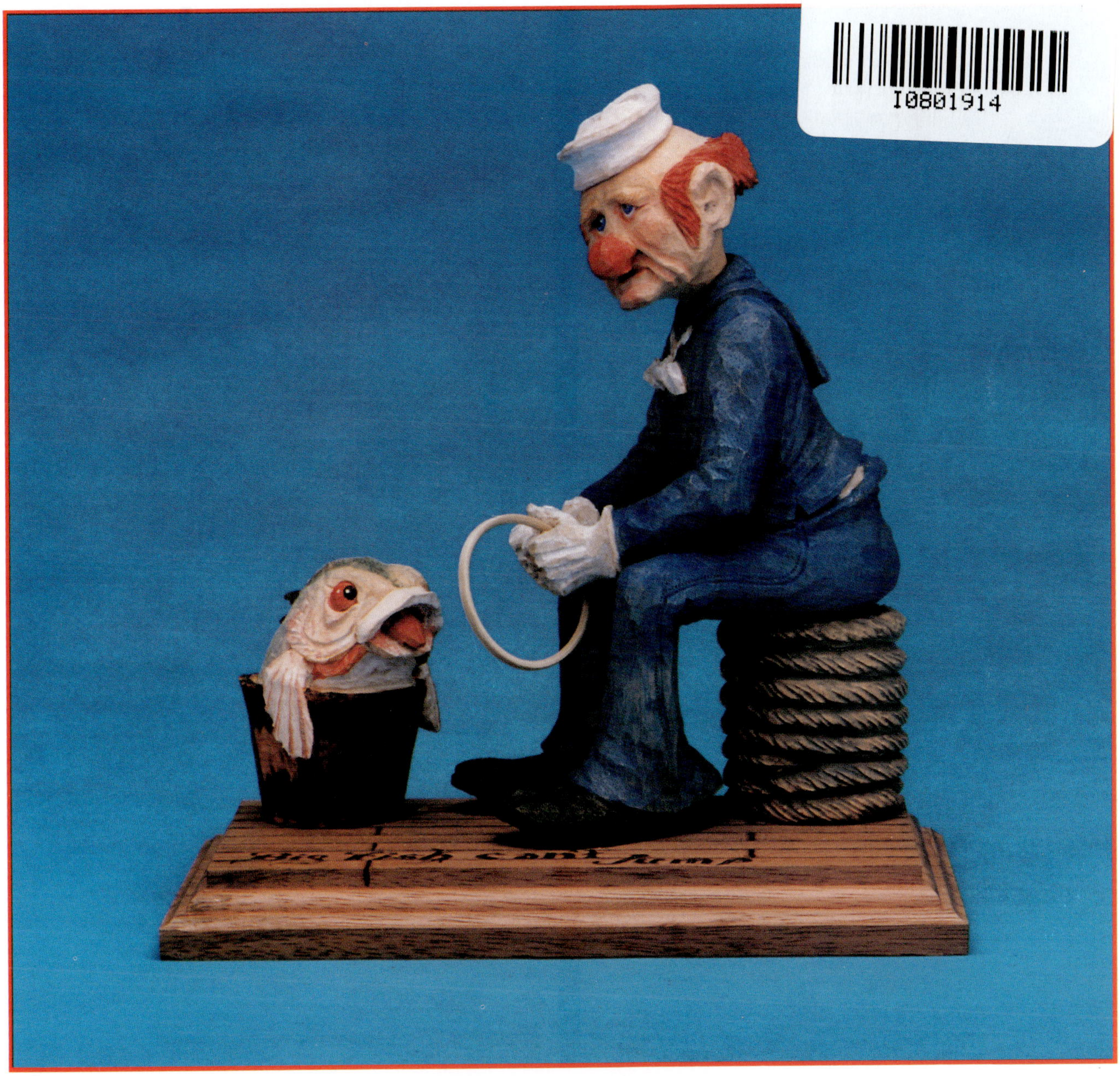

Schiffer Publishing Ltd

77 Lower Valley Road, Atglen, PA 19310

CONTENTS

INTRODUCTION 3
THE PROJECT PATTERN 4
CARVING THE CLOWN 6
PAINTING THE CLOWN 41
A QUICK LESSON IN LETTERING 46
THE GALLERY AND PATTERNS 49

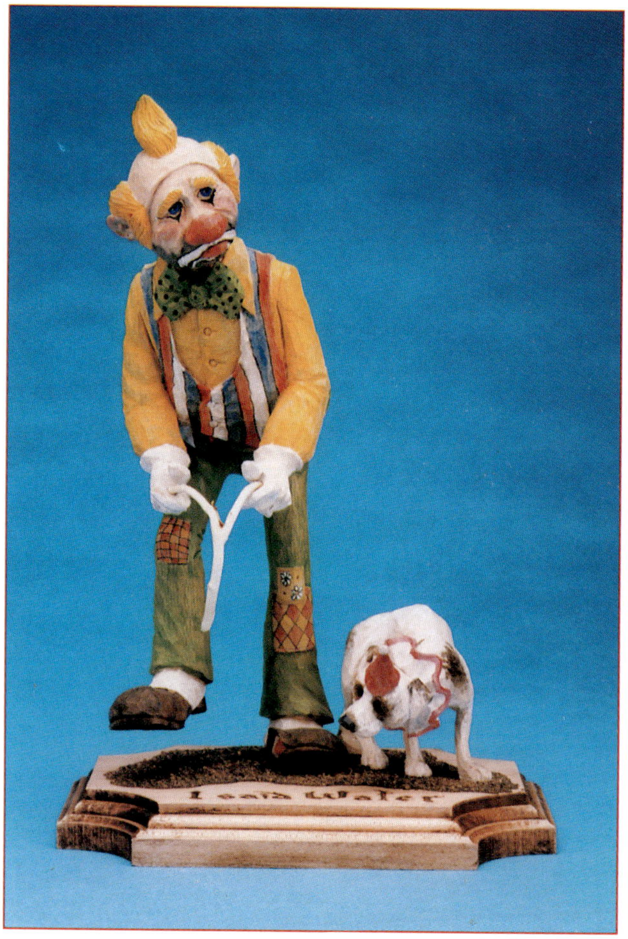

This book is meant only for personal home use and recreation. It is not intended for commercial applications or manufacturing purposes.

Printed in China

ISBN: 0-88740-897-4

Library of Congress Cataloging-in-Publication Data

Wolfe, Tom (Tom James)
Carving clowns with Tom Wolfe/Tom Wolfe.
p. cm.
ISBN 0-88740-897-4 (pbk.)
1. Wood-carving. 2. Wood-carved figurines.
3 Clowns in art. I. Title.
TT199.7.W6383 1996
731.4'62--dc20 95-33682
CIP

Published by Schiffer Publishing, Ltd.
77 Lower Valley Road
Atglen, PA 19310
Please write for a free catalog.
This book may be purchased from the publisher.
Please include $2.95 postage.
Try your bookstore first.

We are interested in hearing from authors with book ideas on related subjects.

INTRODUCTION

This is a book that I have wanted to do for a number of years. I love clowns! They make me laugh, which is pretty important. But, more than that, they can poke fun at the human condition and the things we think are so critical, helping us see them in a new and better way.

For caricature carvers they are the ideal subject. Clowns give the carver a limitless variety of faces and situations to create. The only boundaries are the carver's ability and imagination, and the realities of the human form. While the clown may exaggerate the face, feet, and hands, they still have the basic shape and mechanics of the human body. The carver must remember this, or the figure becomes a cartoon rather than a caricature.

The other thing the carver must be aware of is the paradox of clowns. Beneath their painted grins and bright costumes, you very often can see a solemn, almost sad look. Like all of us, they are complex figures, happy and sad, comic and tragic, all at the same time. Because they capture both sides of us, the clown has been a powerful figure through many years of human history.

I have carved one figure from beginning to end, with each step illustrated to help the carver. Most of the figures are in various comic settings and the gallery has several different clowns in various situations. I have also included a brief section on carving the letters I used to label the pieces.

I hope you enjoy the book and discover in your carving the power of clowns.

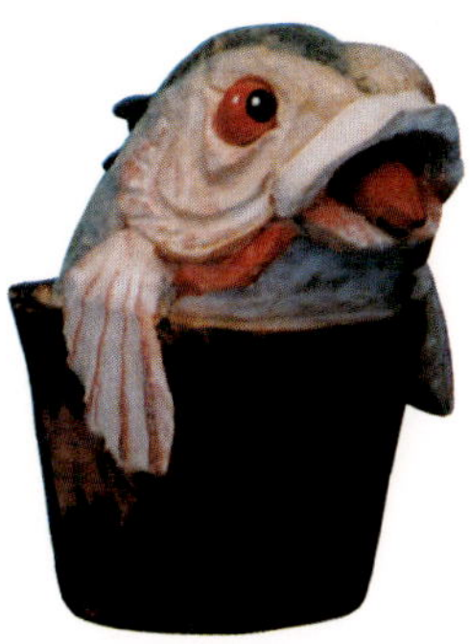

THE PROJECT PATTERN

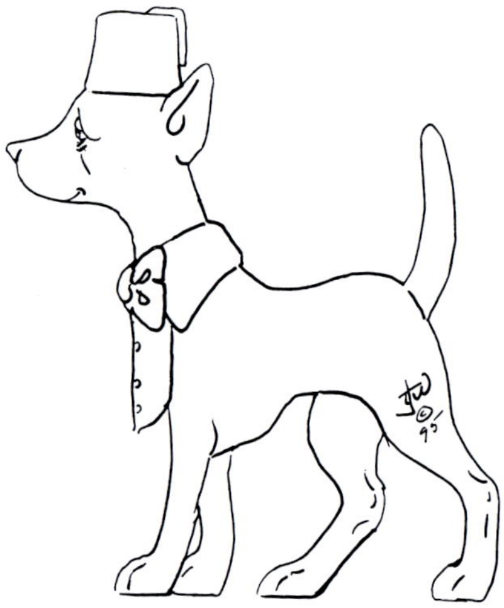

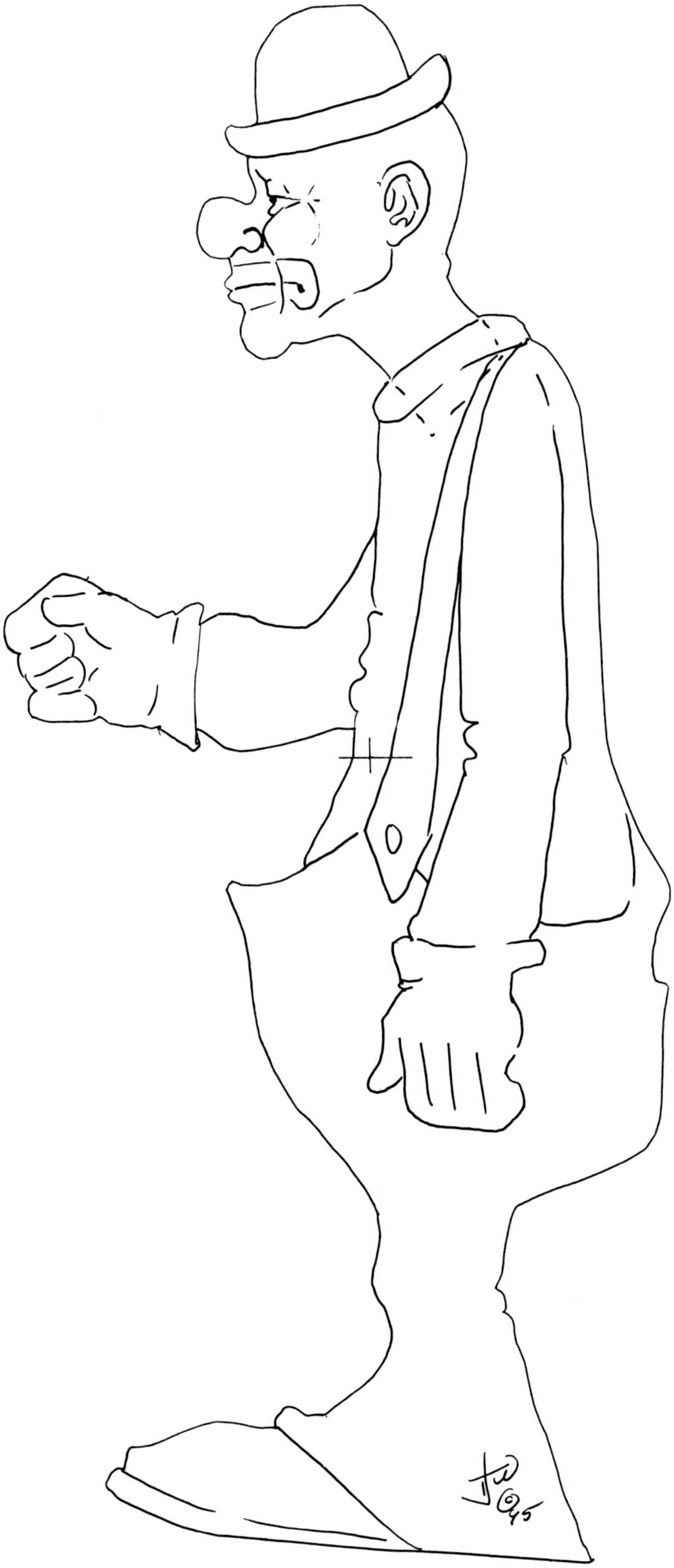

THESE PATTERNS ARE 70% OF ORIGINAL SIZE.

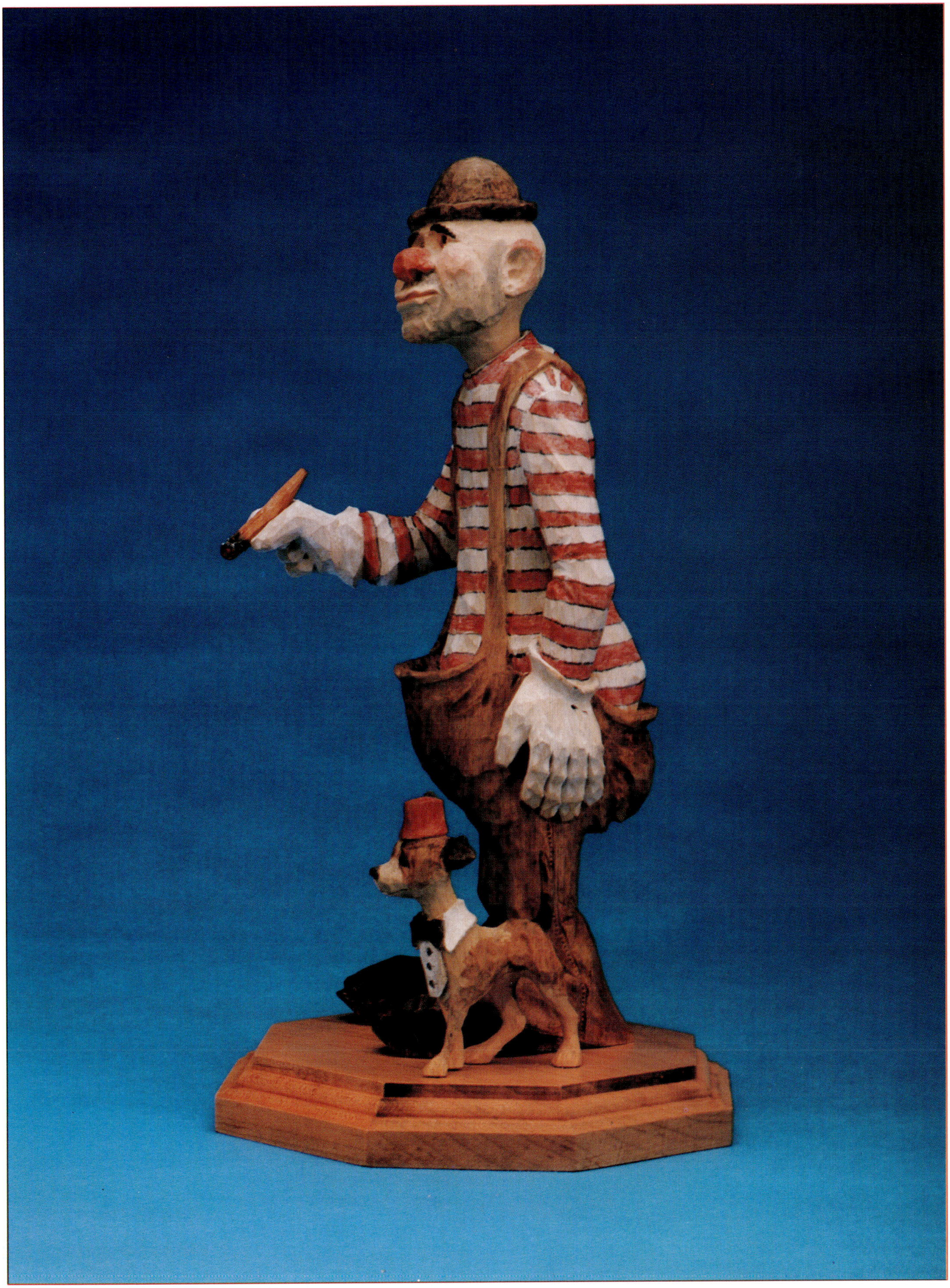

CARVING THE CLOWN

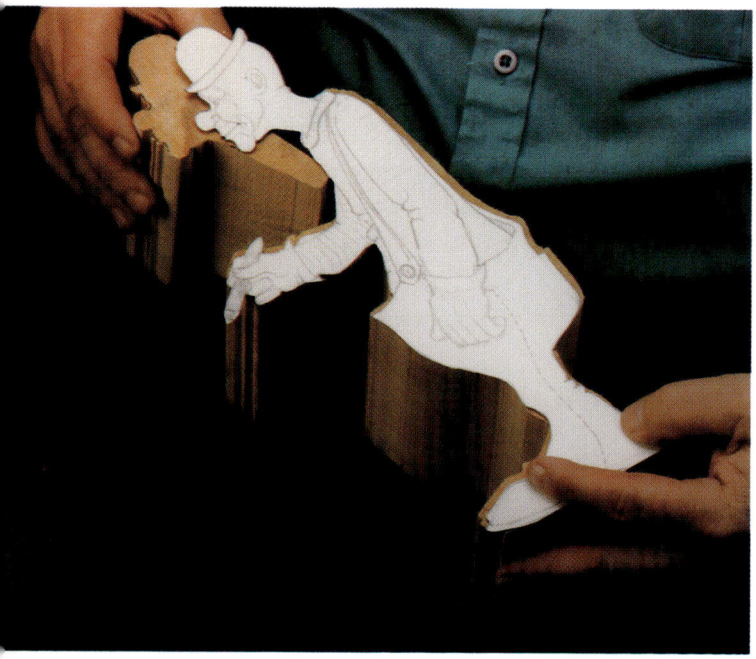

Cut the profile patterns from a wood 4" thick. This wood is jelutong, which I am using because it carves well. It has a nice texture and carves easier than basswood. It is somewhat more splintery, but carves smoother, maybe because of the latex in it. It is grown in Indonesia and is hard to find in thick pieces. If you can't find it you cane use basswood.

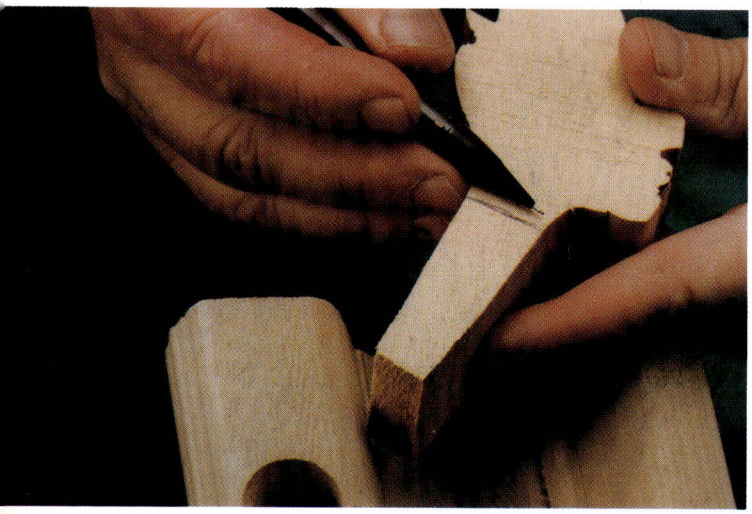

A hole needs to be drilled in center of the shoulder for the neck. Its width is determined by the thickness of the neck at the collar. Cut the head blank first, then pick a drill bit that fits.

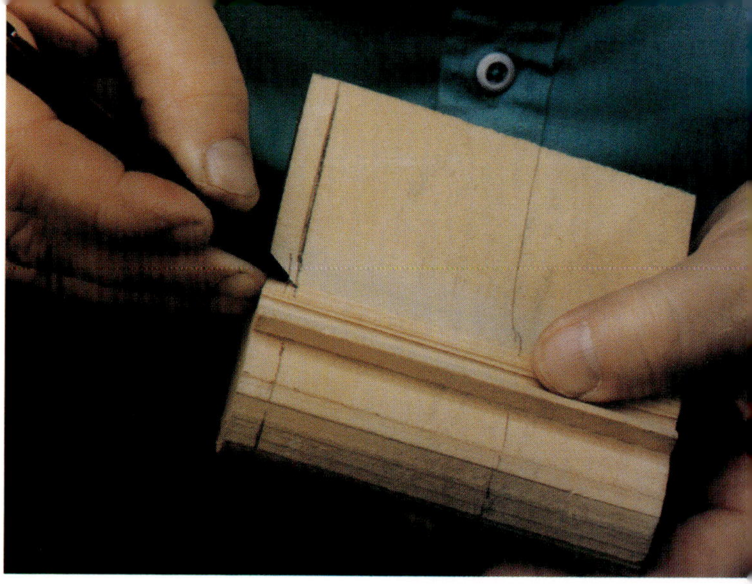

I want to cut off the outside wood on one side...

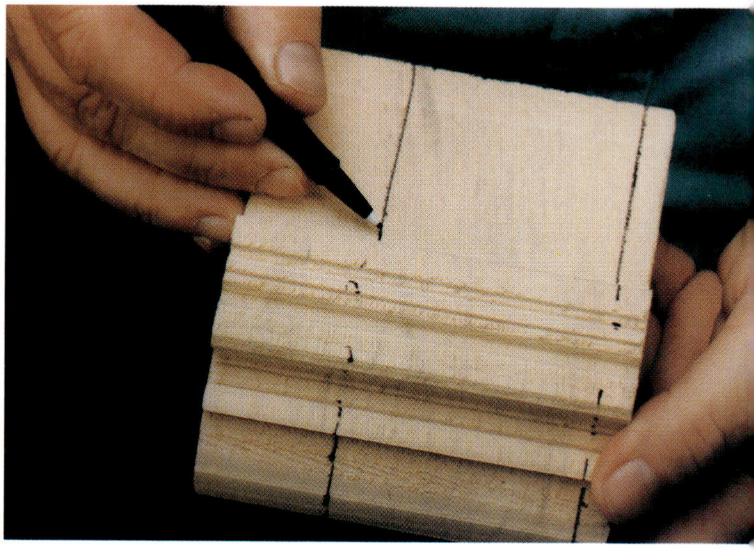

and measure over about 2-3/8" from that line and draw the other line of the head. This gives me a figure that is good and wide. Trim the blank to the lines. I keep the bandsaw near where I carve so I can whack off a quarter inch when necessary. This saves a lot of knife work.

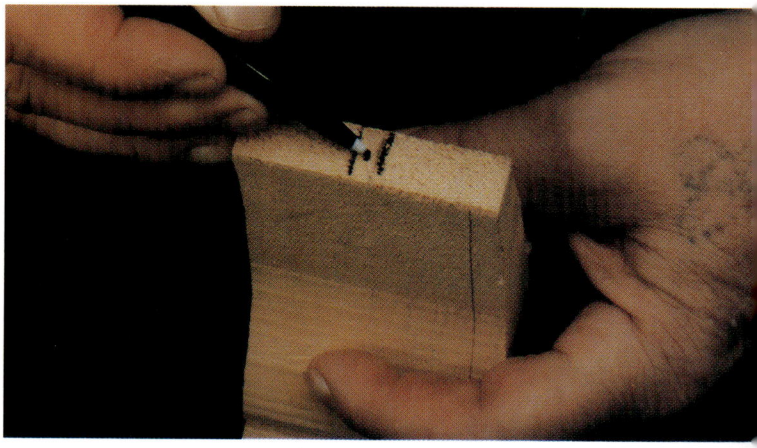

To find the center of the neck I come in the same distance from both sides and make marks. Then I can eyeball the center halfway between these two marks.

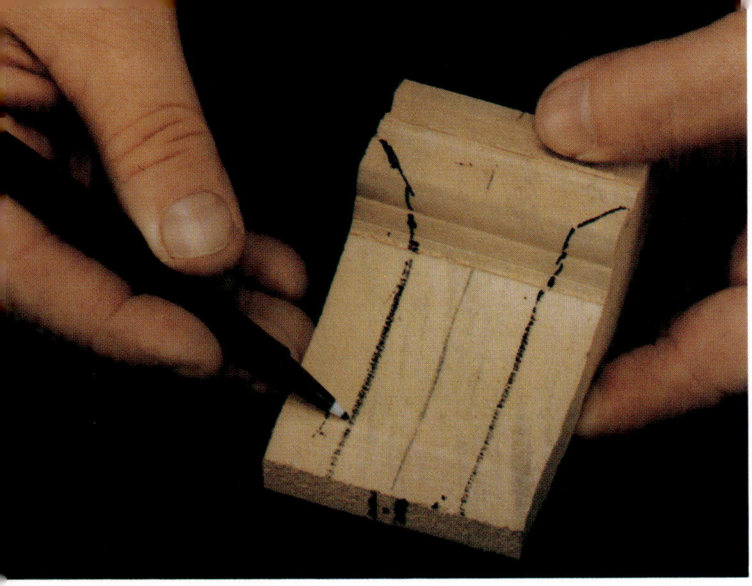

With the center determined, I can draw the line of the neck starting at the chin where it comes in and going down the neck.

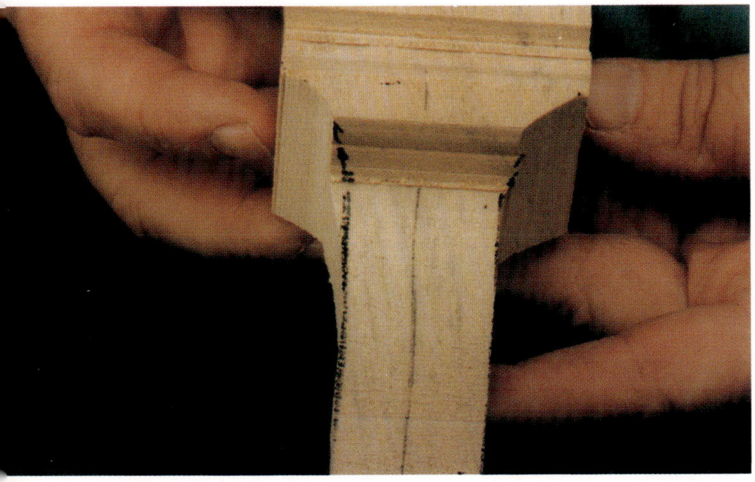

Cut on the lines for this result.

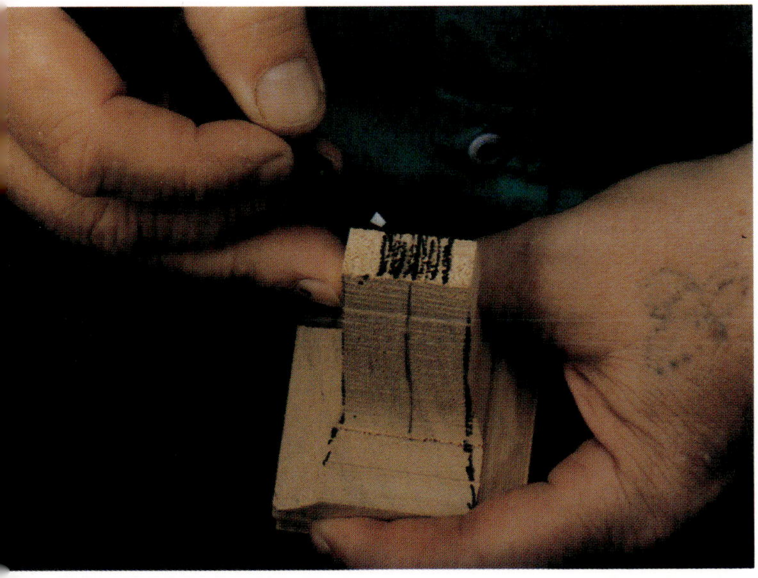

Next we round the neck. First I want to take the neck to square, so I mark it on the base.

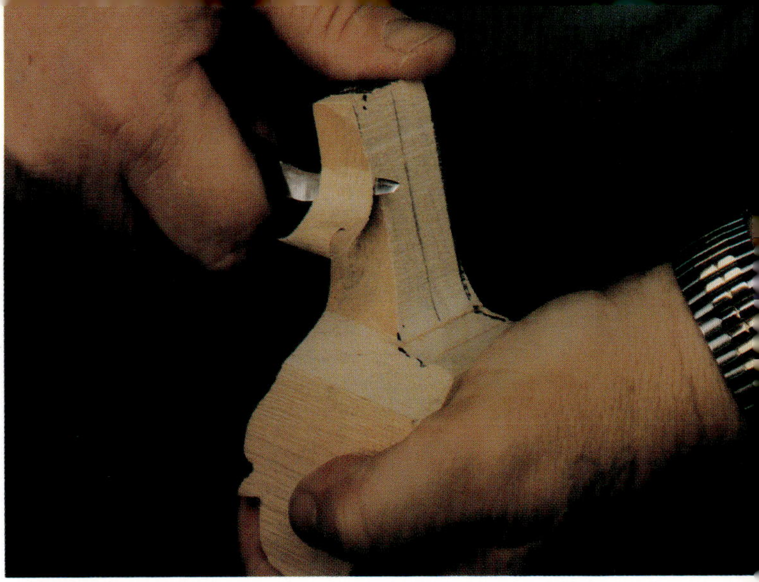

Taper the sides down to the square. I always go to square before going round. If you skip this step, you are likely to get a flattish look.

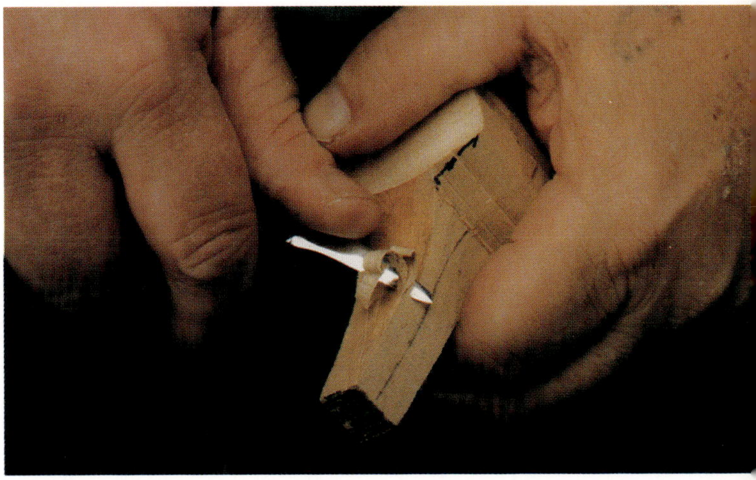

When the square is set, knock off the corners to take the neck to octagonal.

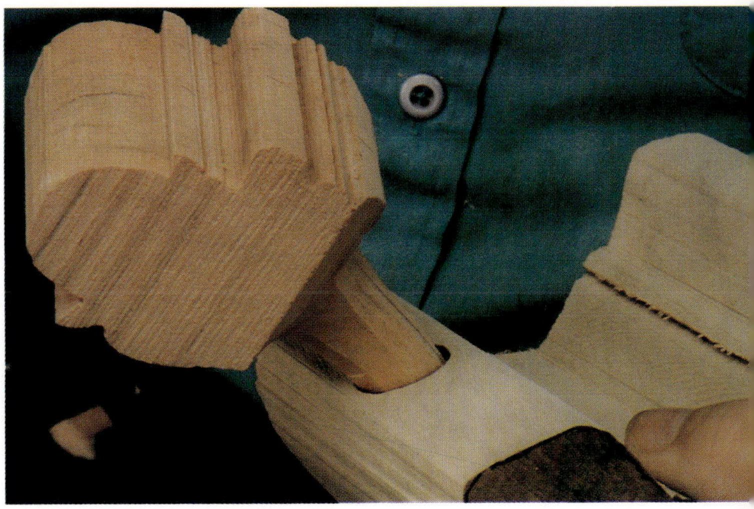

When the neck is shortened later it should fit nicely in the hole in the body. For now I will leave it long so I can use it as a handle.

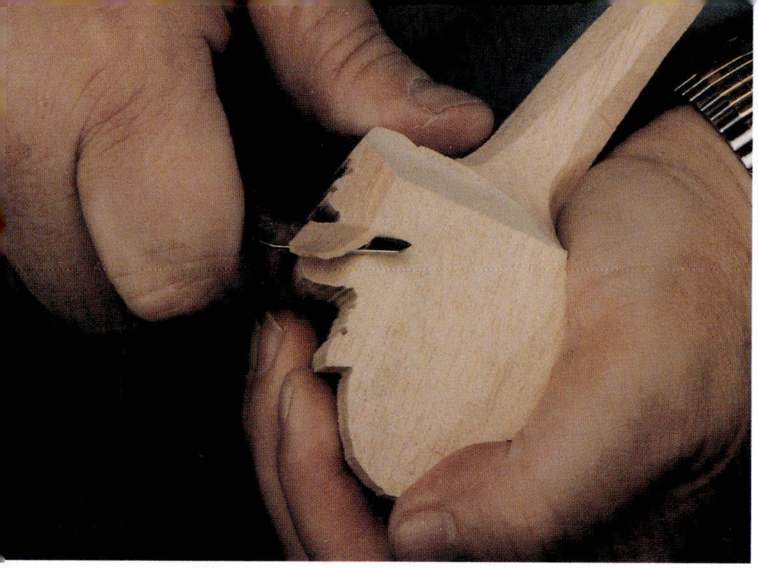

Knock the corners off the head.

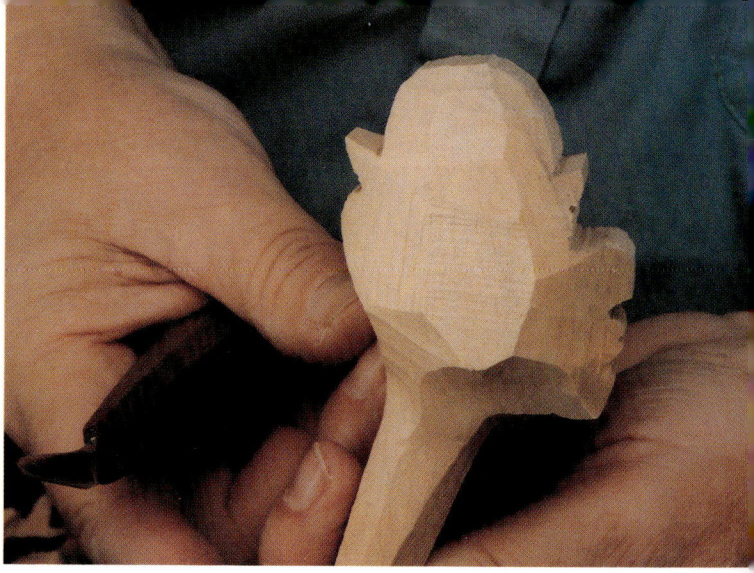

The side view.

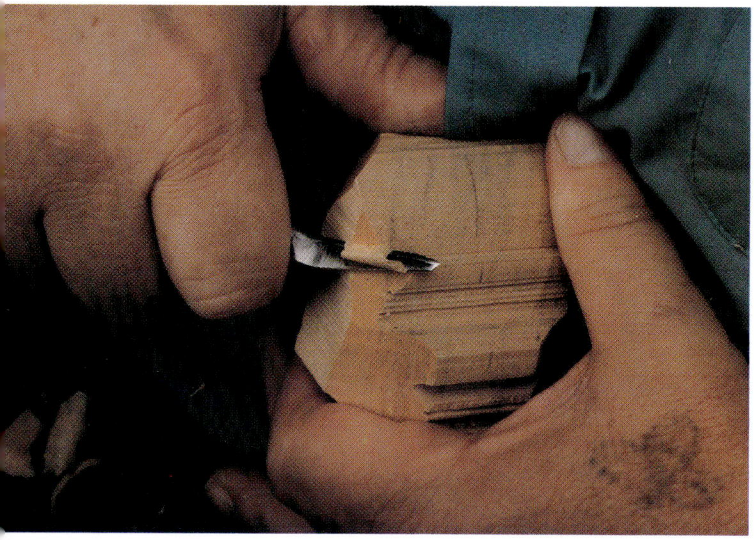

Do all four corners, coming up and over the hat.

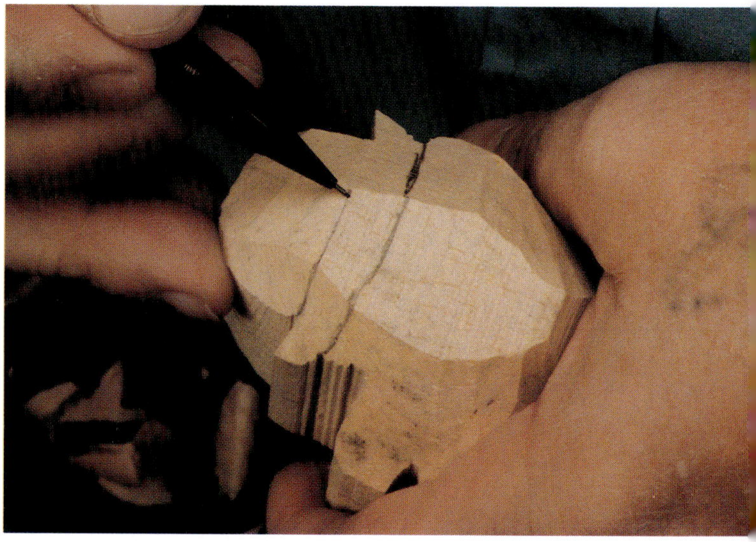

Mark the brim of the hat. This is a clown so the hat doesn't need to fit. It just sort of sits on top of the head.

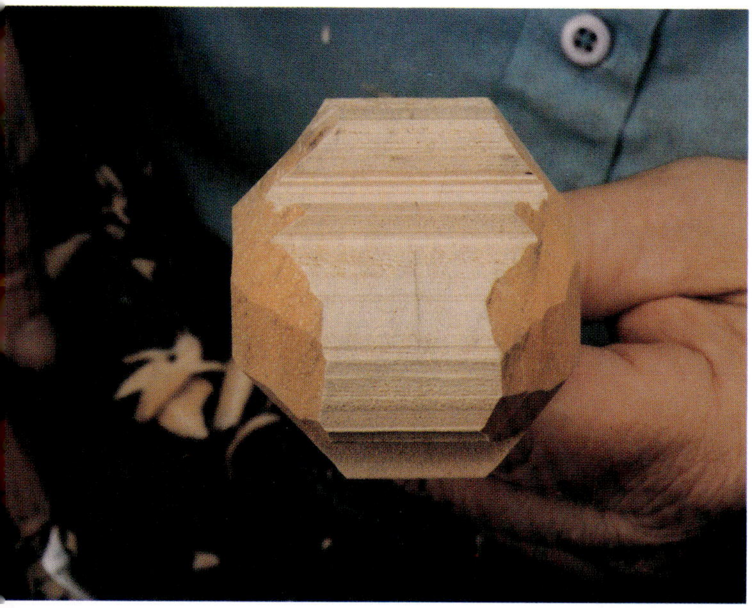

When viewed from the top the head should be octagonal.

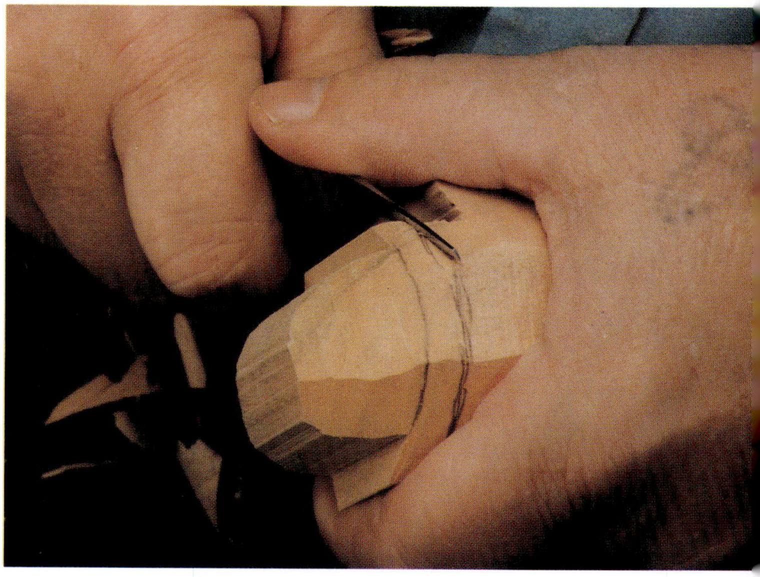

Cut a stop in the lower line of the brim.

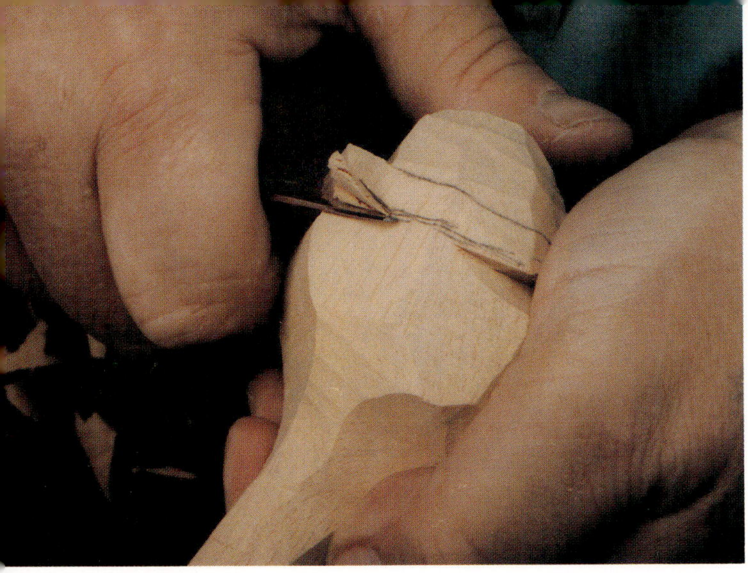

Cut back to the stop from the head. On the side of the head you need to be careful not to crowd the ears.

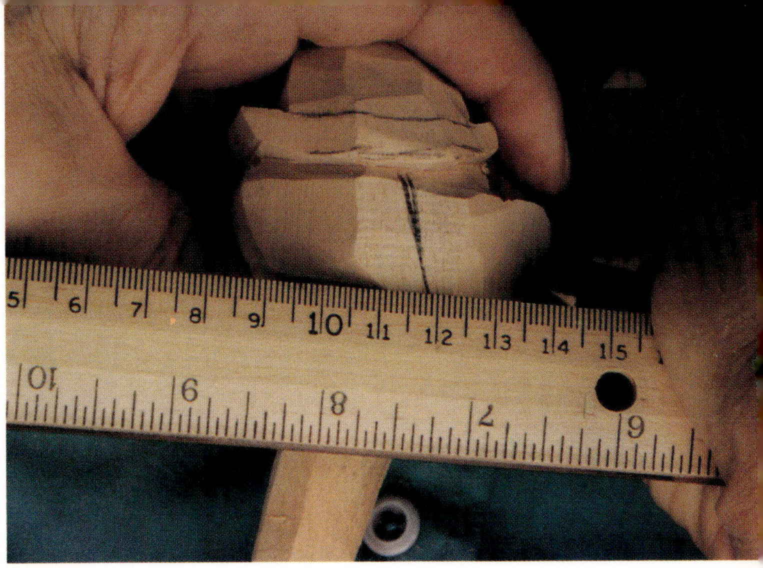

To determine the bottom of the ear, imagine a line from the bottom of the nose to where the skull meets the neck in the back of the head.

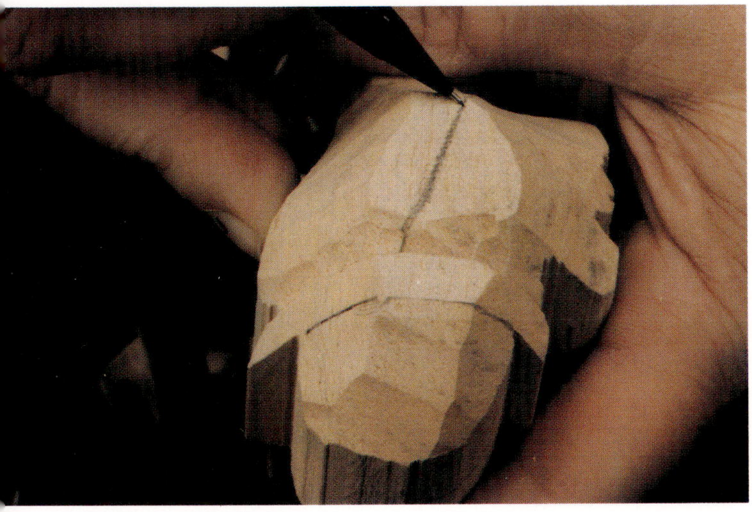

Draw the center line of the side of the head. When you do this ignore the neck; it will just throw you off.

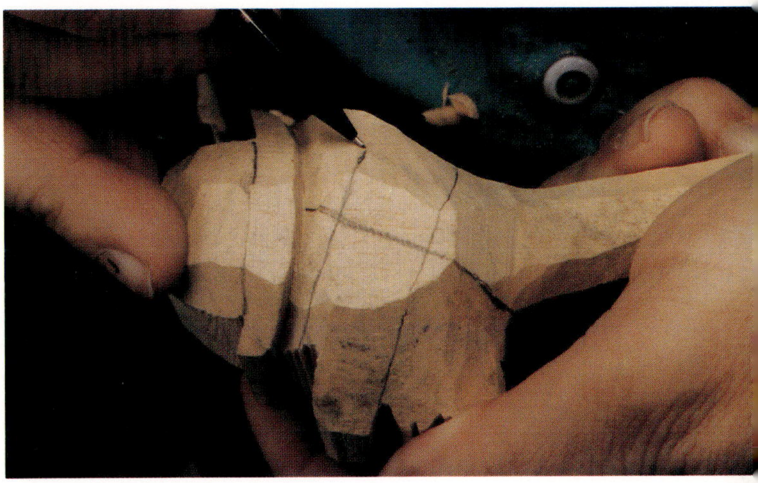

A line back from the center of the eyeball, and parallel to the first, defines the top of the ear.

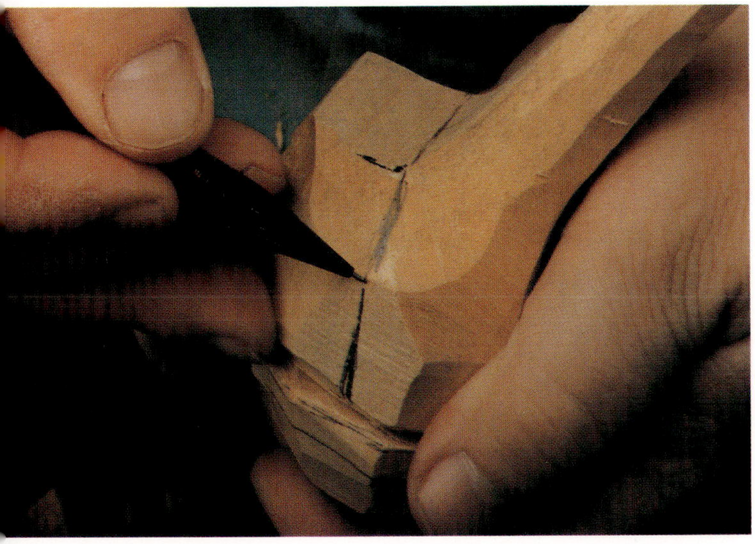

I carry this line all the way under the chin and back up the other side.

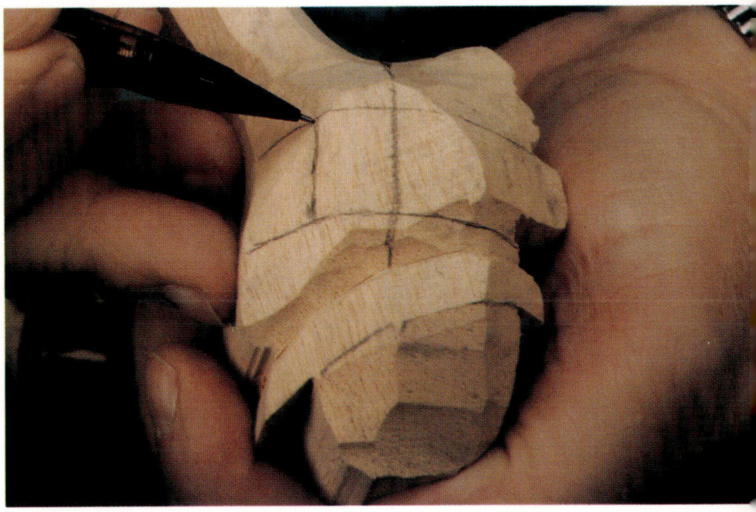

A line drawn halfway back from the center line defines the back of the ear. The ear hole goes in where the jaw bone meets the head.

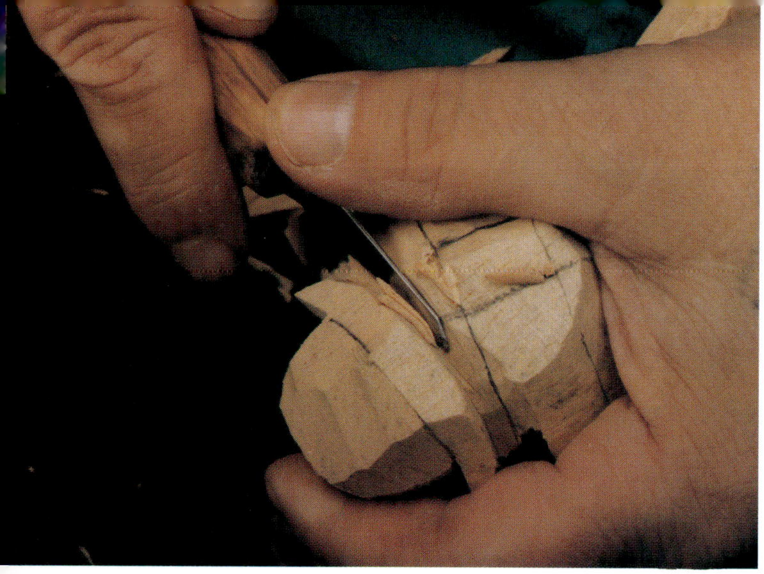

With the area of the ear defined I can go deeper above it.

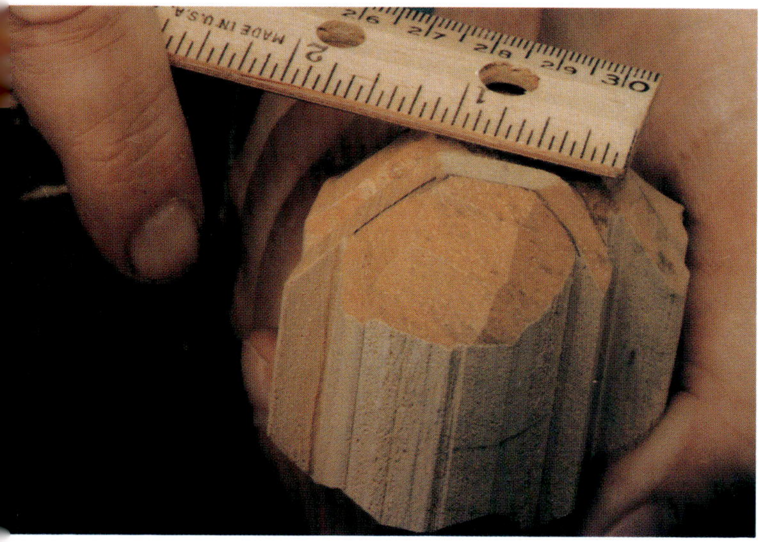

You want to make sure you don't carve too deep. Measure the depth of the head (not including the nose). Here it is 1-3/4".

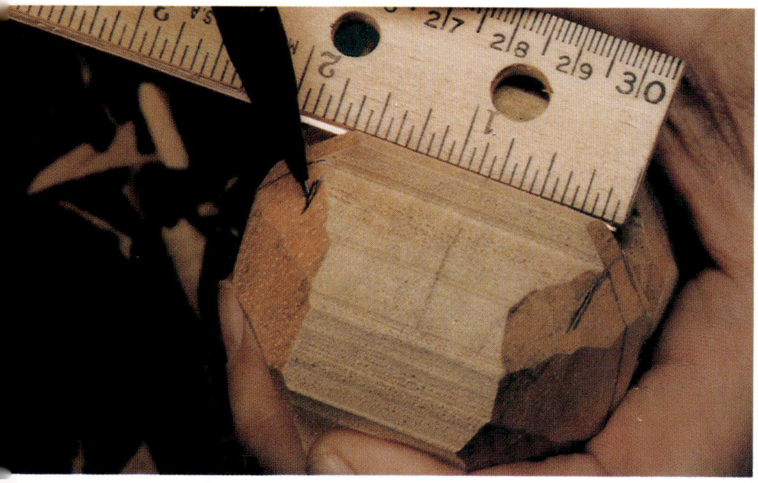

Center the ruler in the front of the head and mark the width to match the depth, 7/8" to either side of center. This is a good estimate that will keep you from disaster.

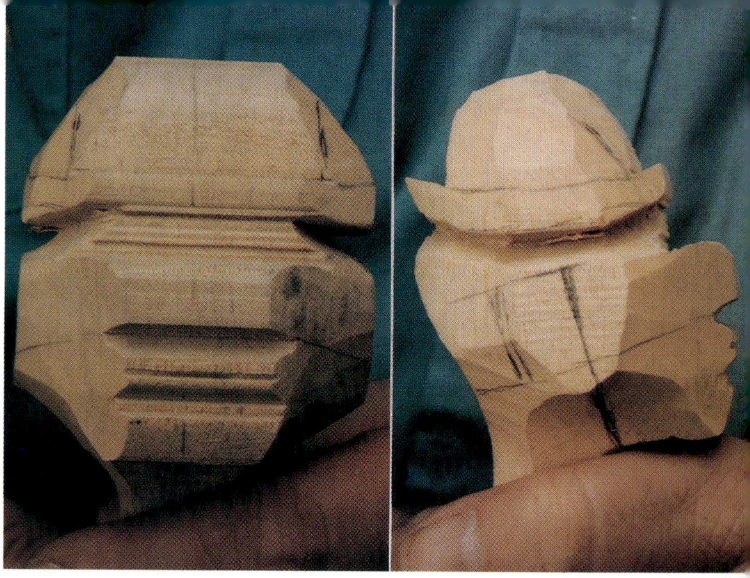

Continue to reduce under the hat brim until you get to this point.

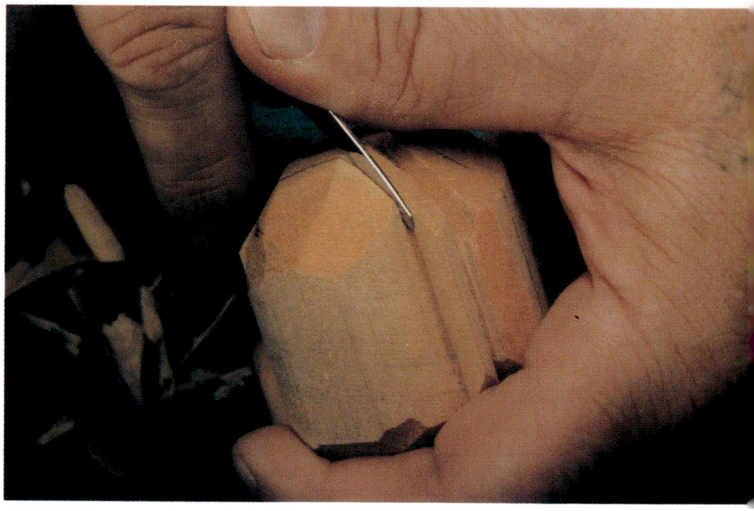

Make a stop in the line of the top of the brim.

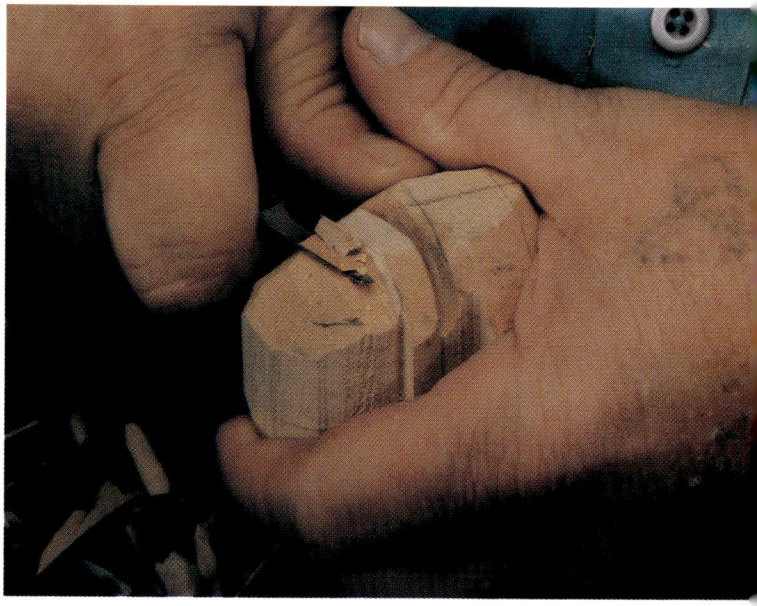

Cut back to the stop to shape the top of the hat.

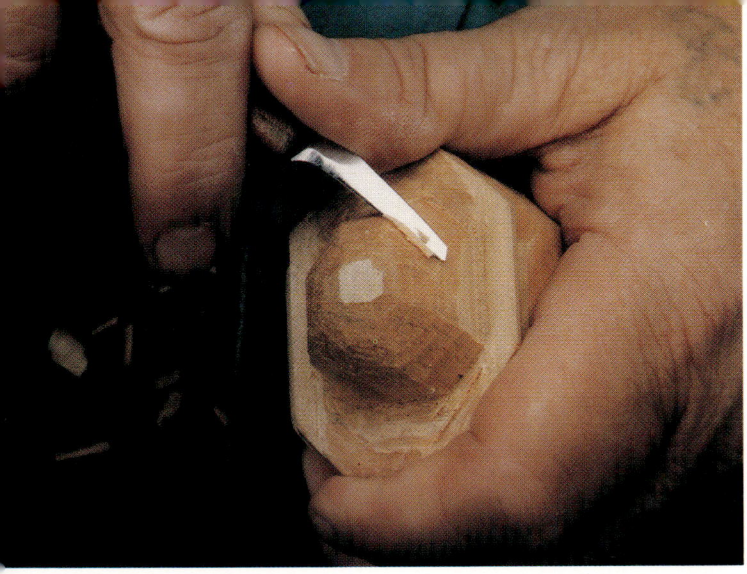

Round the hat up to the top.

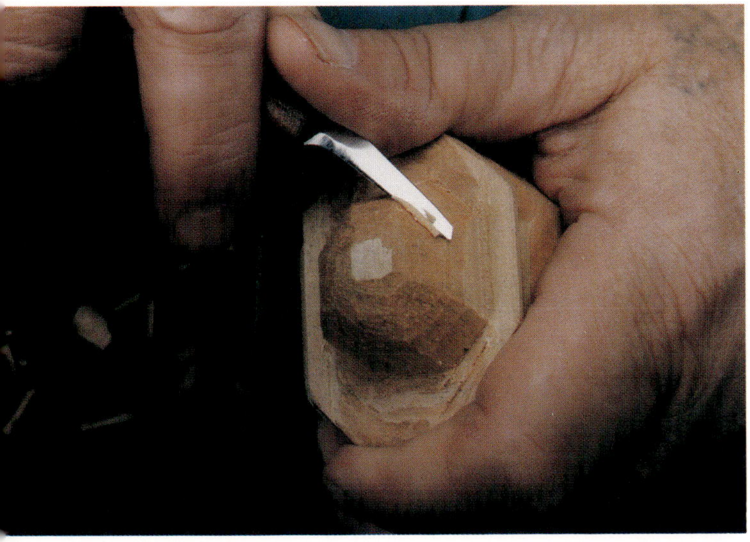

With the crown shaped, I find narrowest thickness of the brim and carry it all around.

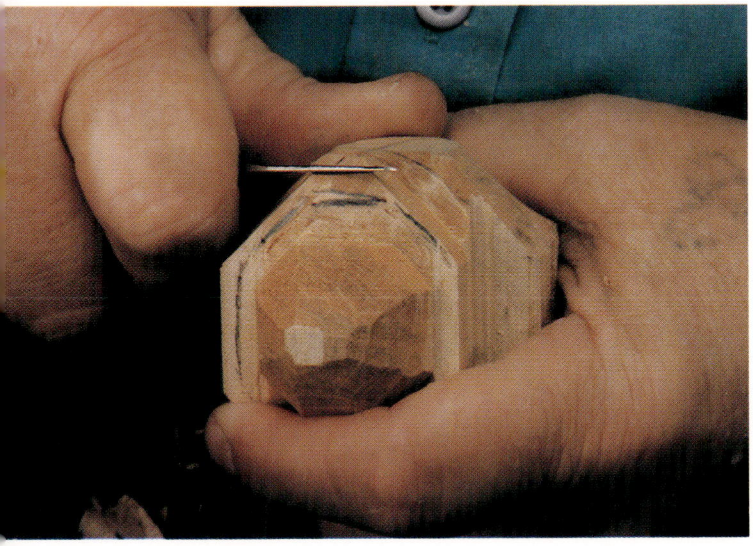

Reduce the brim all around. In places you may need to reestablish the head beneath it.

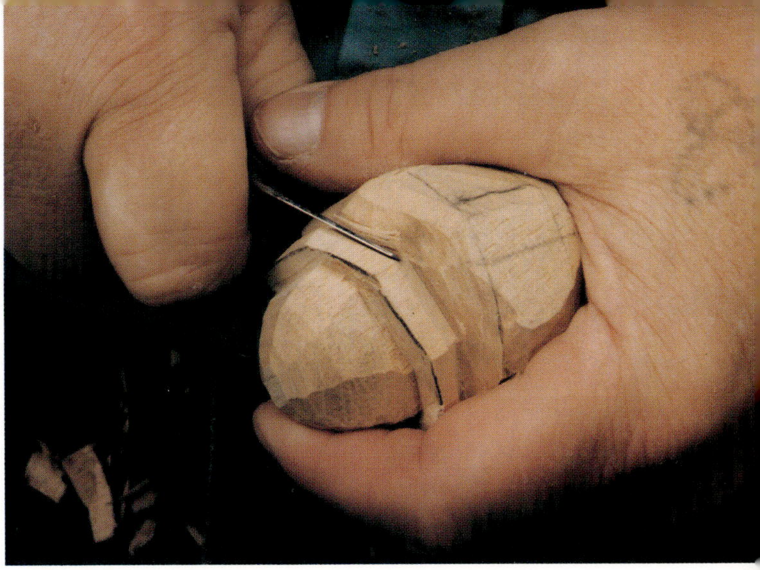

With the brim sized, go back and redo the undercut.

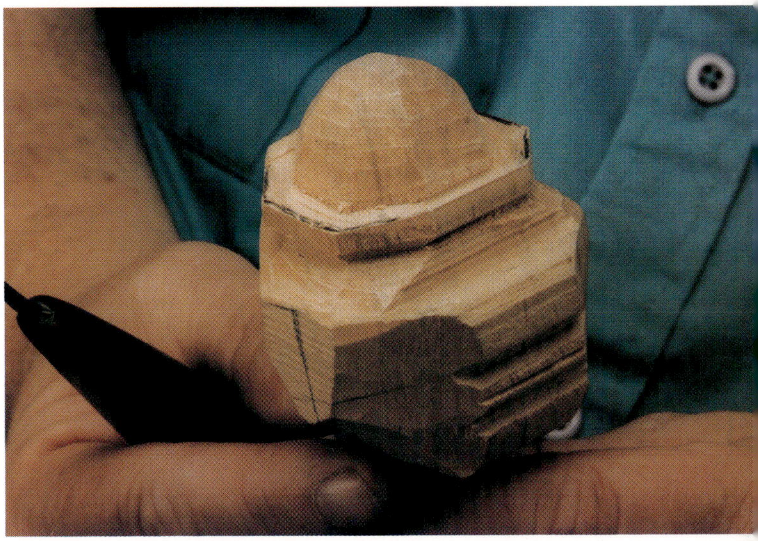

The hat is now sitting on top of the head the way I want it.

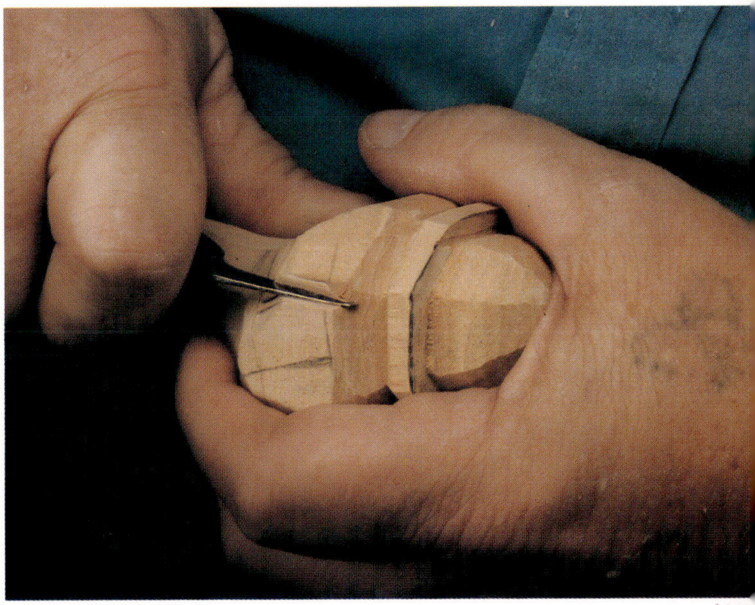

Cut around the ear to let it stand out.

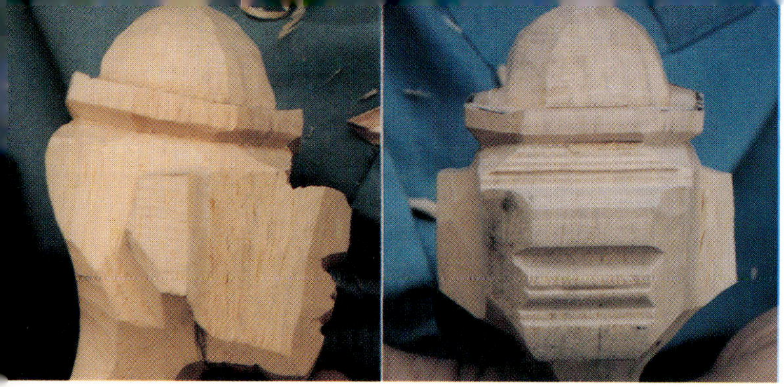

The ears roughed out.

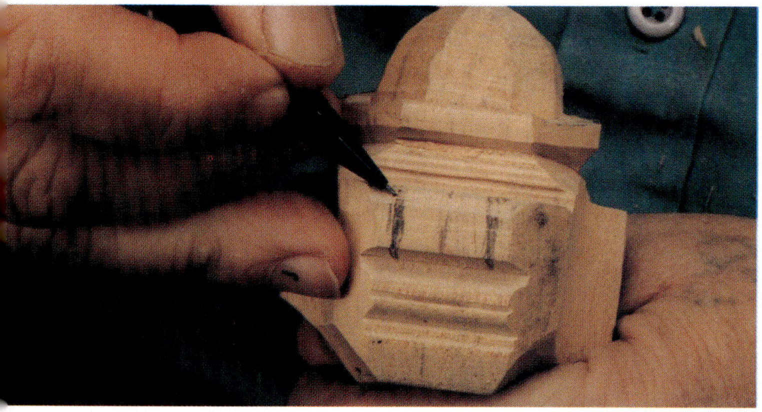

Mark the width of the nose. I want this to be a big artificial nose, so I mark it wide.

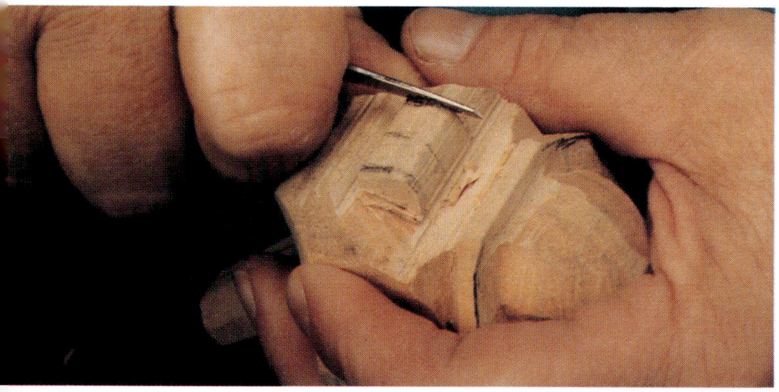

Remove the excess wood by cutting a stop in the line of the nose...

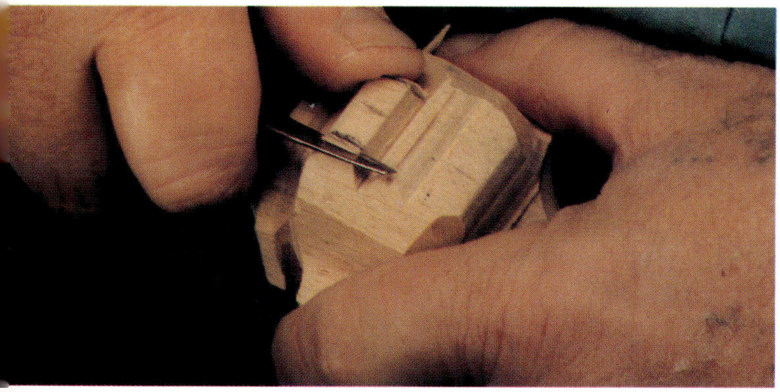

and cutting back to it from the cheek. Continue the process to deepen the cut.

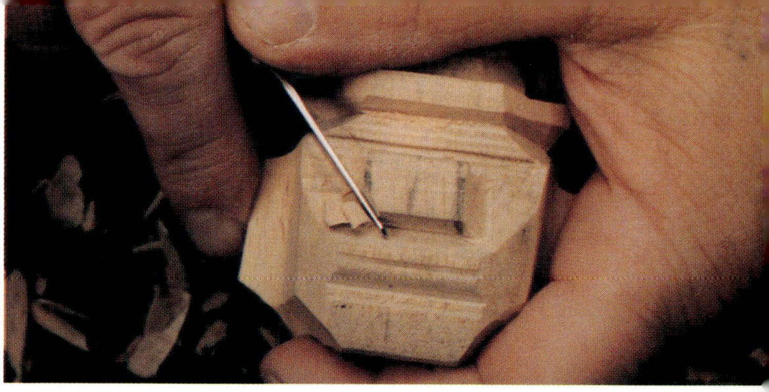

Knock off the four corners of the nose block to take it to octagonal.

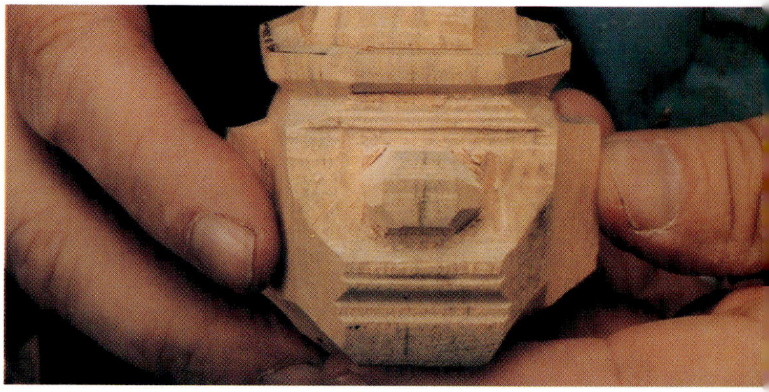

From here it is easy to get to round.

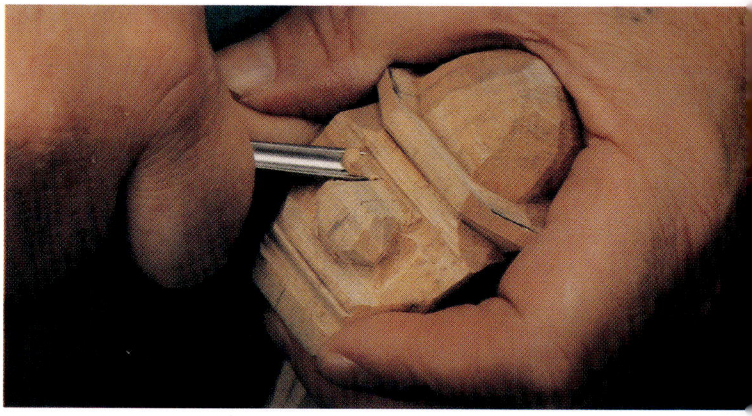

With the gouge, come up beside the nose to create an eyesocket. What we're really doing is bring the nose out more, but we need to bear in mind where the eyes are going.

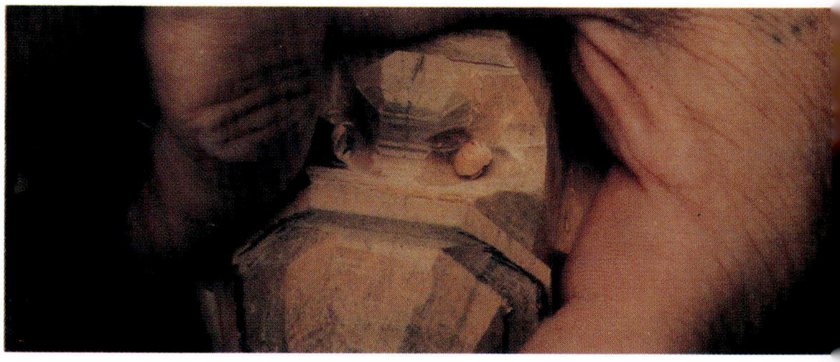

After coming up the side of the nose, come in from the side. With a crumbly wood like this you need to keep the corners of the gouge out of the wood.

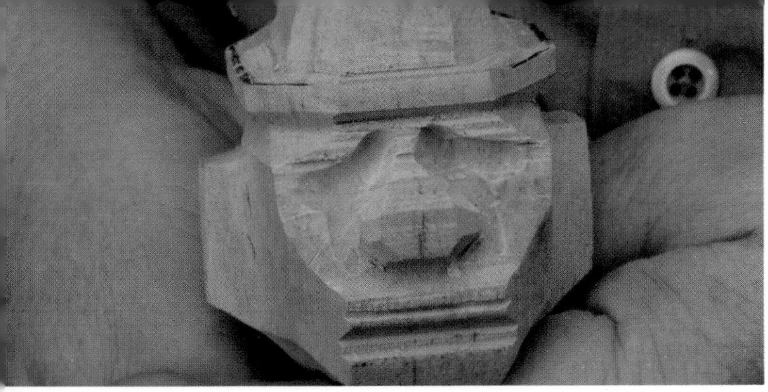

The result.

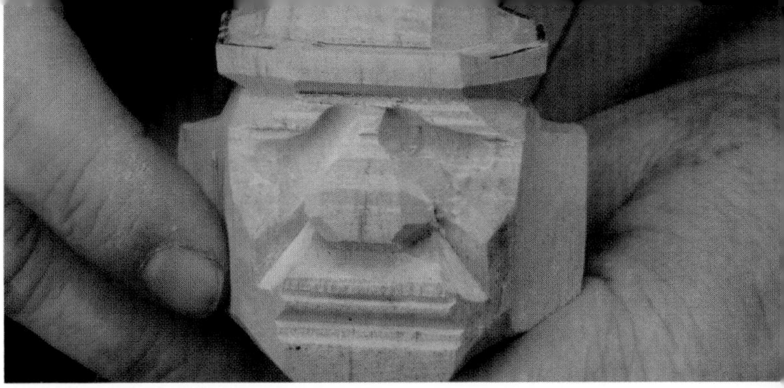

Do the same on the other side for this result.

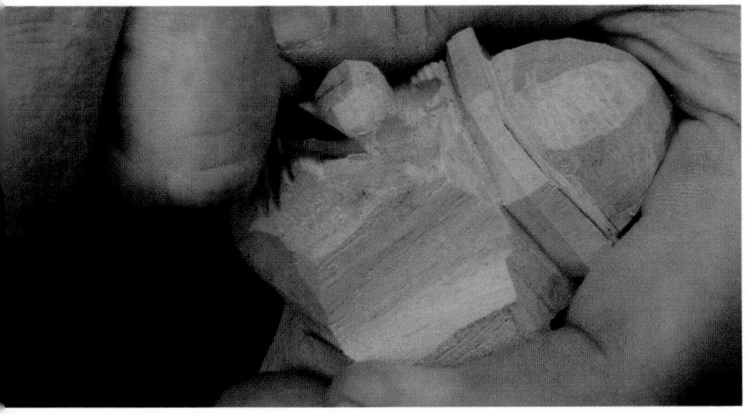

To create the smile line, cut a stop beside the nose.

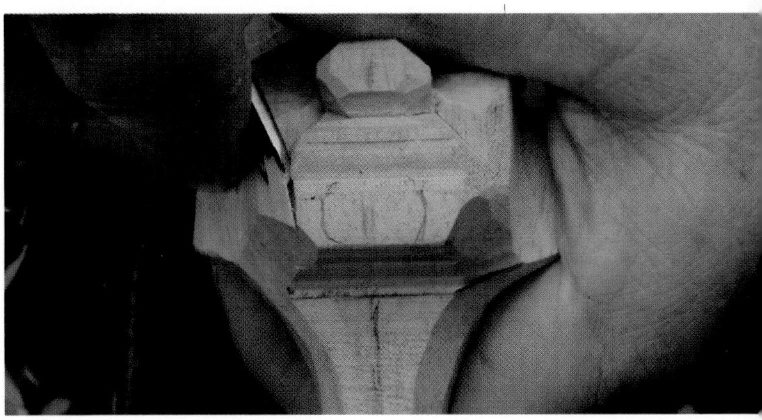

Mark the width of the chin, then carry the smile line down beside the chin with a gouge.

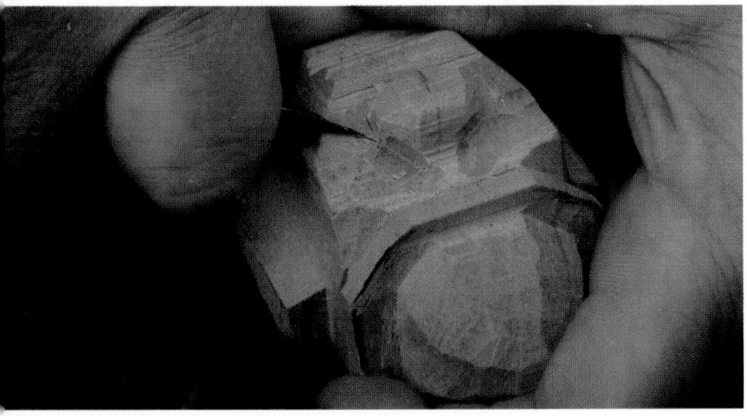

Then cut down on the line of the cheek...

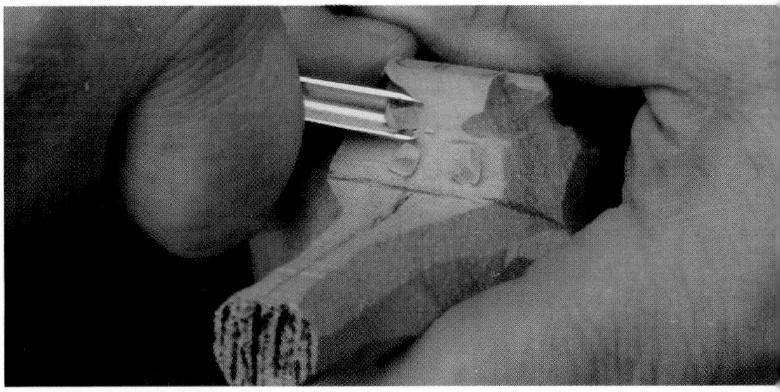

Continue the line underneath the chin.

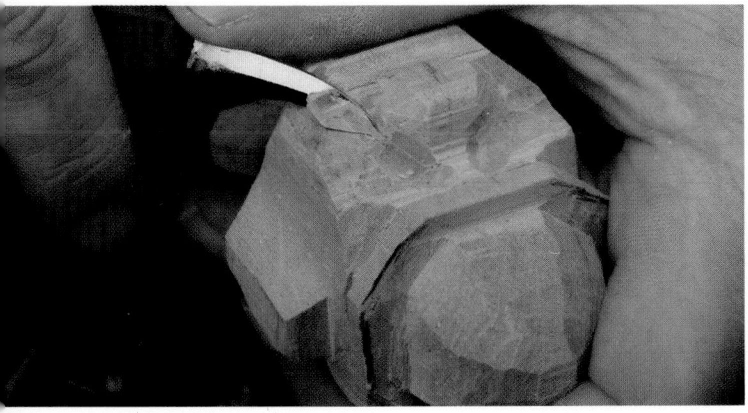

and back into the corner from the lip with the knife following the lip surface.

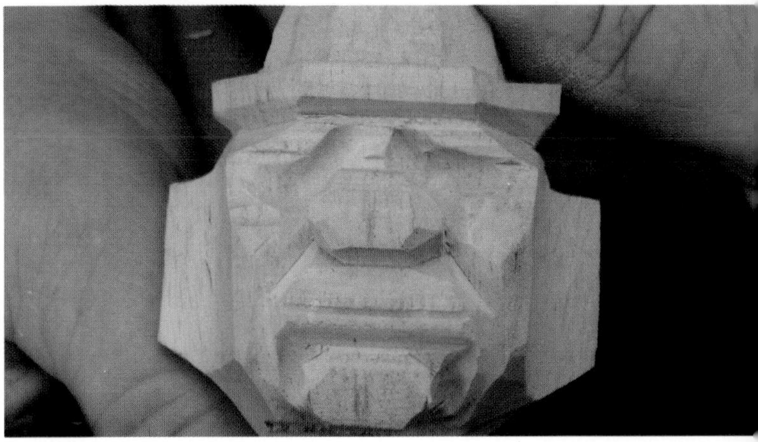

Progress.

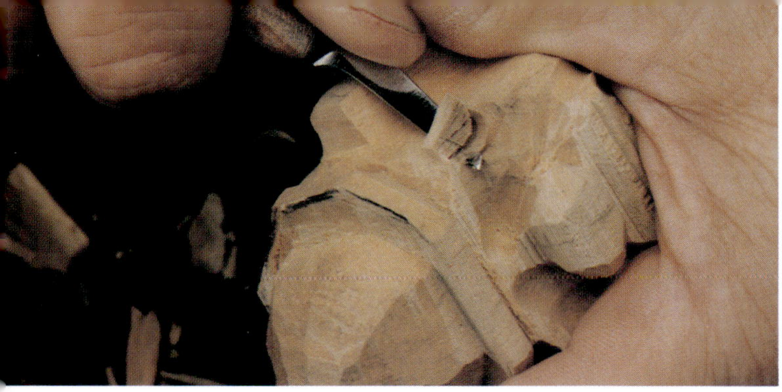

Create the plane of the temples.

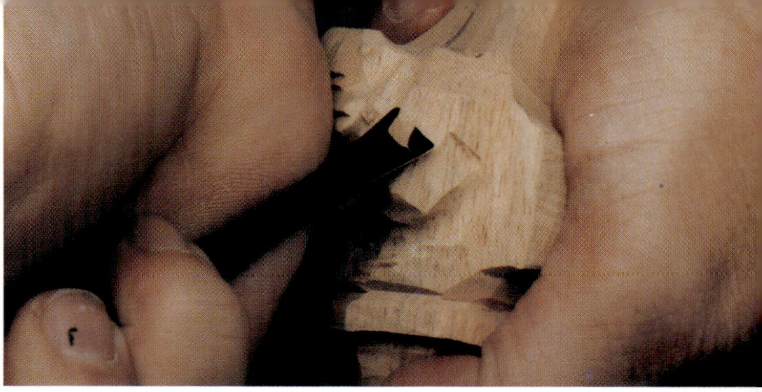

With a flatter gouge I create the sunken contour of the cheeks.

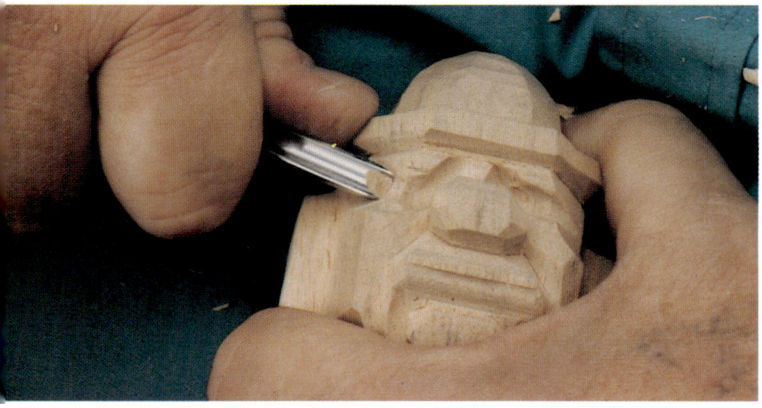

Carry the eyesocket into the temples with a gouge.

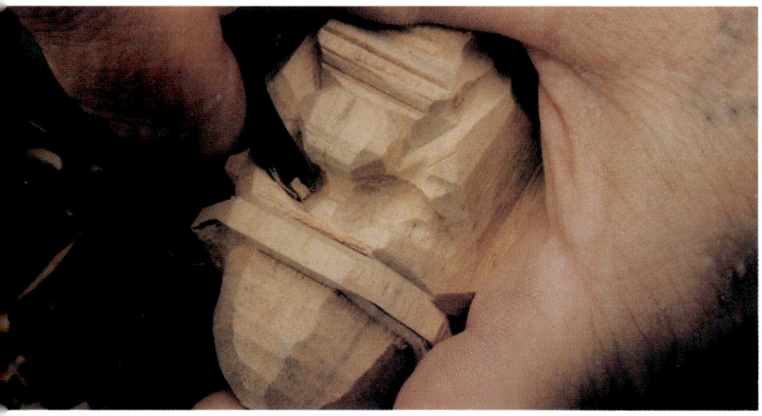

I use a thin half-round gouge to undercut the eyebrows a little bit.

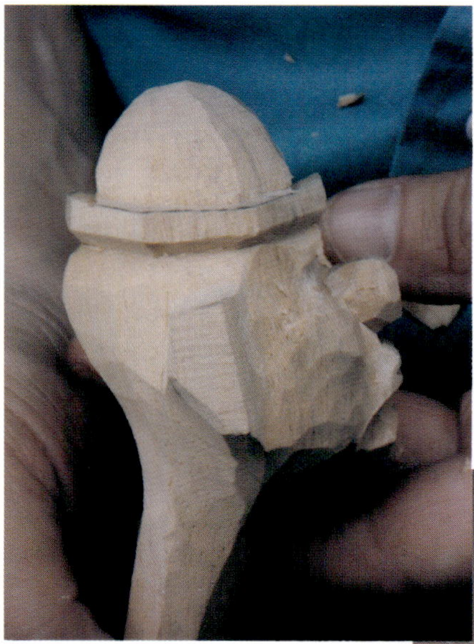

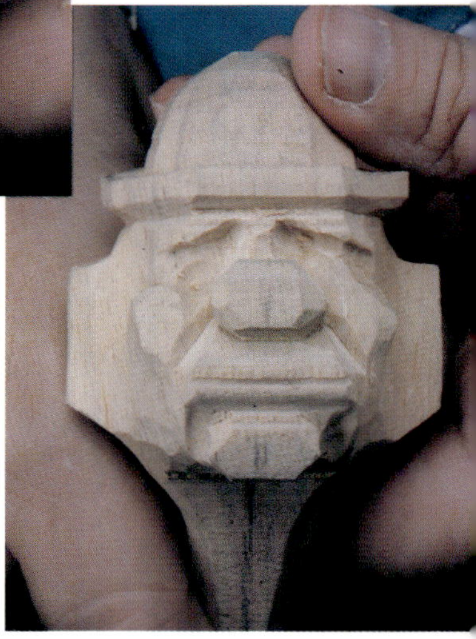

Progress

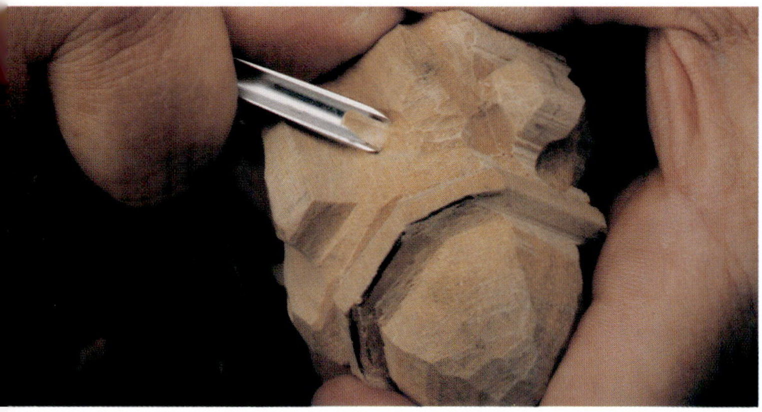

A gouge cut around the back of the cheek brings it out more.

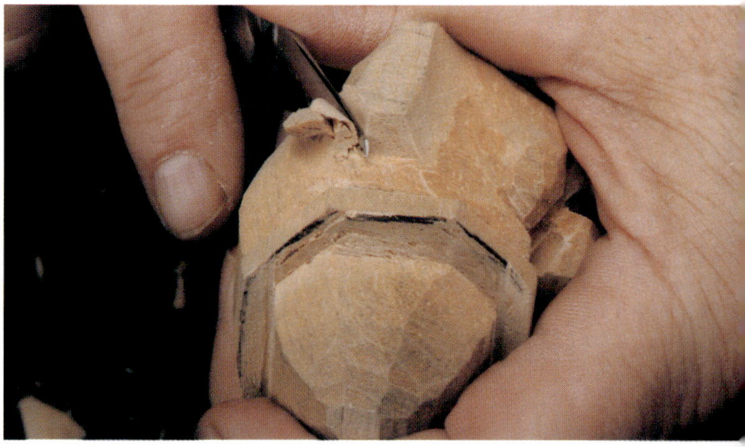

Cut off the back upper corner of the ear.

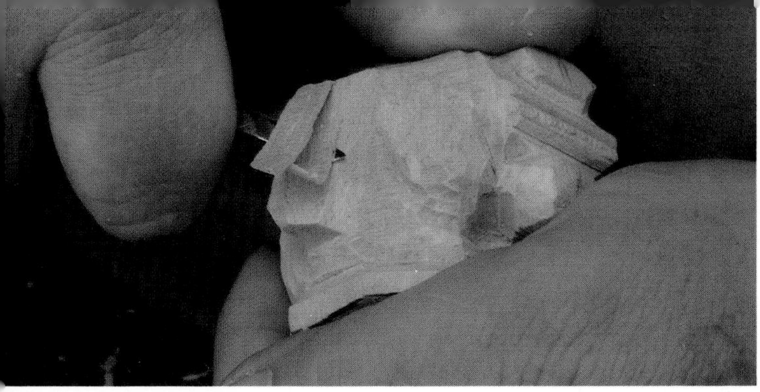

Cut the surface of the ear so it slopes from the back edge down to nothing on the front edge.

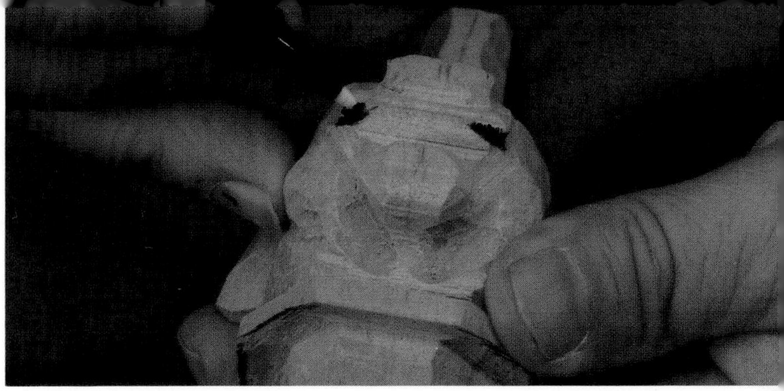

Mark the corners of the lips to be cut off.

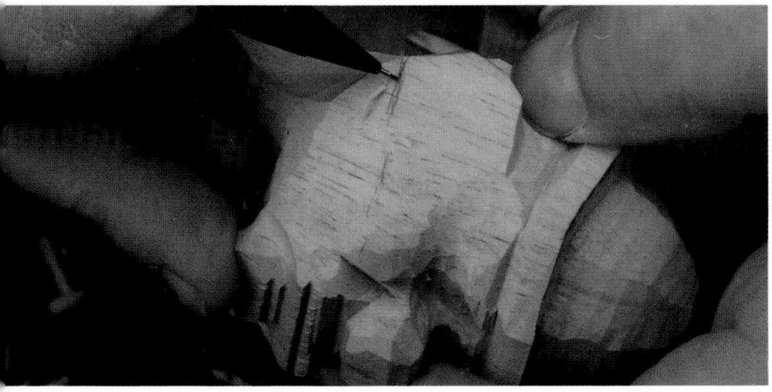

Redraw the line from the bottom of the nose to the nape of the neck.

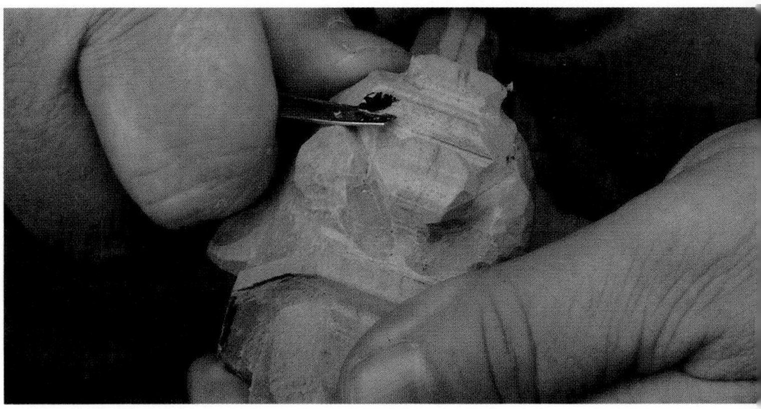

Cut them off to round the mouth mound. The ends should pop right off with a knife.

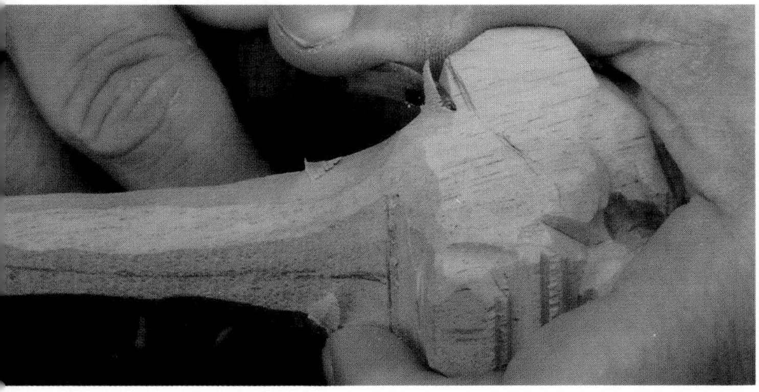

Trim the bottom of the ear up to the line.

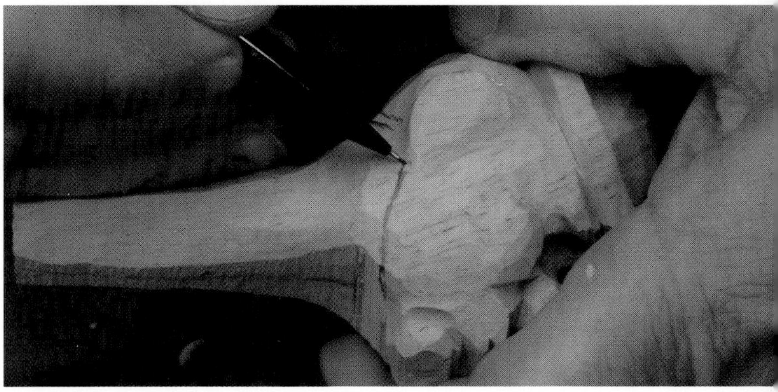

Draw the jaw line.

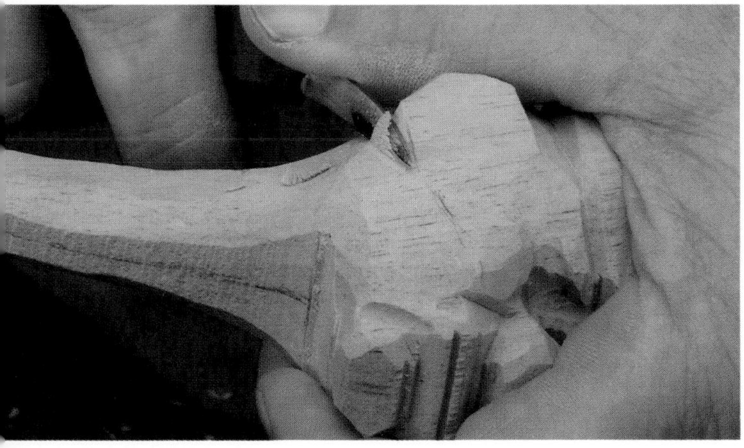

Shape the back of the jaw beneath it.

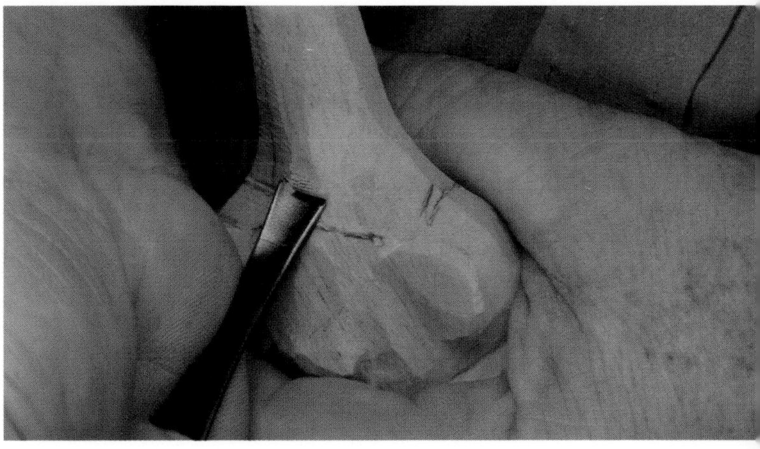

Use a knife or a gouge to cut behind the jaw line.

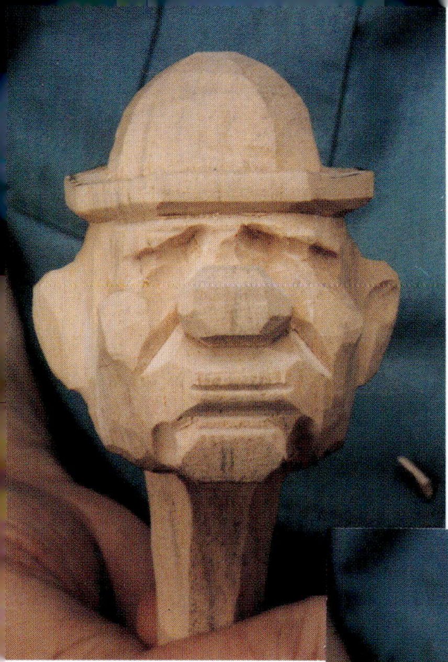

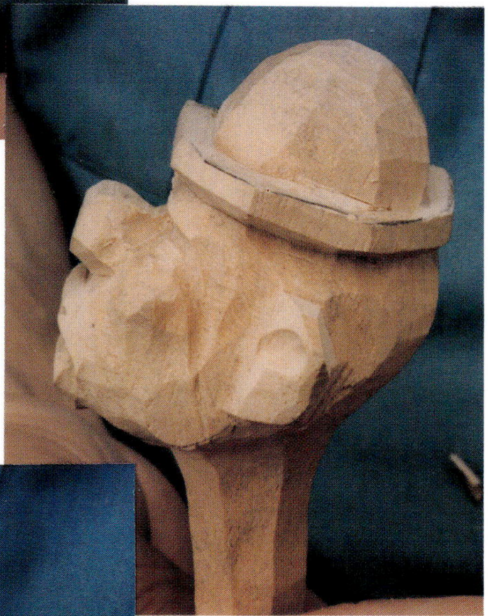

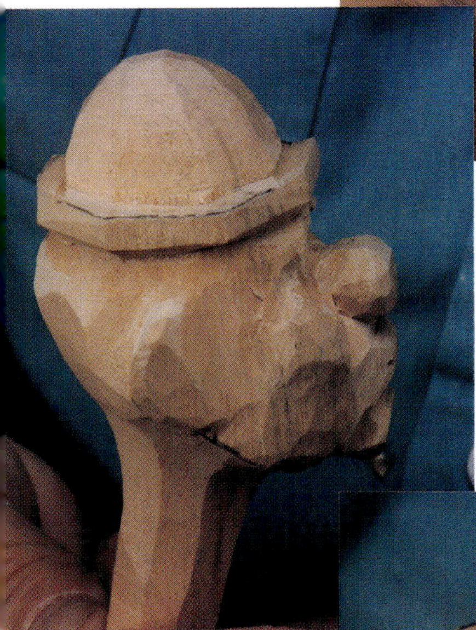

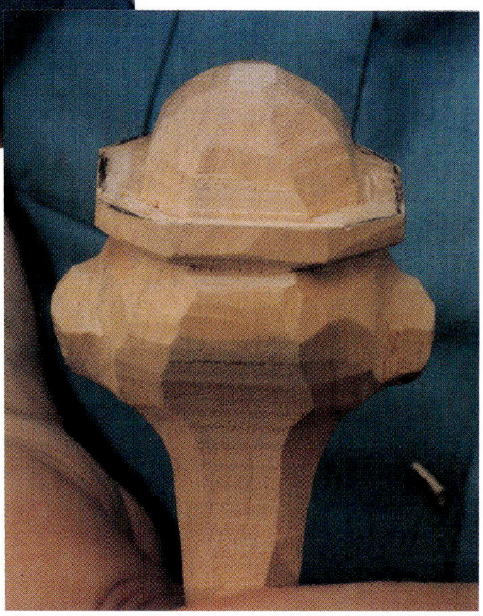

Progress.

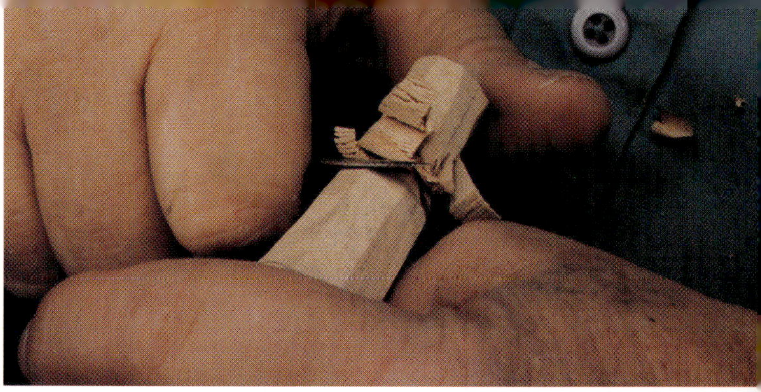

Shorten the neck in preparation for fitting.

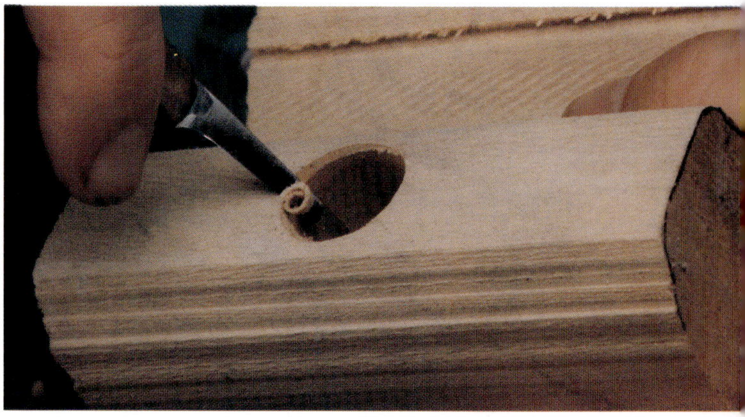

The edge of hole in the body is knocked down just a little.

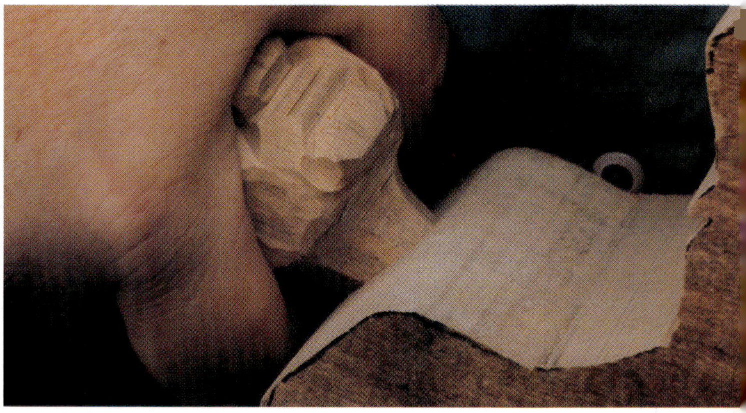

Put the neck in the hole and apply pressure while rotating it back and forth.

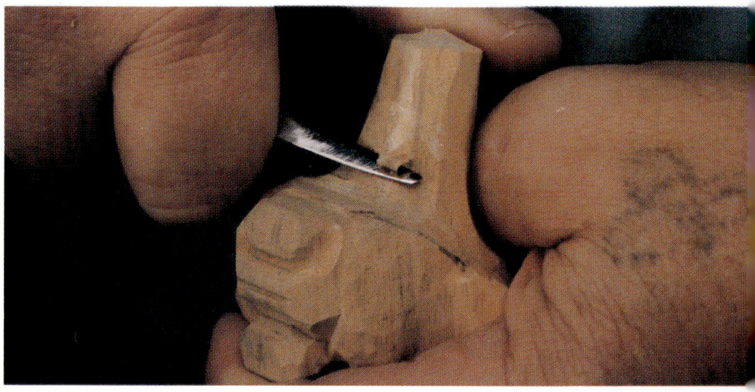

This will make the high places shiny so you can knock them off.

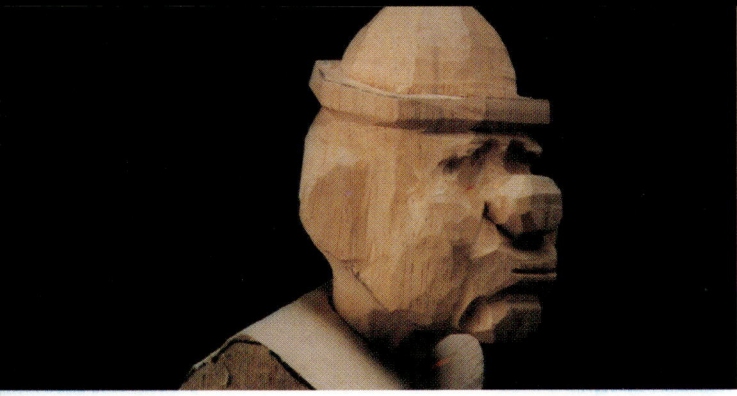

A good fit.

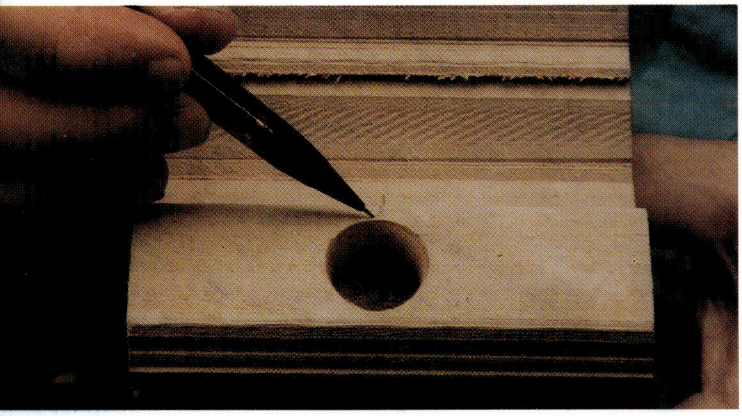

Use your fingers as a depth gauge...

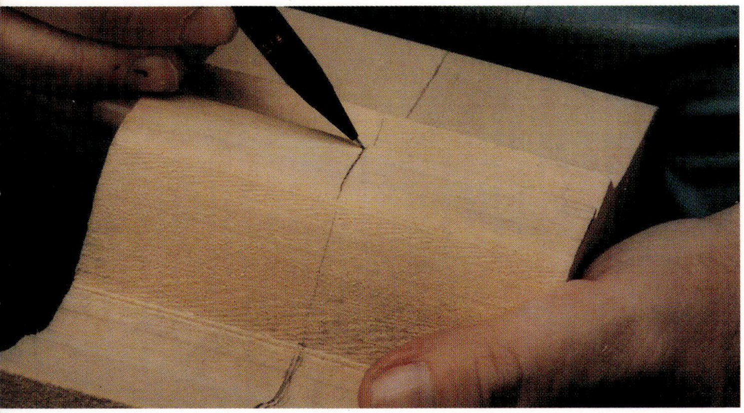

and draw a center line all the way around.

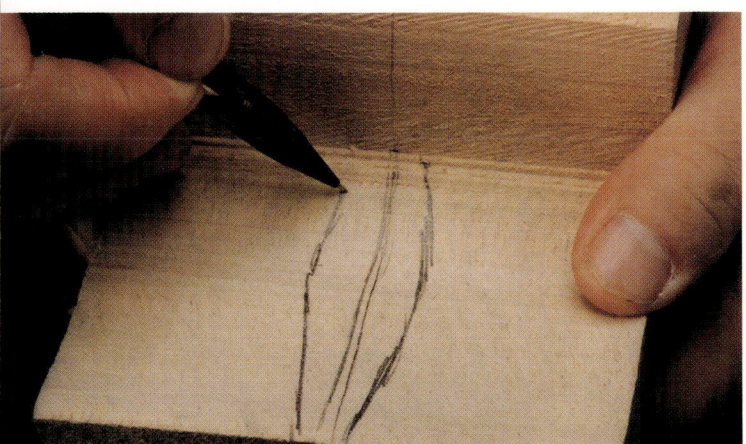

Draw the bow of the legs.

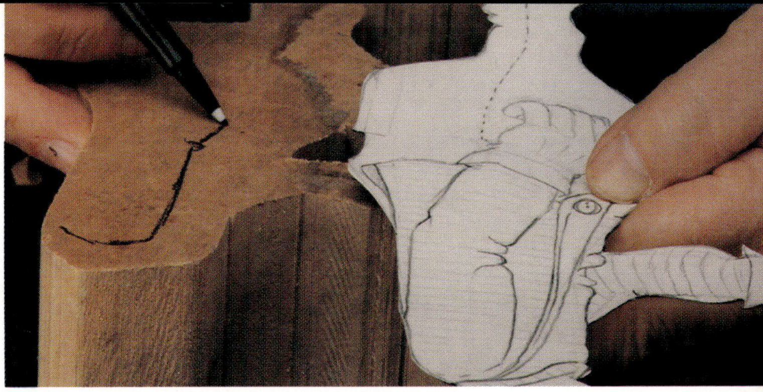

Referring to the pattern, draw in the shape and position of the arms.

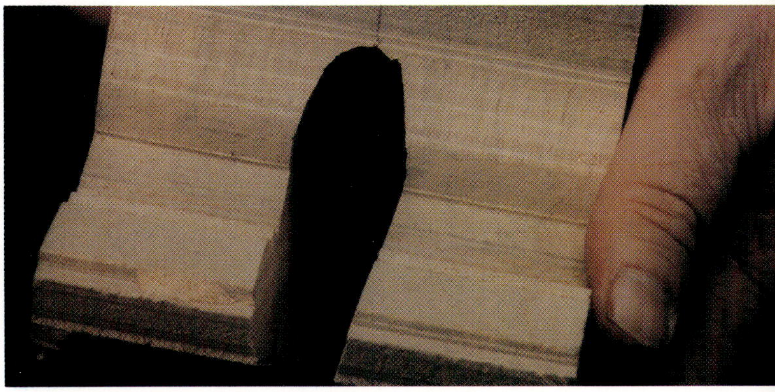

Saw the bow of the legs on the bandsaw for this result.

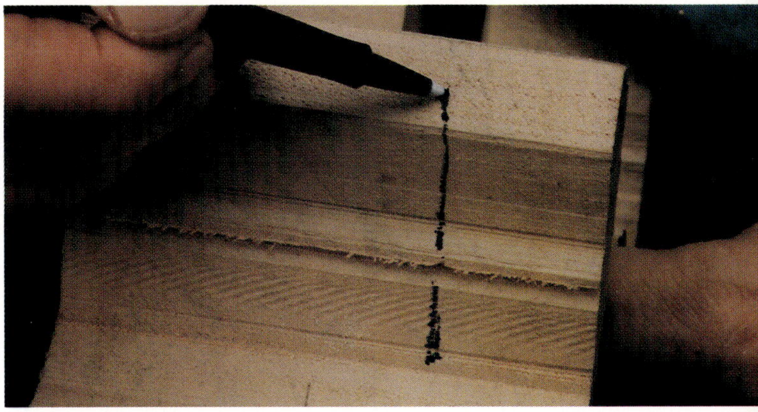

Mark the inside edge of the right arm.

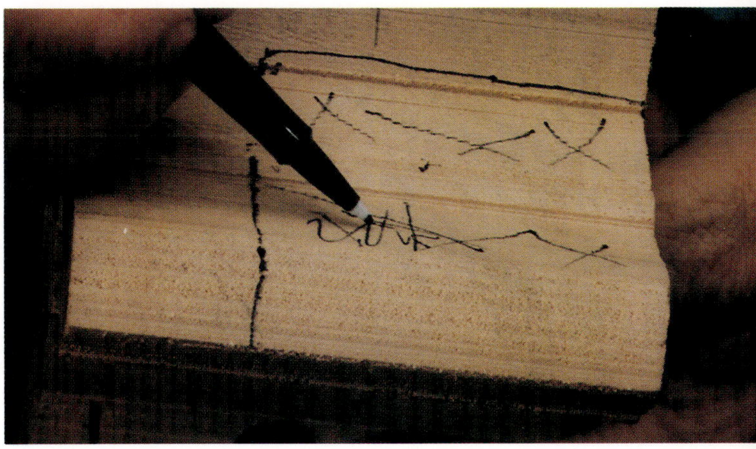

Mark the area to be removed.

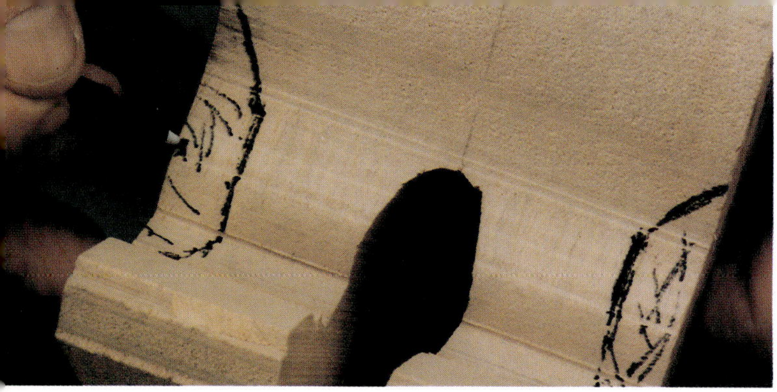

The outside line of the legs. This will be cut on the bandsaw.

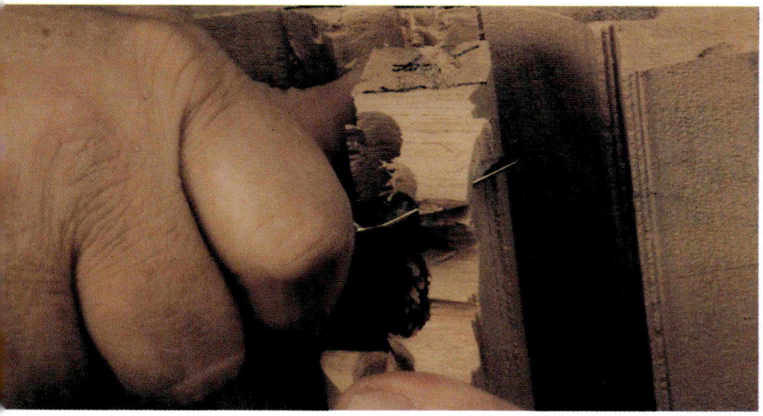

The unwanted wood in the arm area can either be carved away, or to make work easier, drilled away on a press. Clean up is done with a knife. The drill makes a good stop and reduces the effort needed to carve.

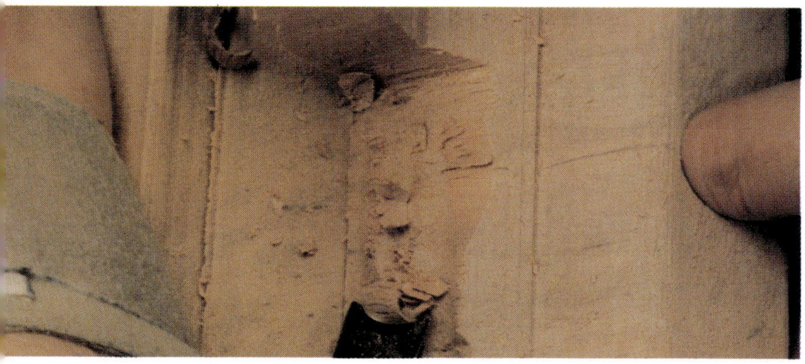

Clean up the chest area with a gouge.

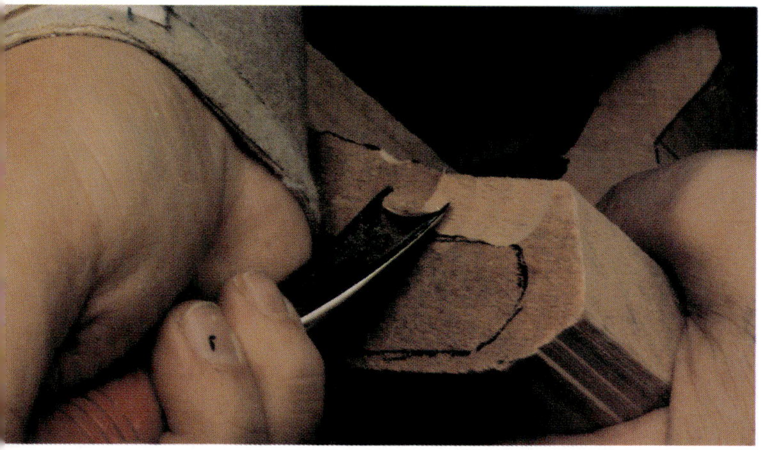

Use the gouge to carve around the left arm, bringing it out.

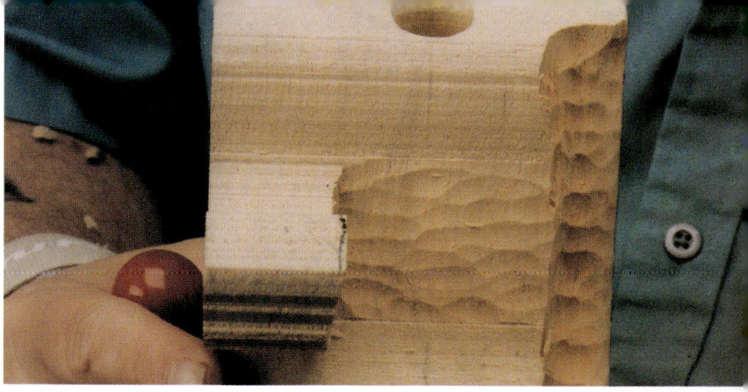

Continue to about this depth.

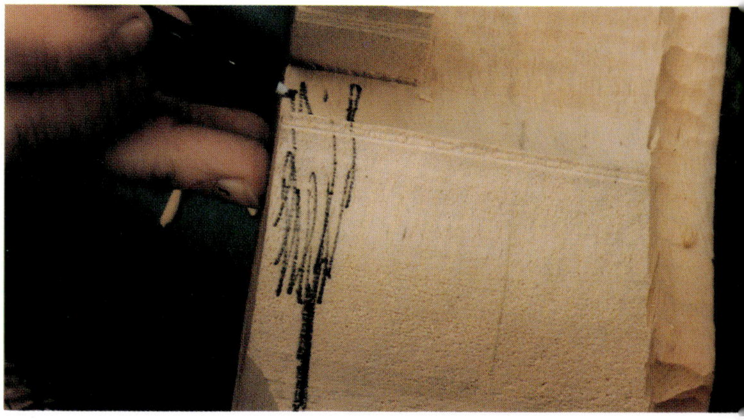

Do the same thing on the other side. Mark it for symmetry.

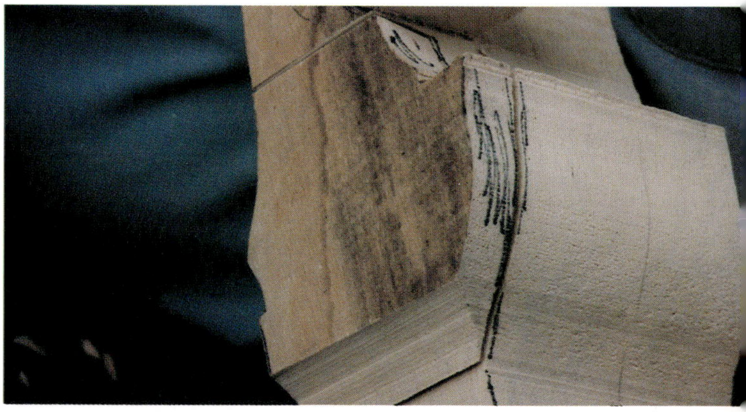

Some of this can be done on the bandsaw if you wish.

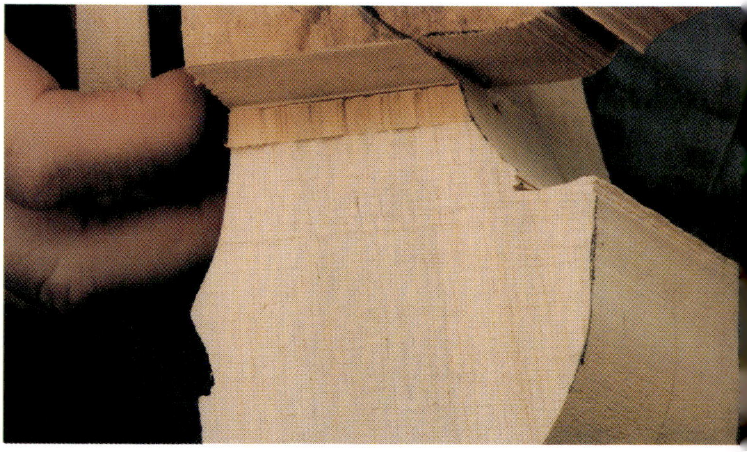

Pop off the piece for this result.

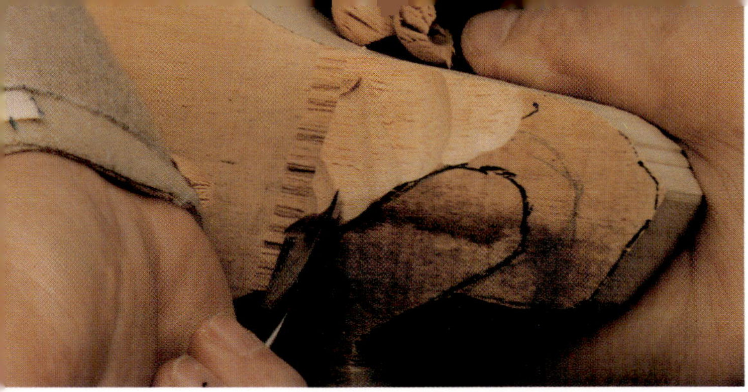

With a gouge take the chest down to the same level.

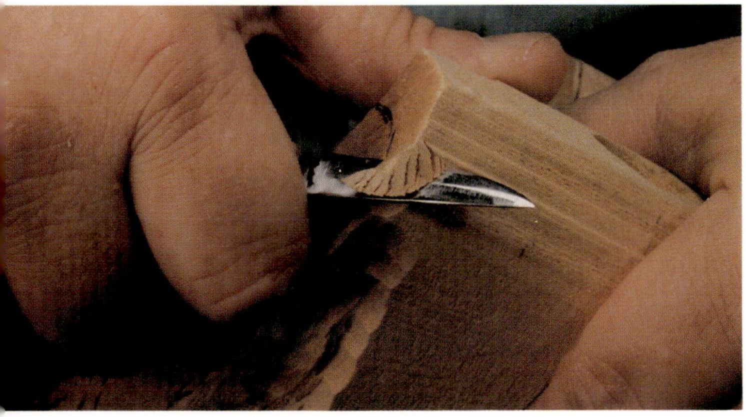

Drop the shoulders down.

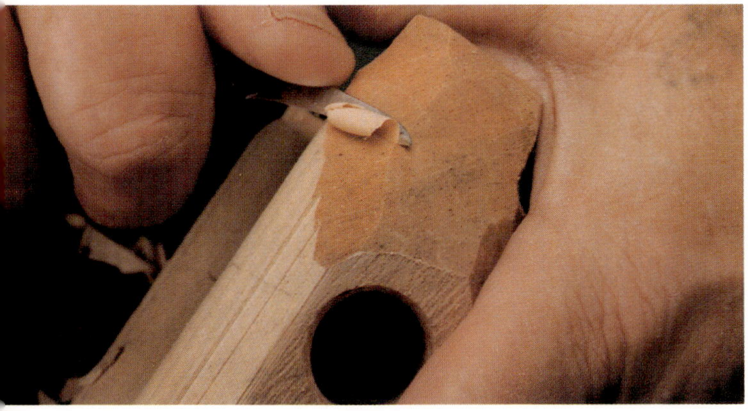

Slope the shoulders up to the neck, leaving a little rim at the neck. Round the chest and the back as you go.

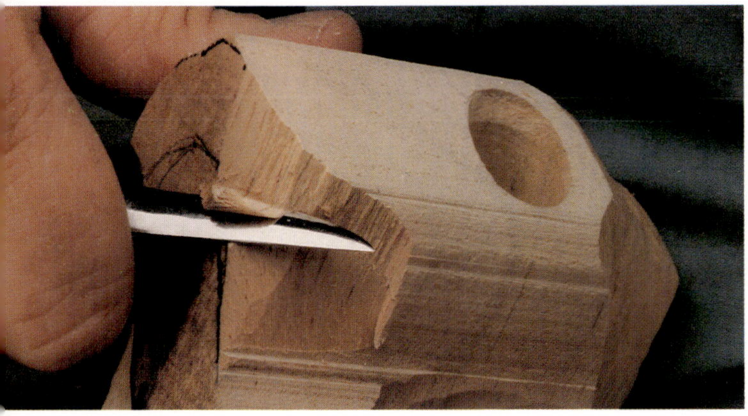

With one side done, do the other.

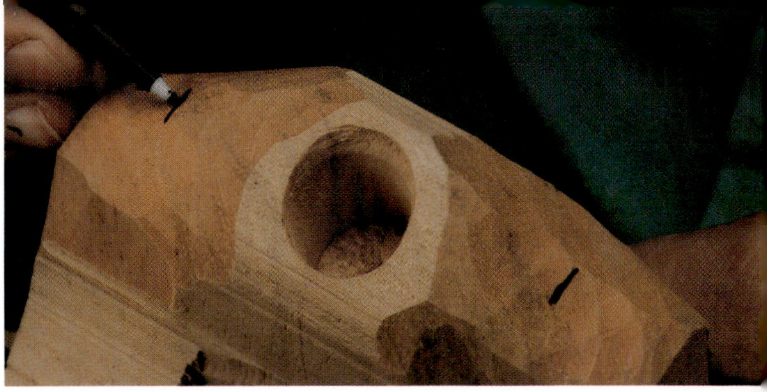

Reestablish the width of the shoulders, bringing them in.

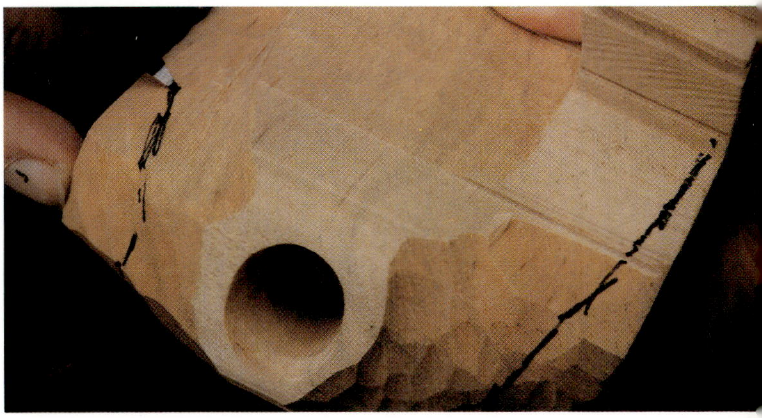

From there draw the line of the upper arms. This will give the clown a more humorous droopy look.

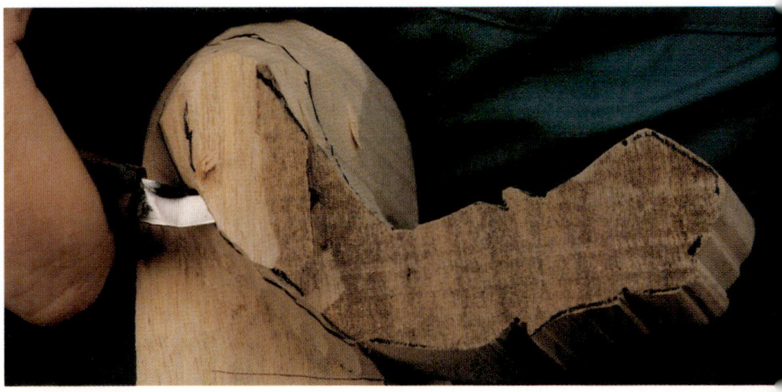

Pop off the outer surface of the upper arm.

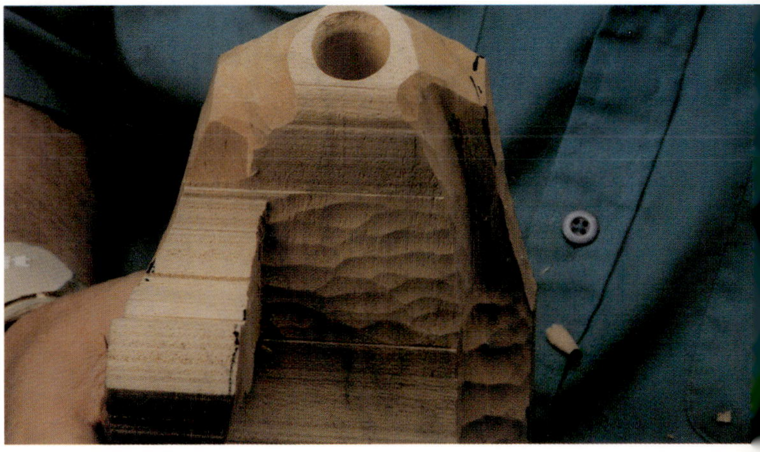

The result.

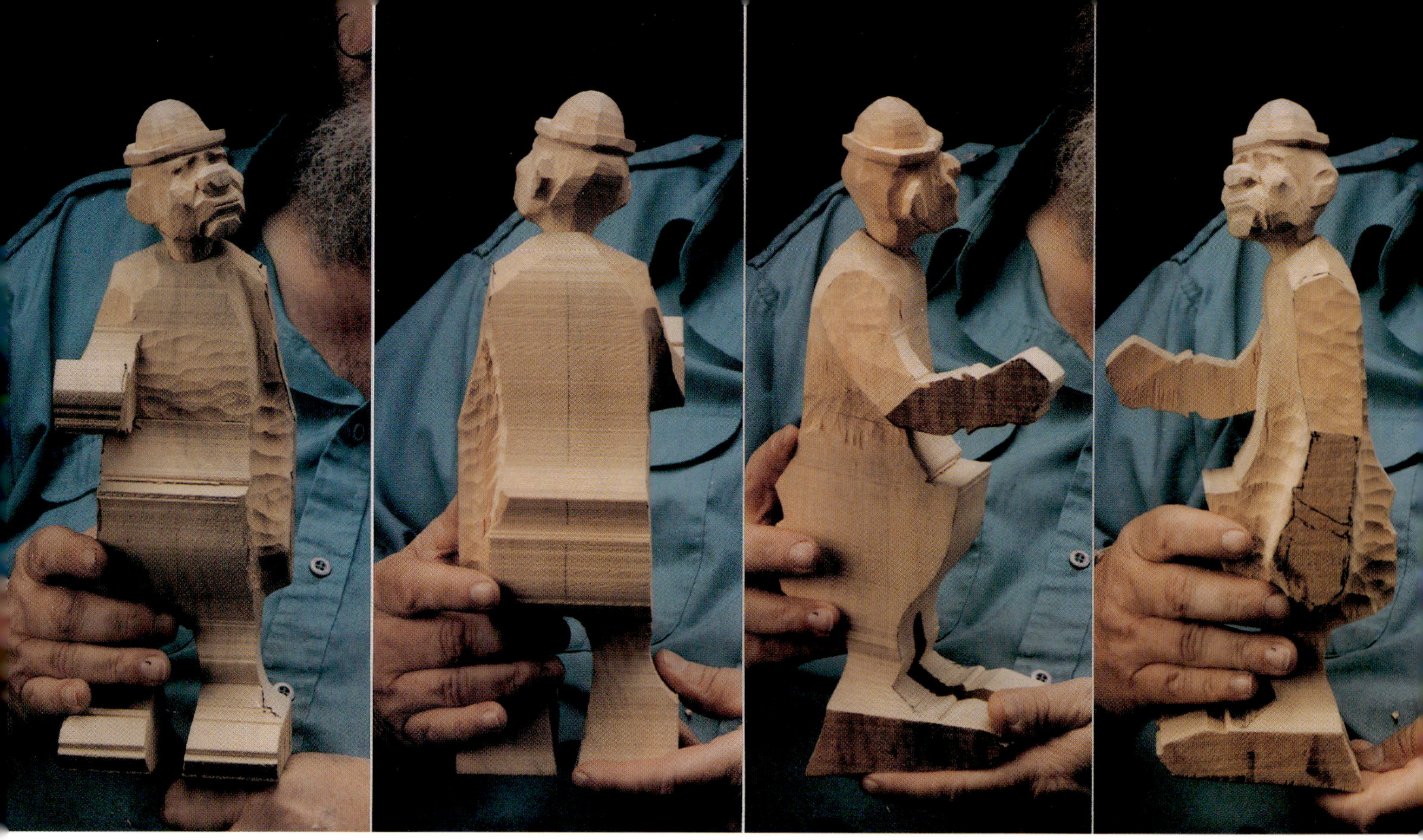

The basic shape of the body is set. Notice that all the corners are square.

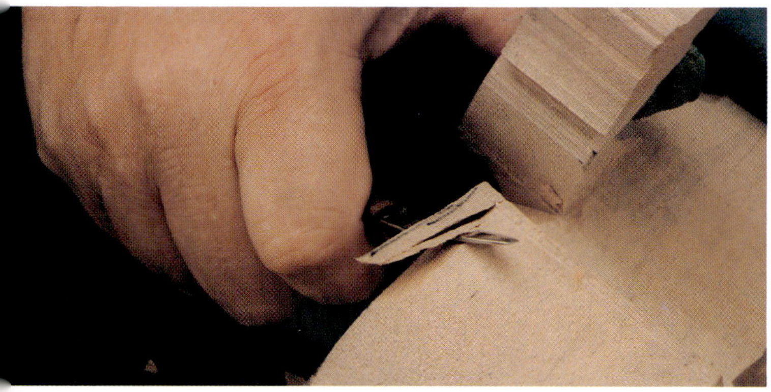

Knock off the corners. Always go to octagon before going to round.

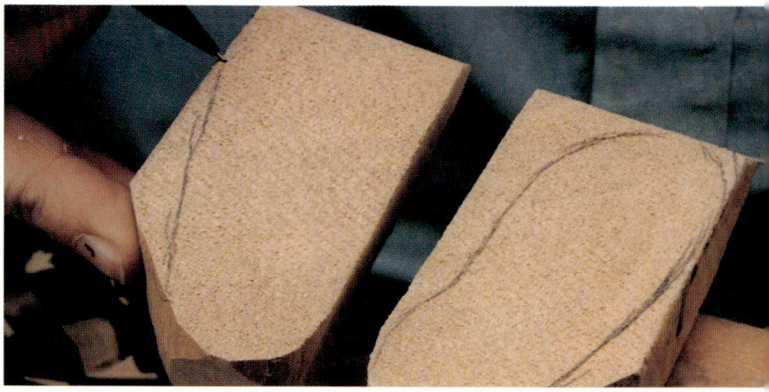

Draw the outline of the soles of the shoes.

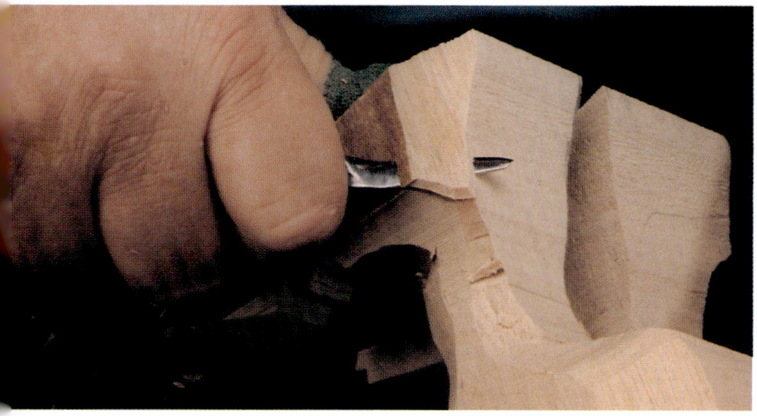

Continue down the legs and the back of the feet.

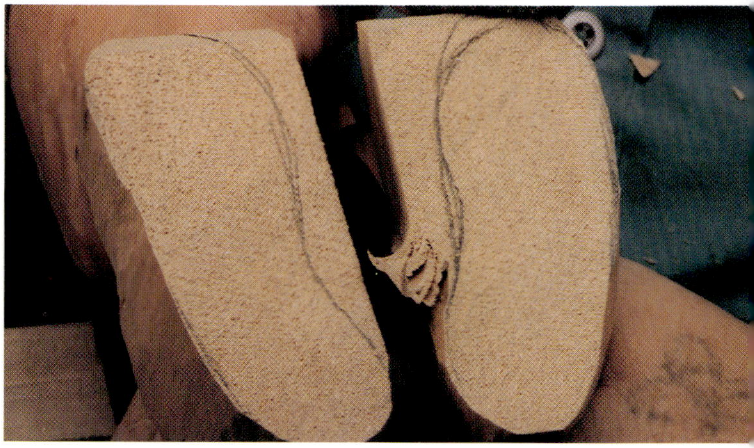

Trim the foot down to the outline.

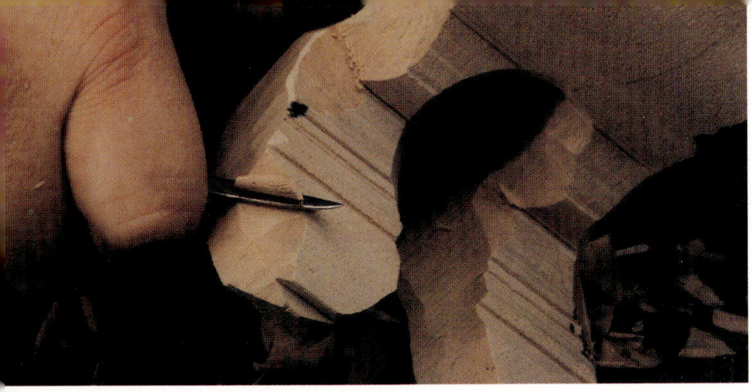

When the shape of the shoes is set, knock off the corners.

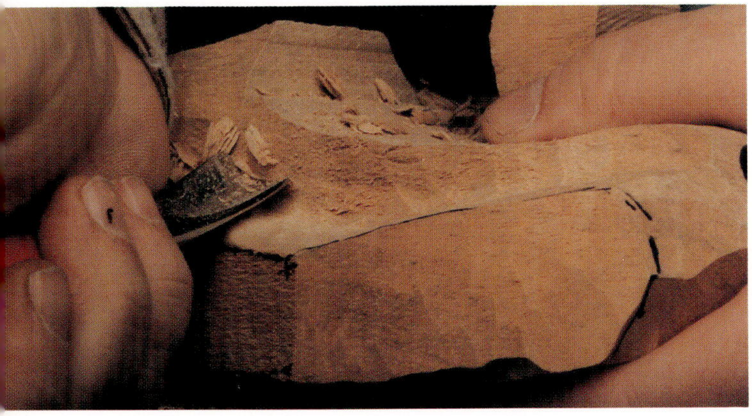

I want some daylight to show between the left arm and the body, so I need to narrow the body. This will make the upper body kind of skinny, but I think I'll like it.

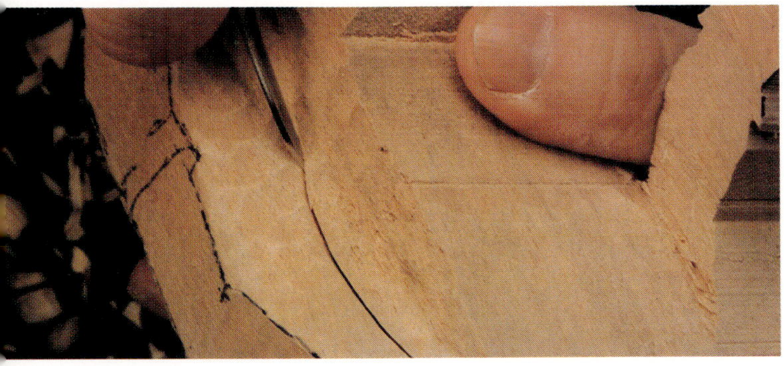

Make a cut along the line of the inside of the arm...

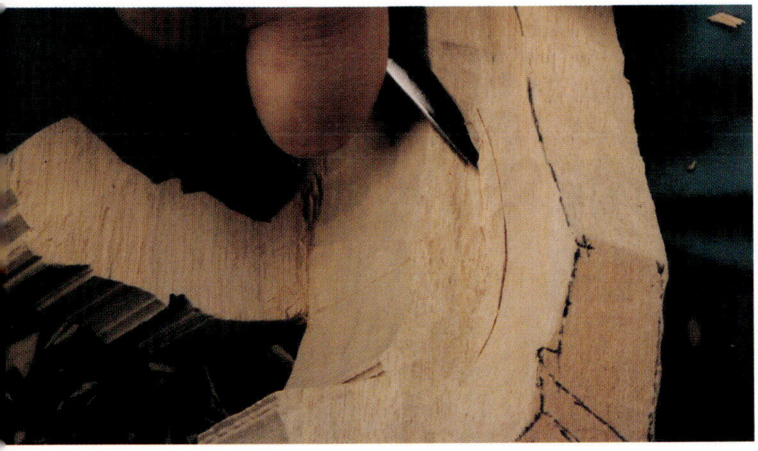

and back along the body.

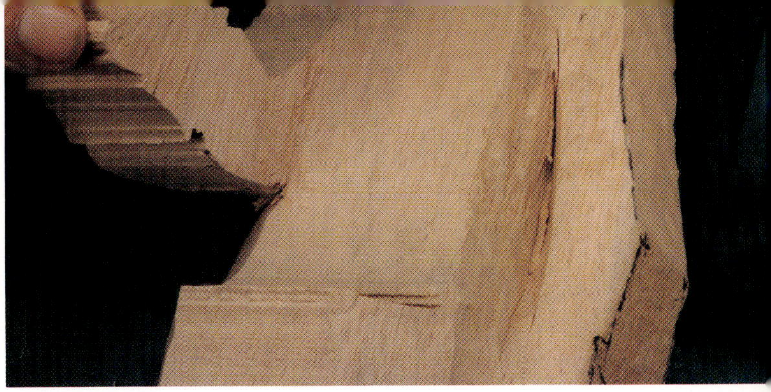

Go over it until the slice pops out. Repeat the process going deeper and deeper.

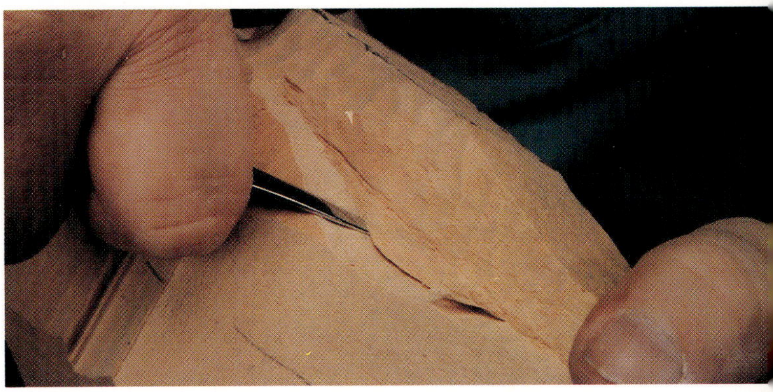

Do the same on the back.

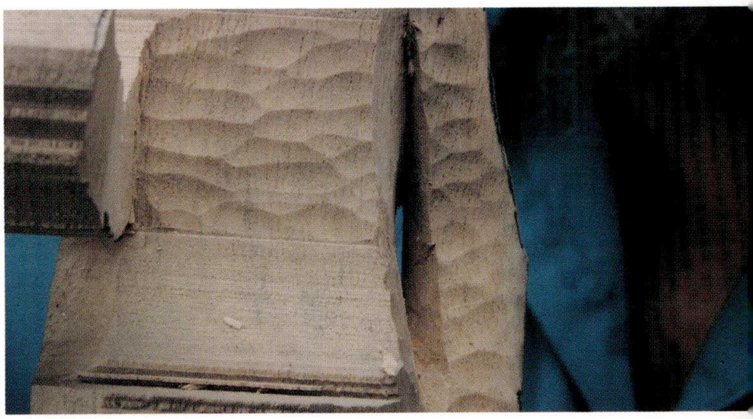

Continue until you break through.

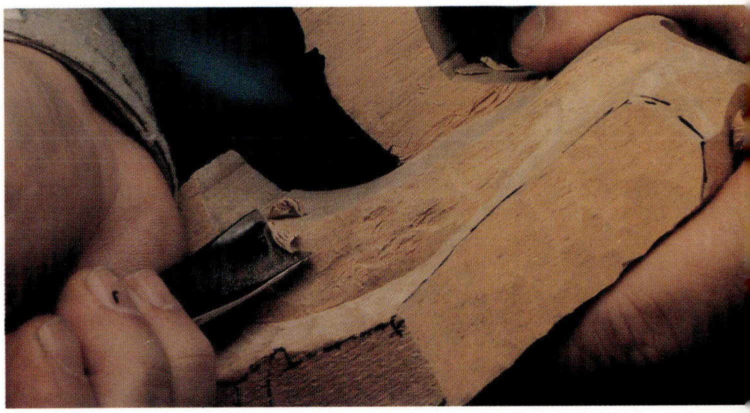

Round off the corner of the upper body again. I'm going to leave the trousers because I want them to look comically big.

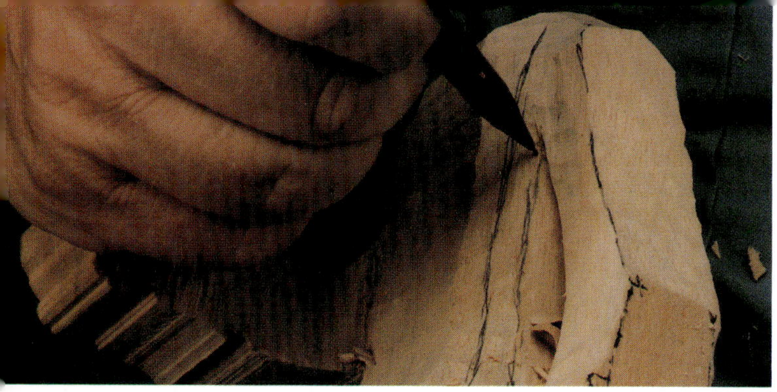

Draw in the straps or suspenders for the trousers.

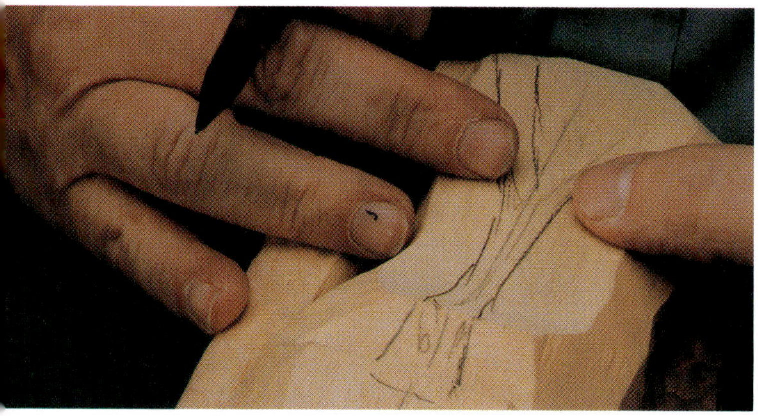

Do the same on the back.

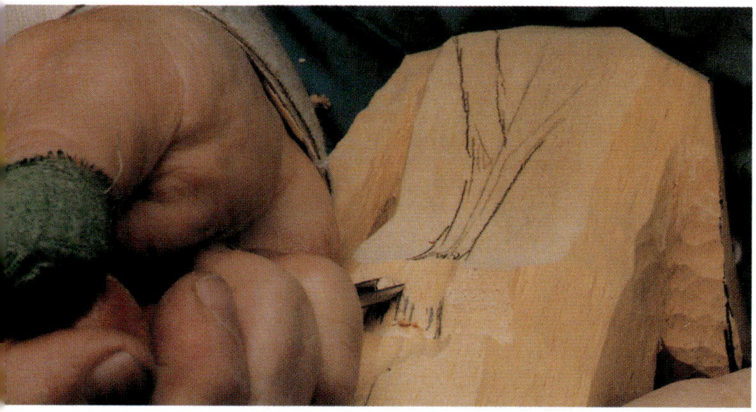

The shirt will blouse out on either side of the strap in the back, so I need to reduce the strap area to create this effect.

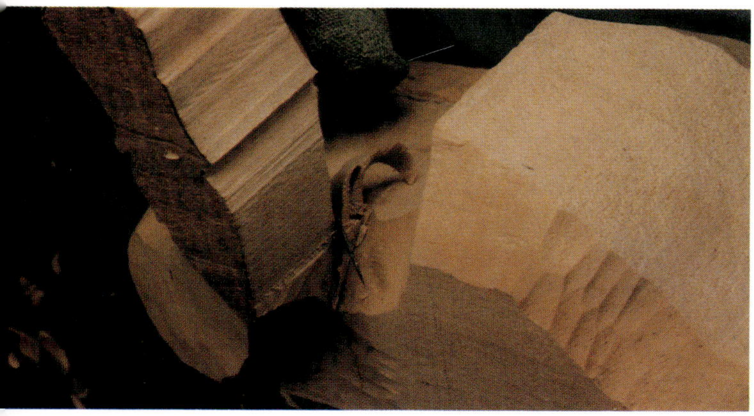

Trim the outside of the extended arm.

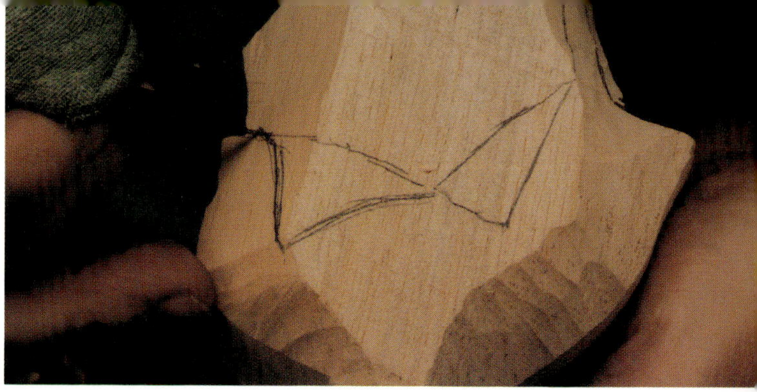

Draw the strap and the side of the trousers. This is where the buttons are undone and the straps folded down.

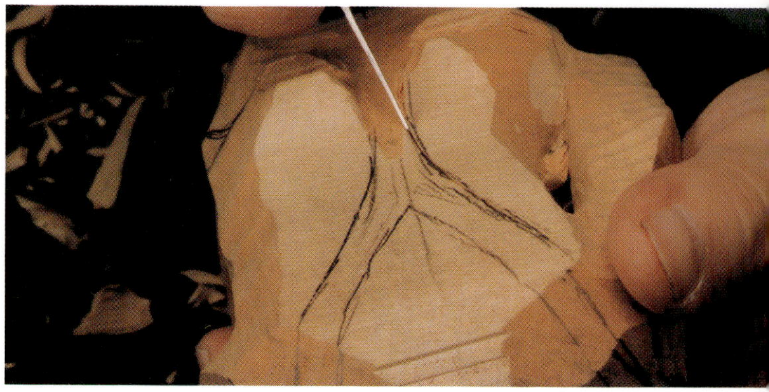

Normally I wouldn't do clothing this early in the carving, but with clown pants it is important that the straps be preserved during the other carving. Run stops on the lines.

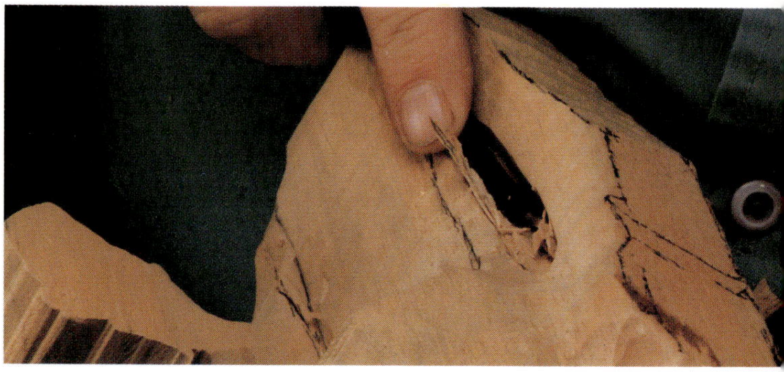

Trim back to the stop. Here under the arm I slice back to the stop with a gouge.

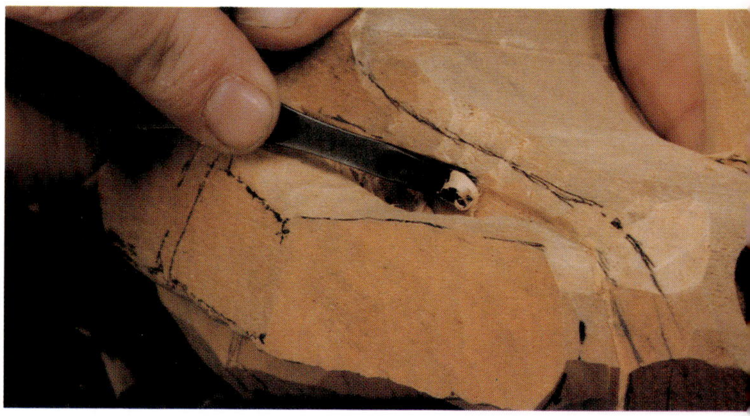

A v-tool may work as well or better.

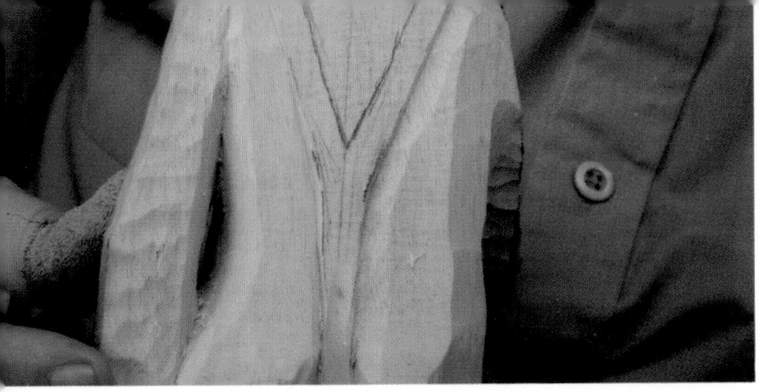

Continue around the back.

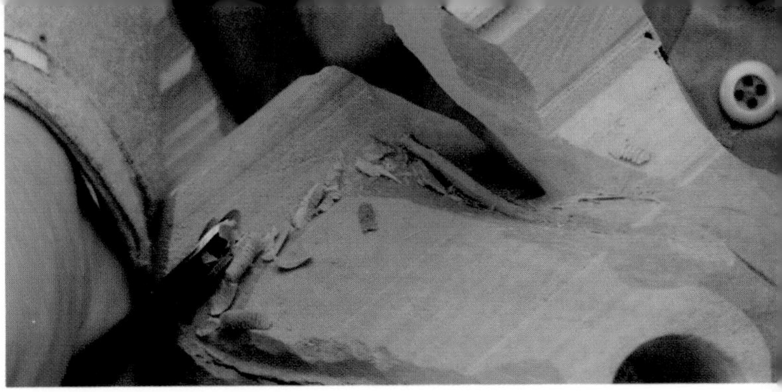

Clean out the top of the trousers with a narrow deep gouge.

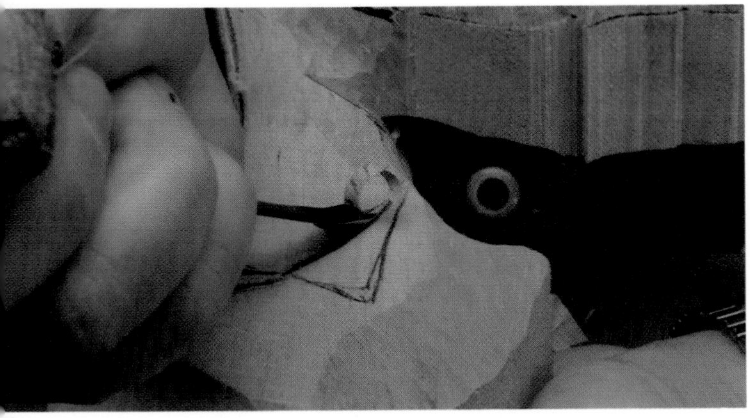

With a v-tool set the line at the top of the trousers.

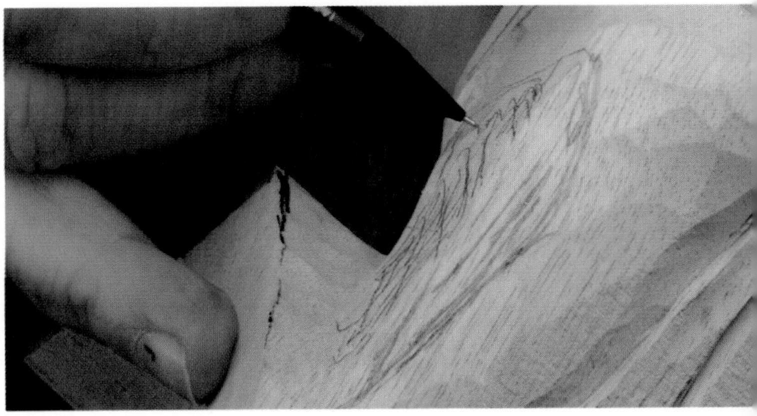

To match the other side I need to remove some from here.

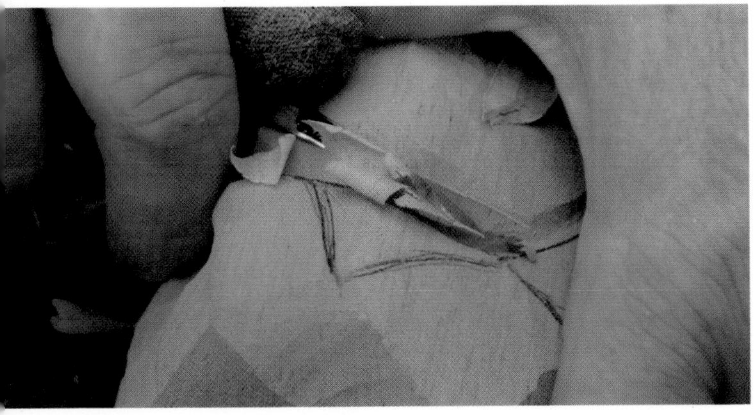

Reduce the upper body to the trousers.

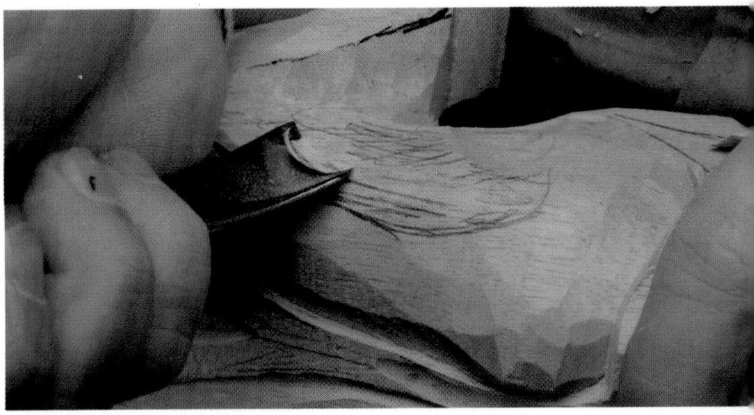

Remove it with a gouge.

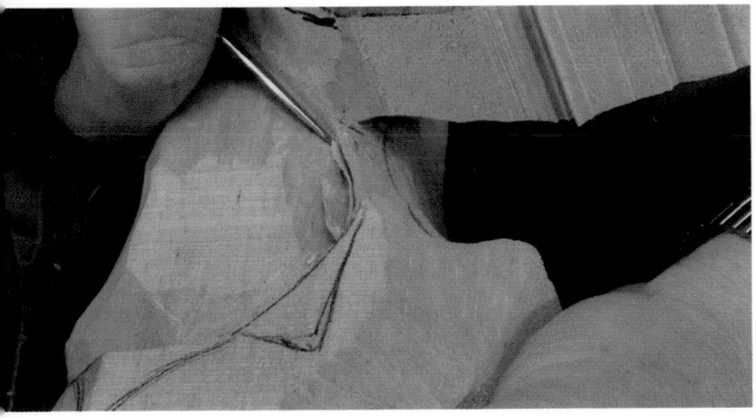

I want to undercut the front straps to make them stand out and seem more believable.

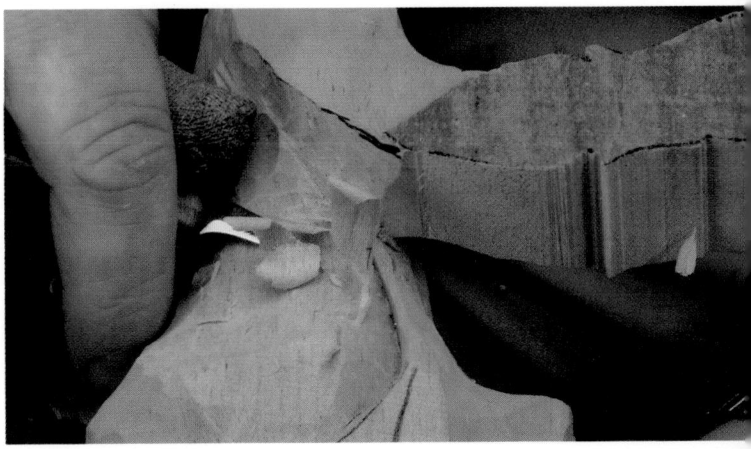

Clean and blend with a knife.

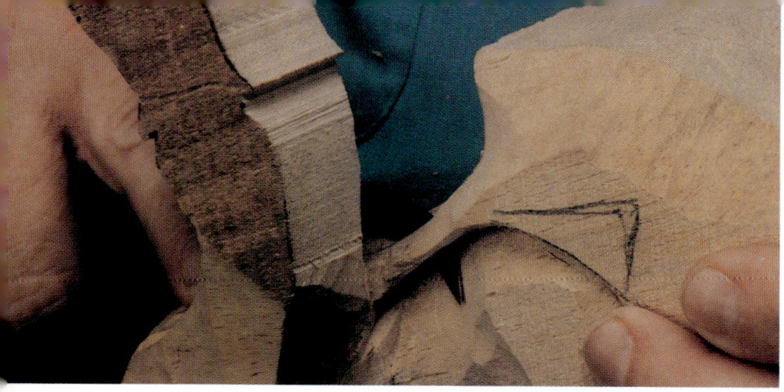

I've carved far enough to get a cut through behind the strap. It adds interest to the piece, but at the same time creates a week spot that I'll need to be careful of.

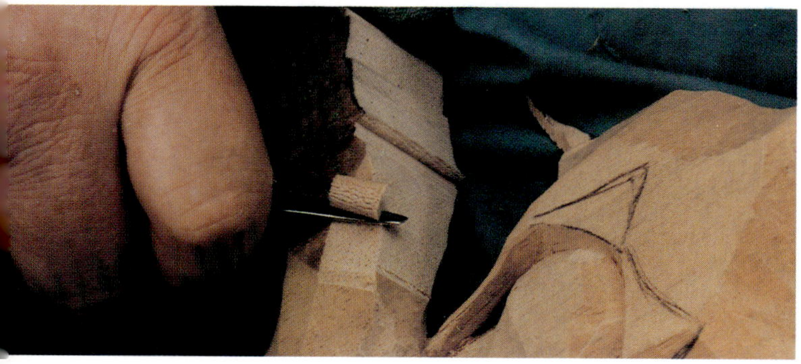

Knock the corners off the arms, leaving the gloves kind of whole for a while.

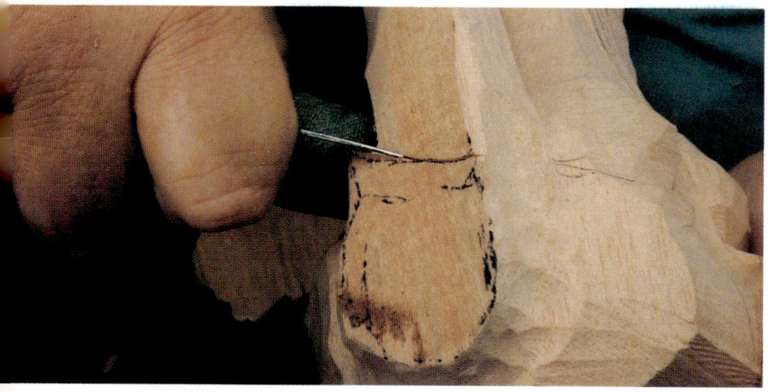

Cut a stop in the cuff of the glove...

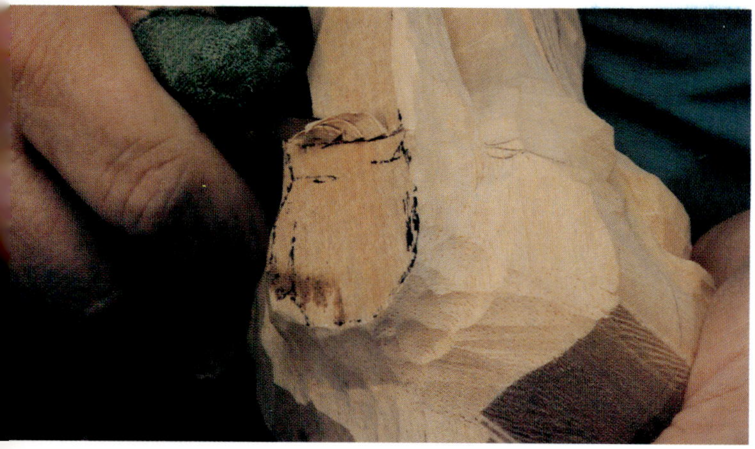

and come back to it from the arm.

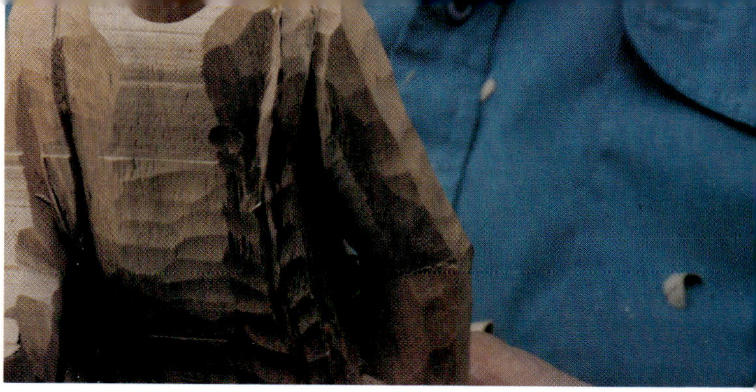

Continue working on the arm. I want it to be believable all the way around, and I think it needs to be a little thinner.

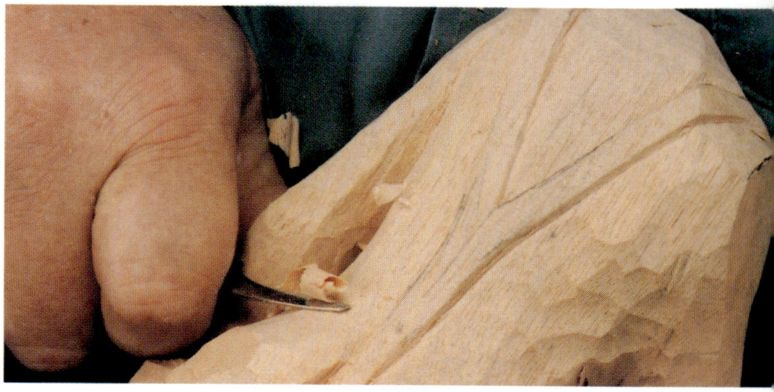

Shape and smooth the back of the shirt.

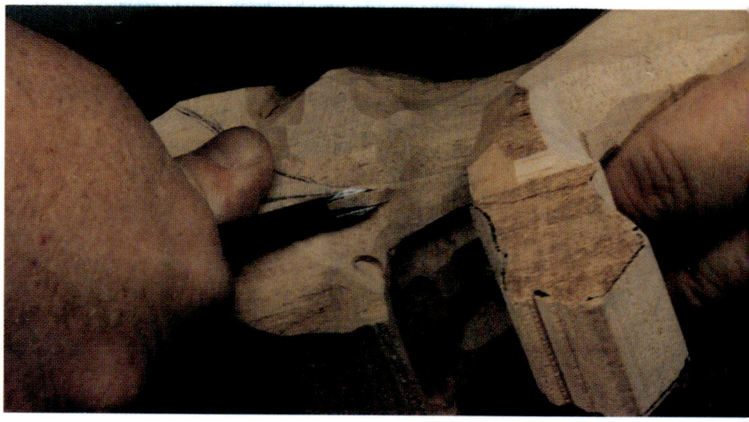

Use a v-tool to create the underside of the fold. This gives the strap a thinner look without making it weaker.

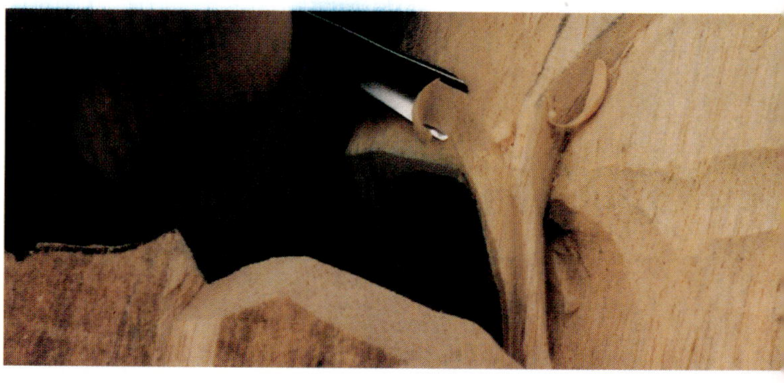

A channel running under the front of the trouser top does the same thing, giving the effect of thinness without losing strength.

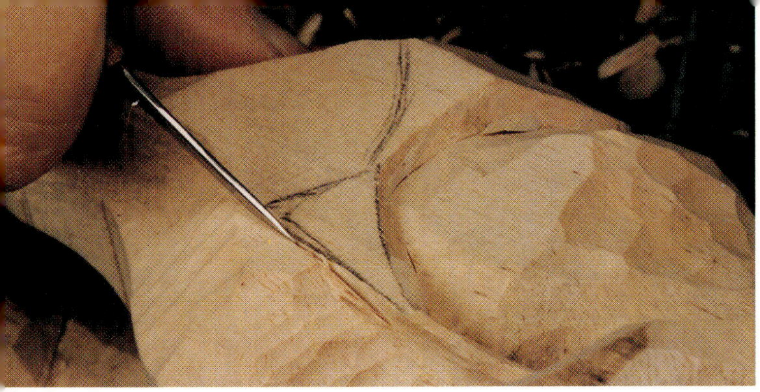

Now cut a stop along the edge of the fold-over.

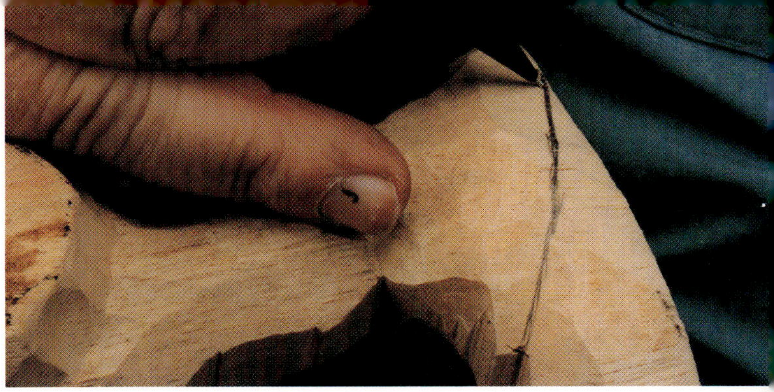

The pants hang over the shoes, so draw the line.

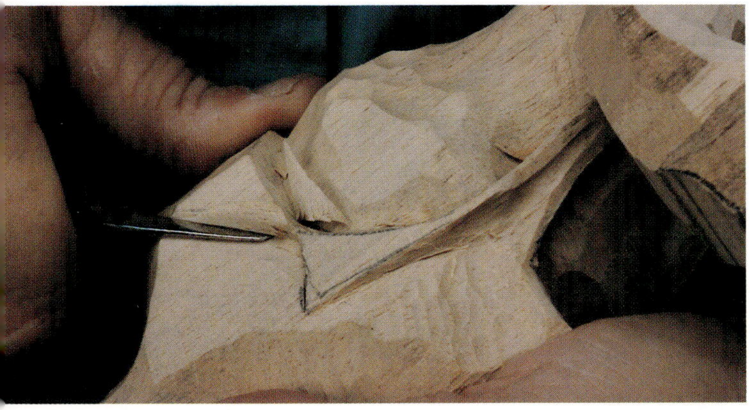

Cut back to it from the trousers.

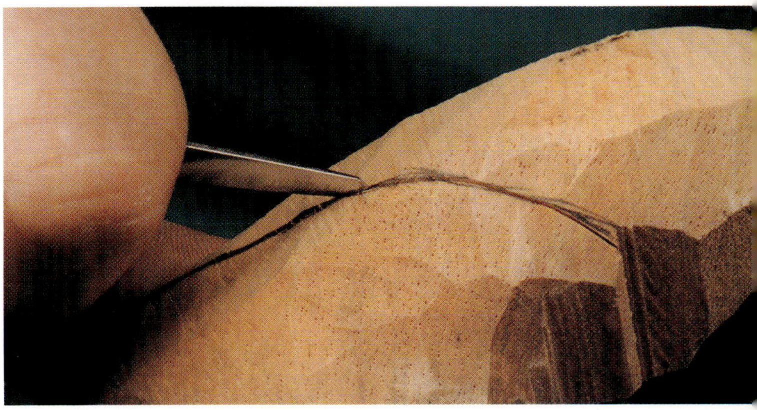

Cut a stop on the line...

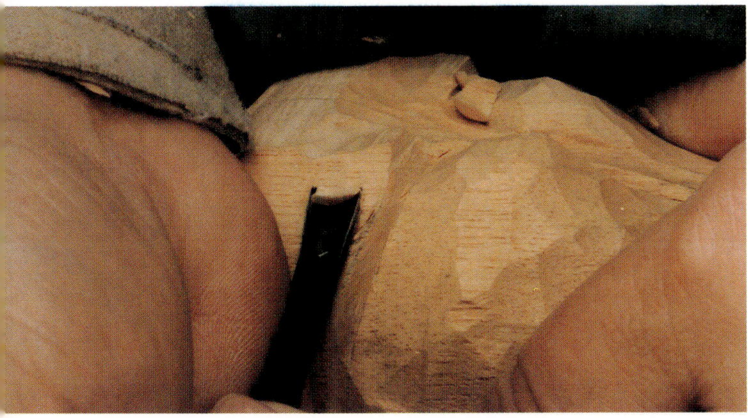

Run a channel under the back edge of the trousers as you did in the front.

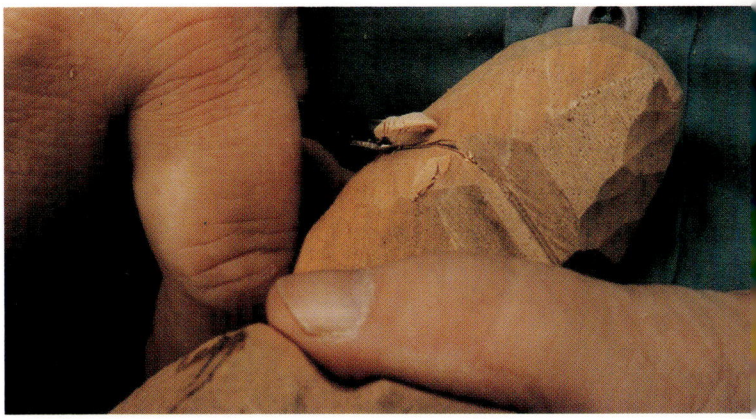

and cut back along from the shoe with a v-tool.

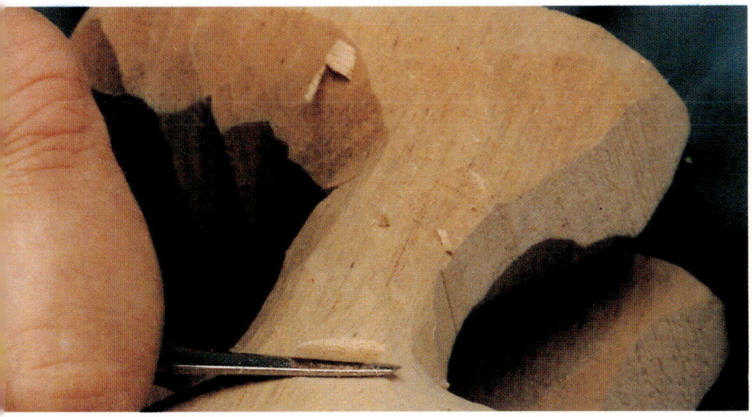

Smooth the legs.

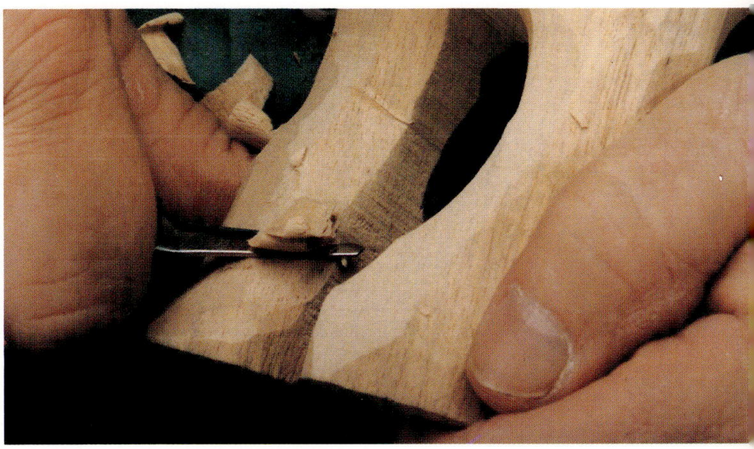

Continue softening and rounding the lower leg.

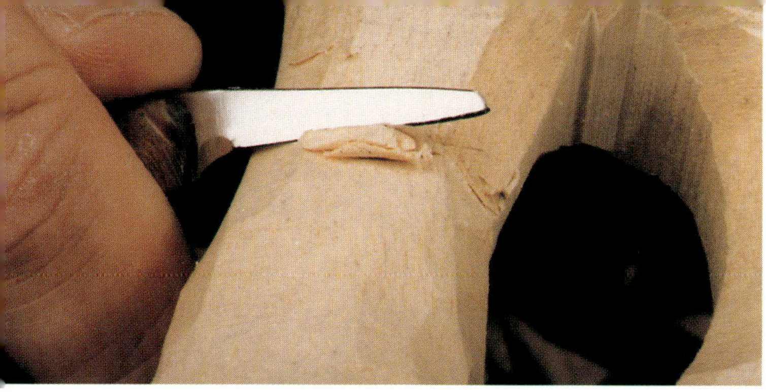

Cut a crease across the back of the knee, cutting down and up.

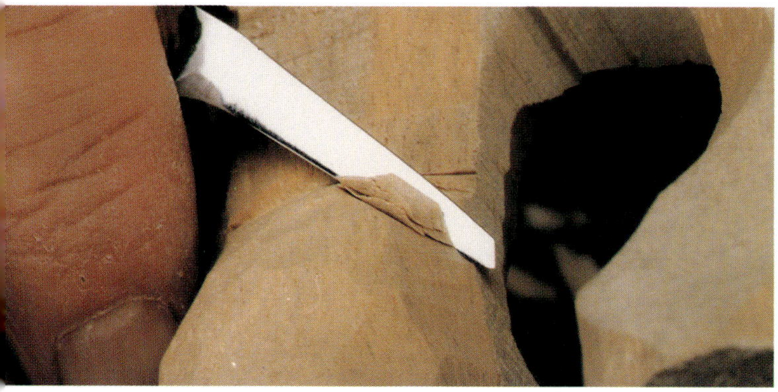

Three smaller creases radiate from the end of the main crease...

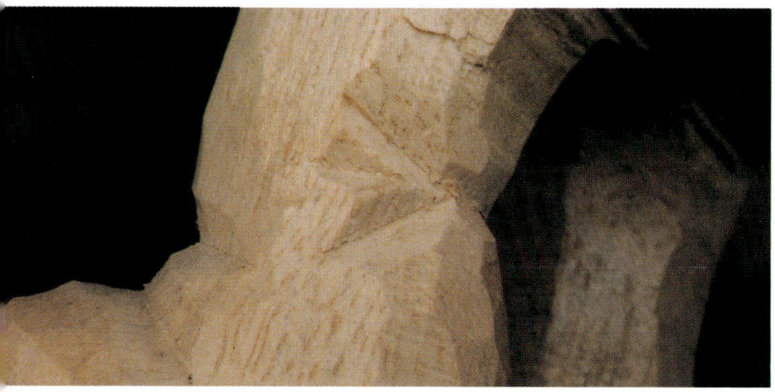

to create this "crow's foot" effect.

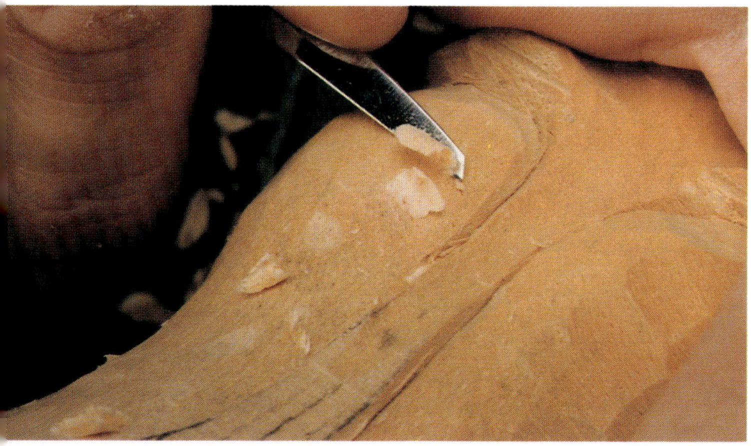

Trim the butt.

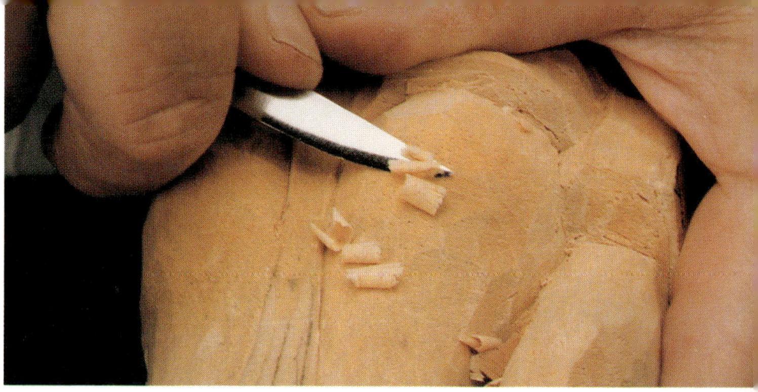

Do the other side so it is balanced.

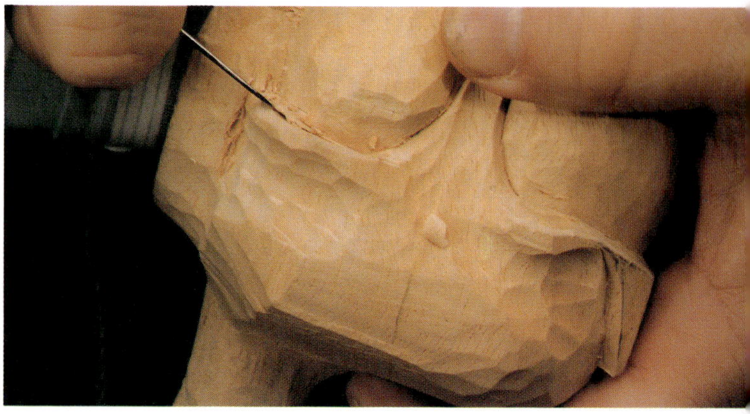

Undercut the back of the pants so it looks like it is hanging away from the body. This will help give it the floppy look we're after.

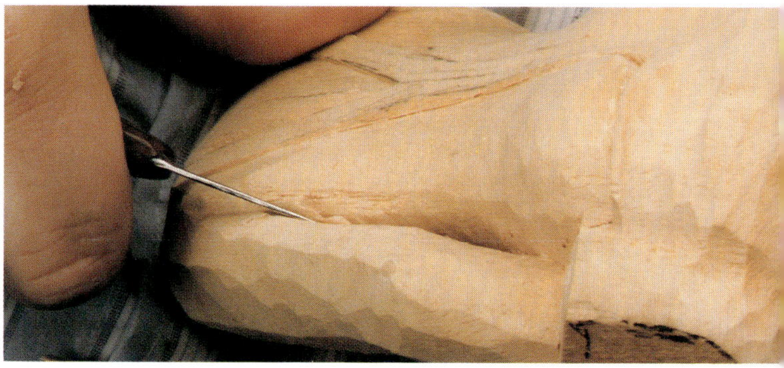

Thin the left arm on the inside as much as possible, but keep it looking realistic. This will emphasize the opening you worked so hard to achieve.

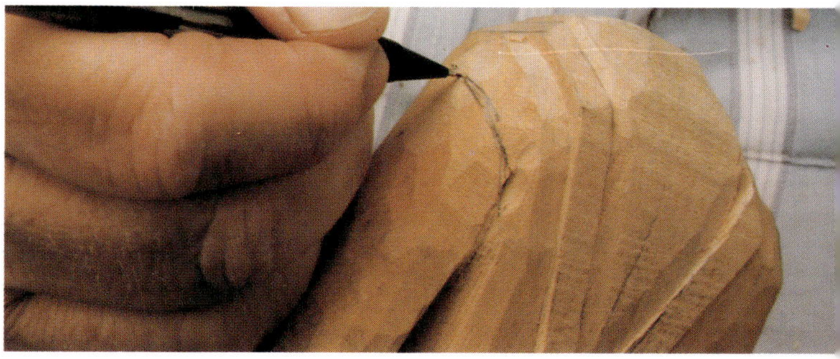

Sometimes things just don't look right and you have to make adjustments. The shoulders on this guy are just too square, so I'm going to lower them a little to create more slope.

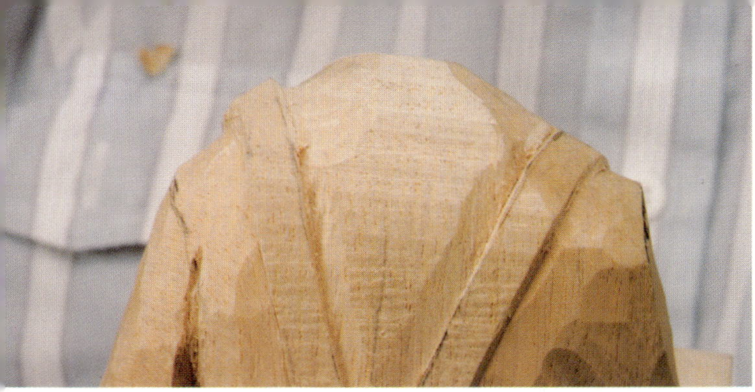

That's better.

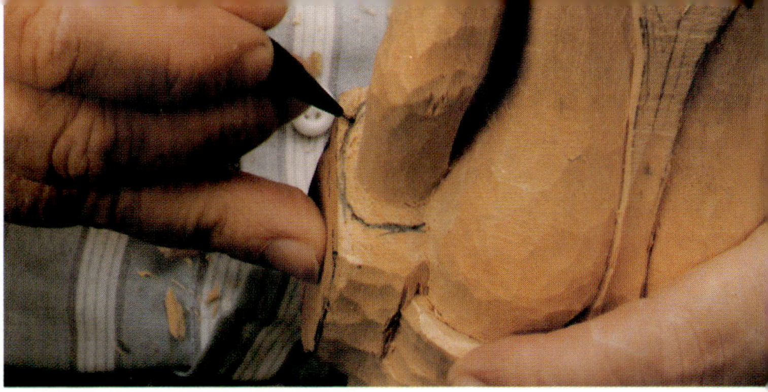

At the wrist mark the cuff of the glove.

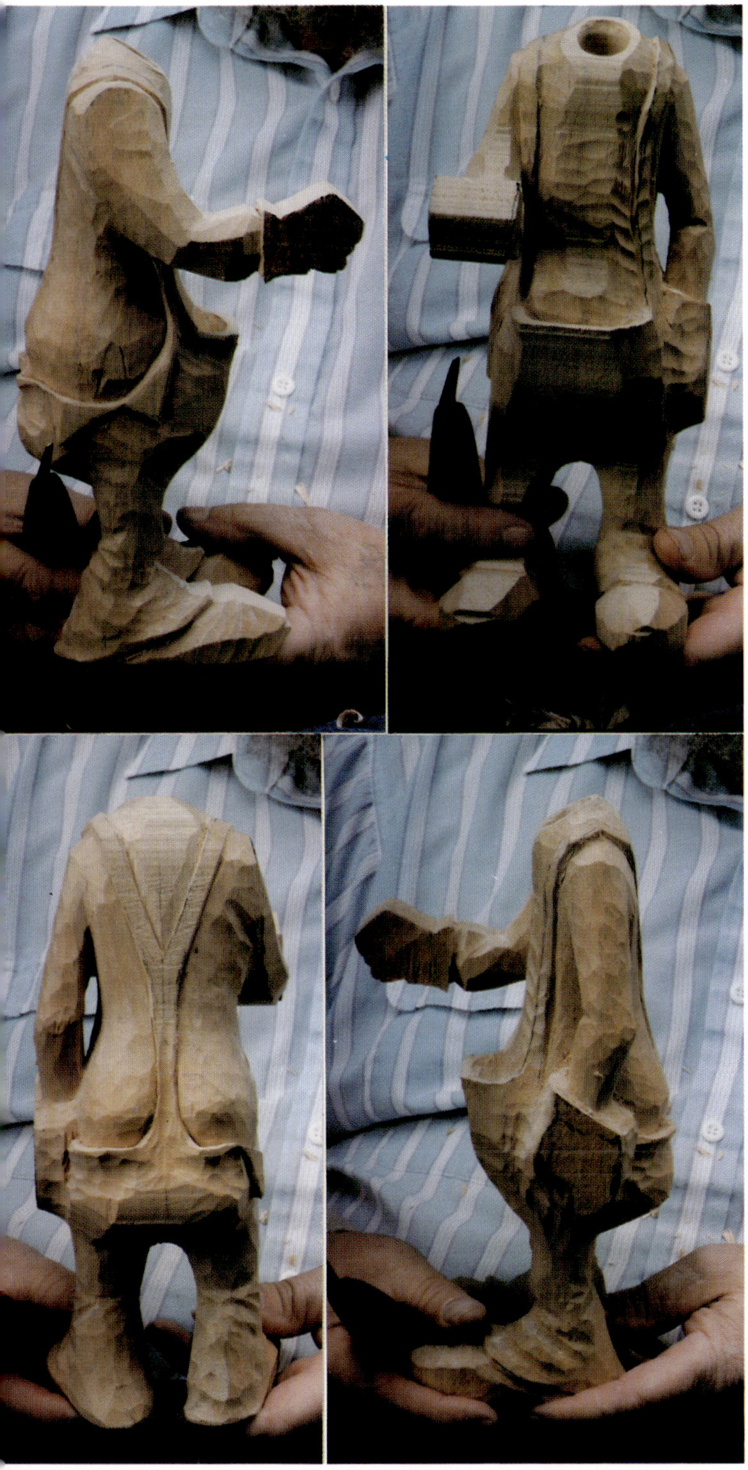

Progress. I'll do the left glove before starting on the right arm.

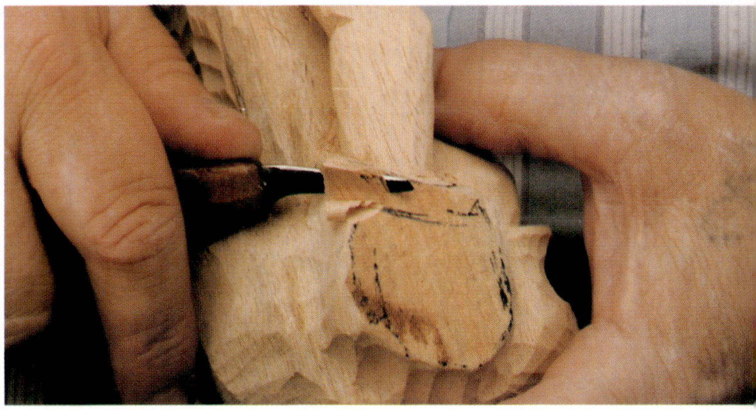

Trim the cuff down to the mark.

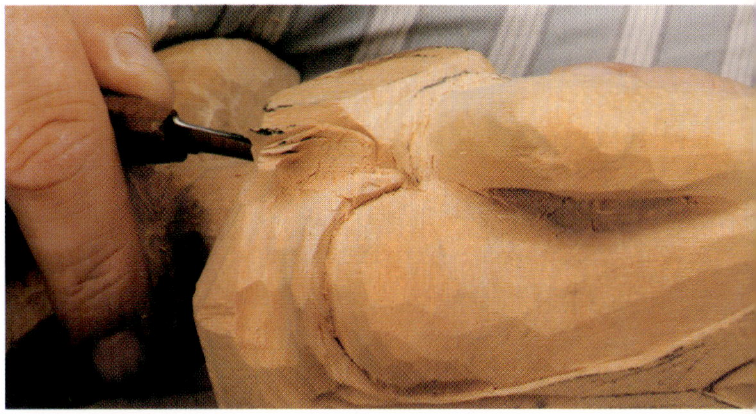

The back edge of the glove is too big, so I'm knocking it off.

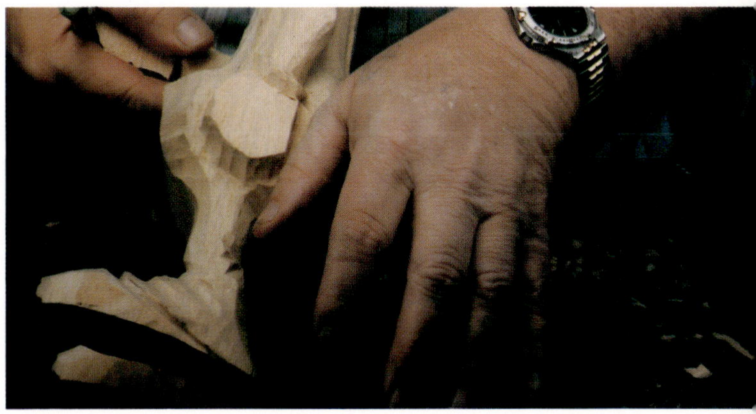

The hand will be in a position something like this, so I look at it before...

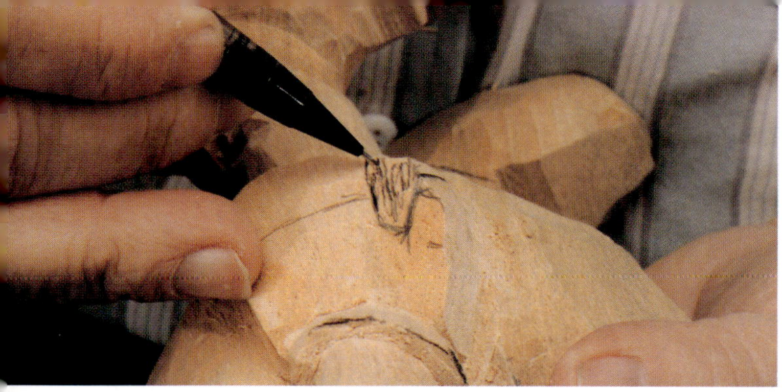

drawing in the thumb.

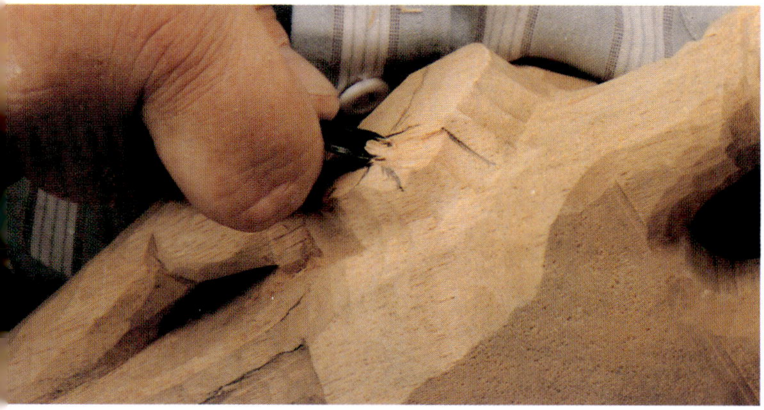

Begin carving the space between the thumb and forefinger with a gouge.

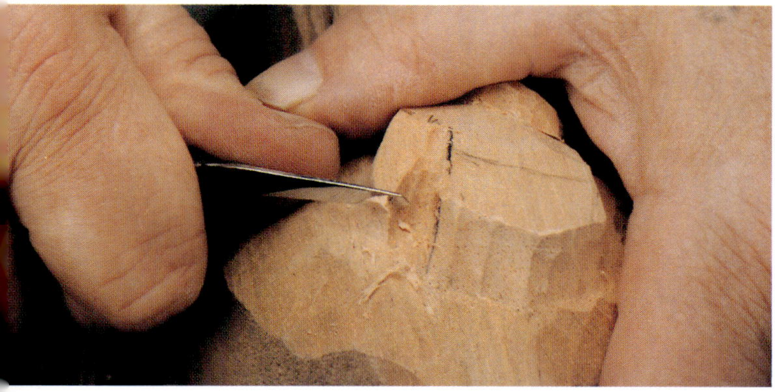

With a knife, thin the thumb and set its overall shape.

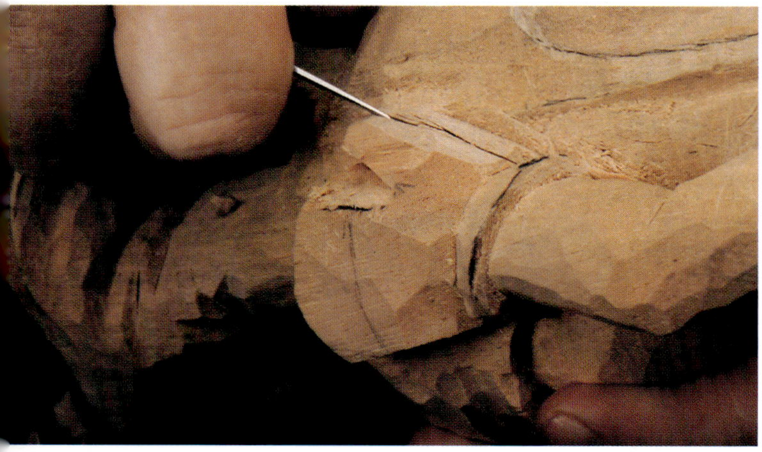

Undercut a stop around the thumb.

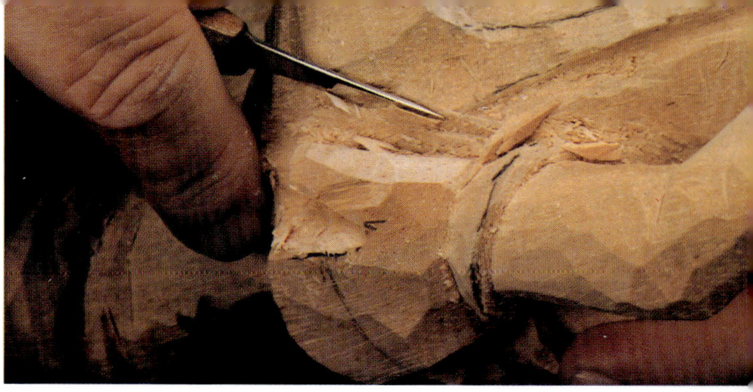

Cut back into the stop along the surface of the trousers. This will lift the thumb away from the body.

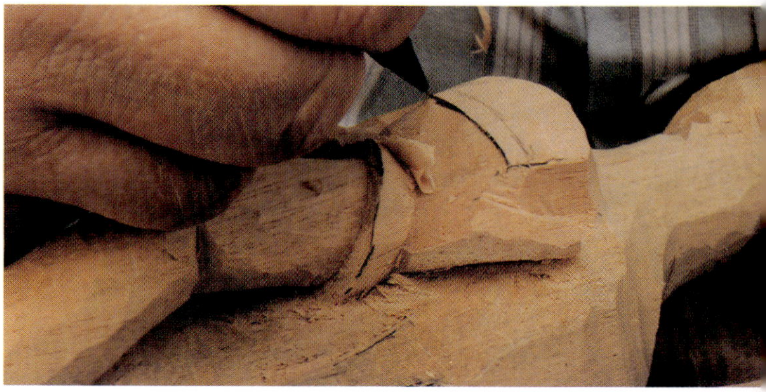

The flat plane of the back of the hand ends at about the knuckle of the thumb.

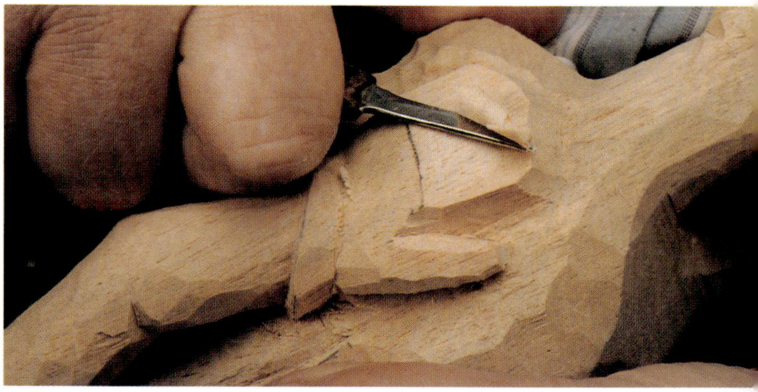

Establish a plane from the line back to the cuff and one from the line to the end of the fingers.

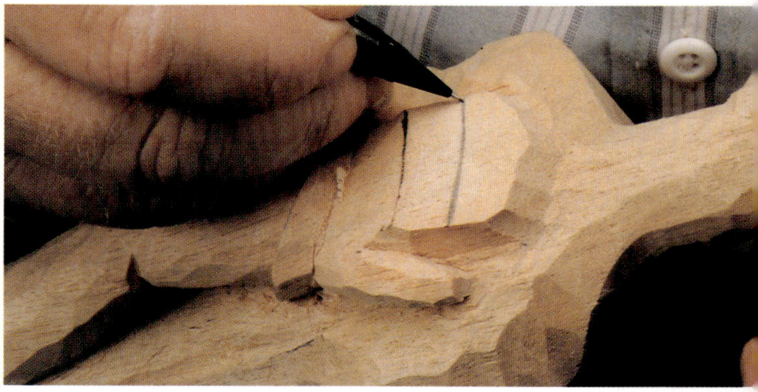

The finger plane is divided again at the line of the finger knuckles.

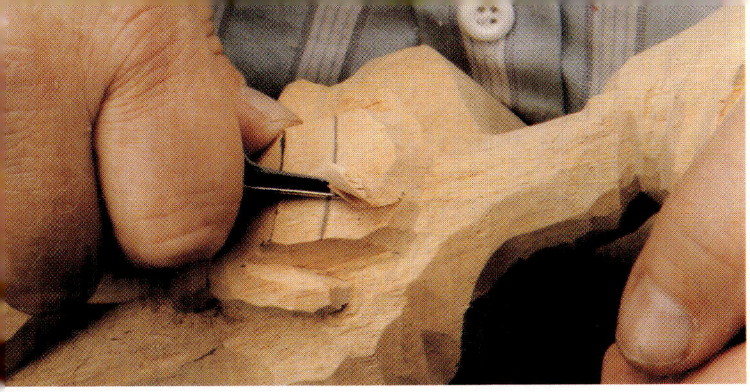

Carve from there to the end of the fingers creating a third plane.

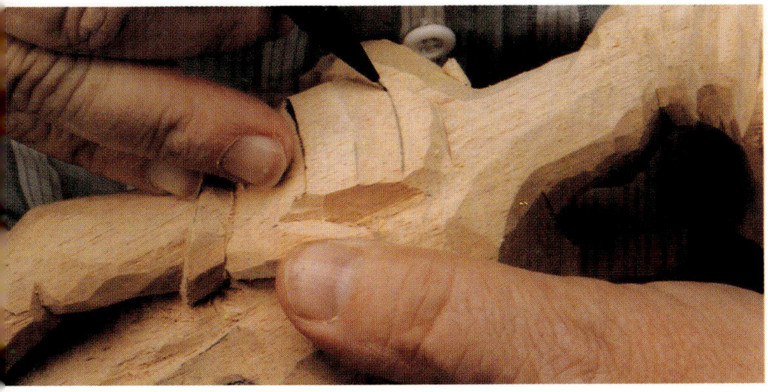

One more plane, the tips of the fingers, starts at the last joint.

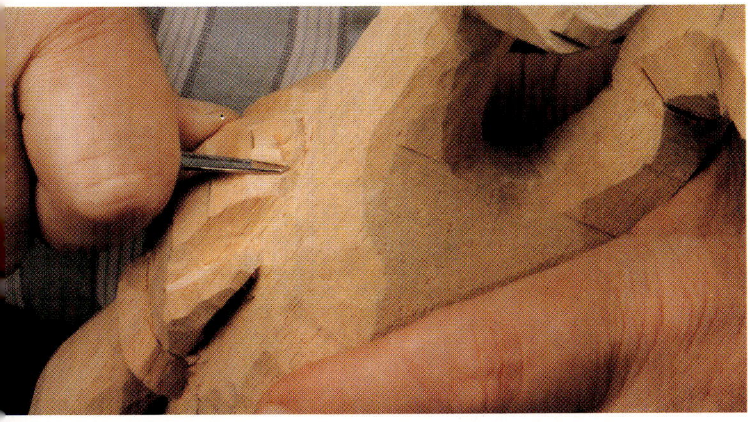

Carve the last plane to the end of the fingers.

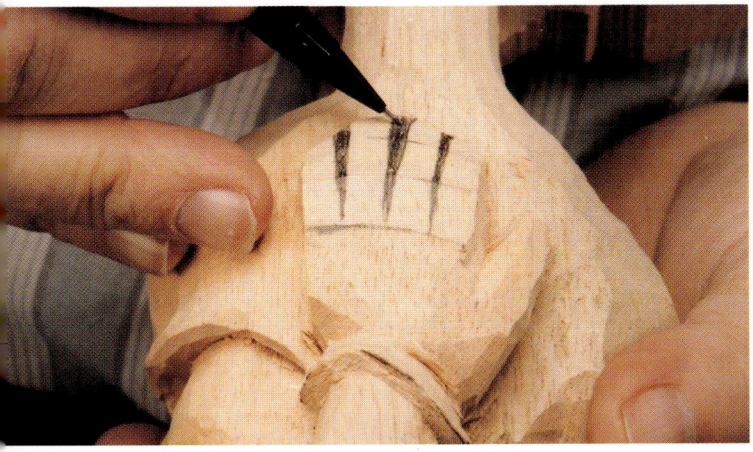

Draw the spaces between the fingers.

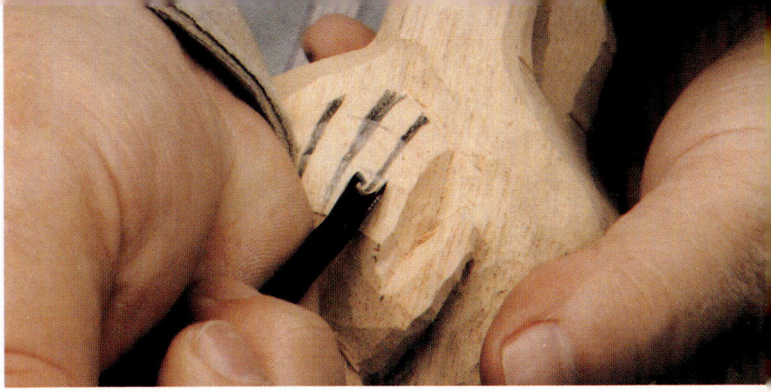

Carve the spaces...

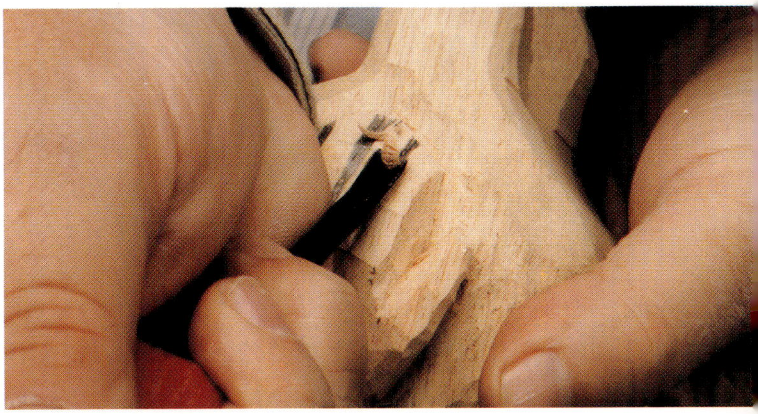

one segment at a time.

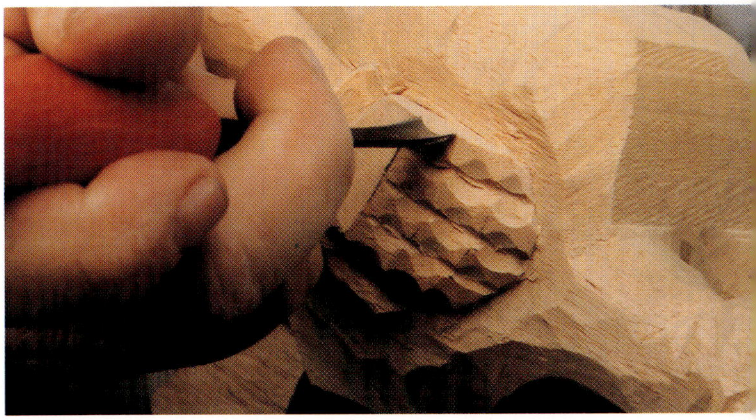

Carve the edge of each joint with a gouge to give it shape.

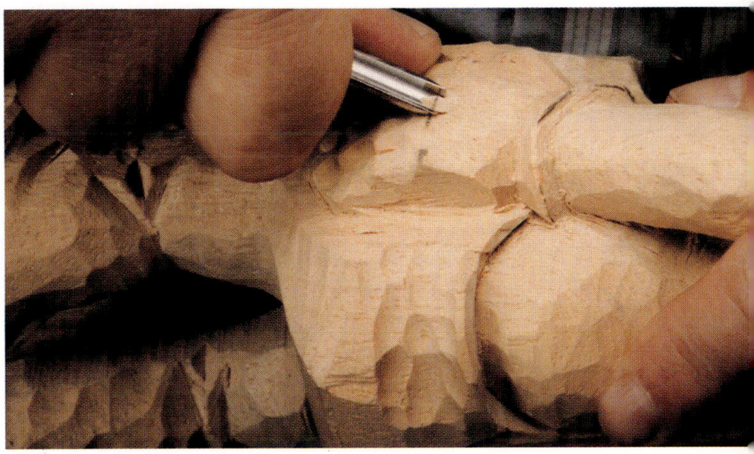

Run the gouge between the knuckles at the back of the glove.

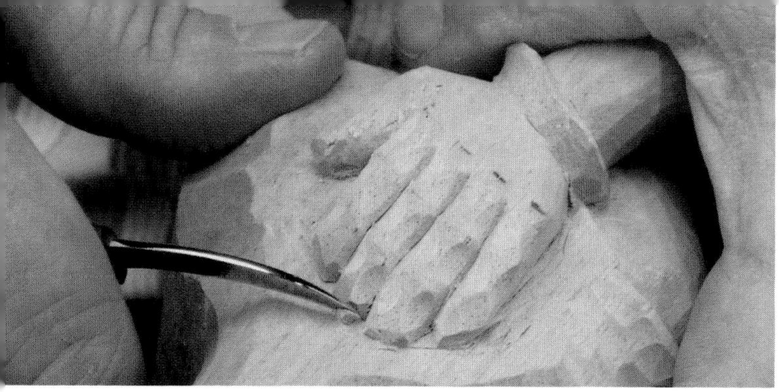

Go back and refine the glove, rounding off things like the fingertips.

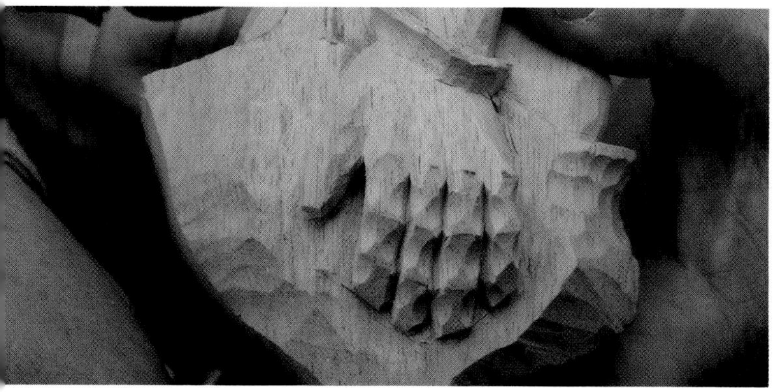

Progress.

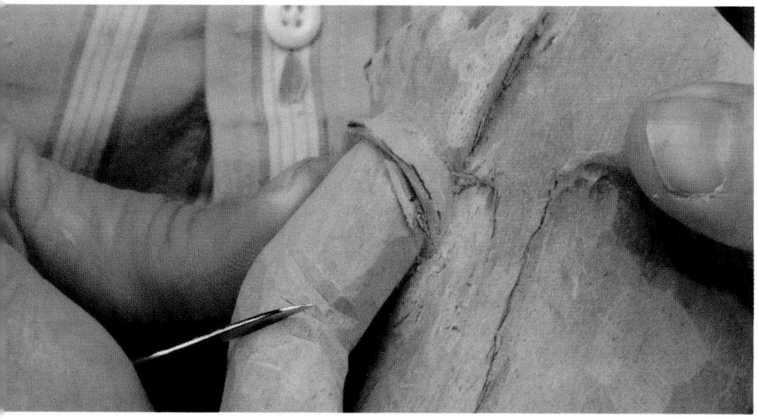

Cut slices at the elbow to create stress wrinkles.

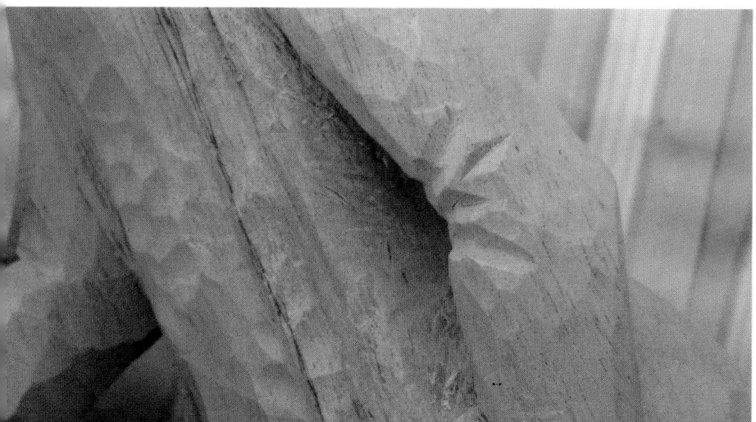

The result.

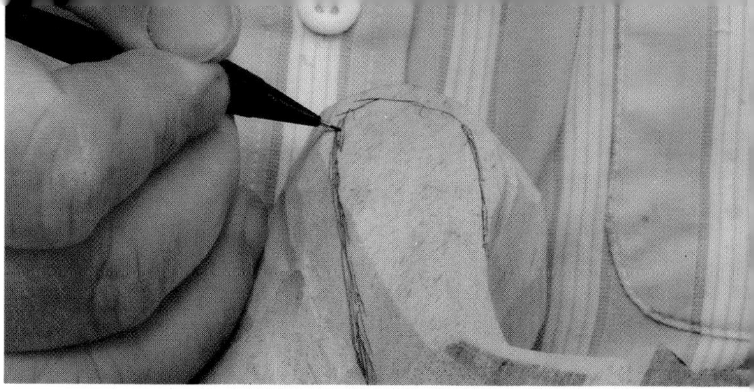

Moving to the right arm, we need to thin it to match the left. The line gives me some idea where I'm heading.

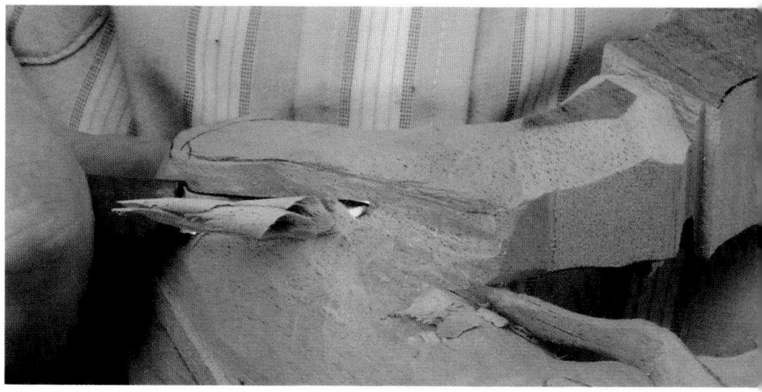

Trim the arm down to size.

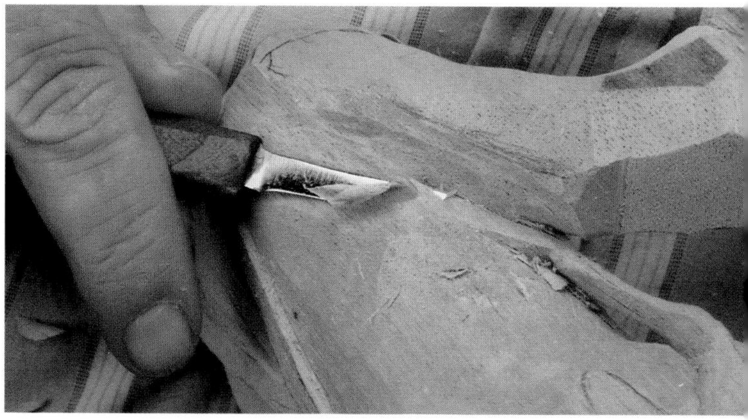

Narrow the back to blend.

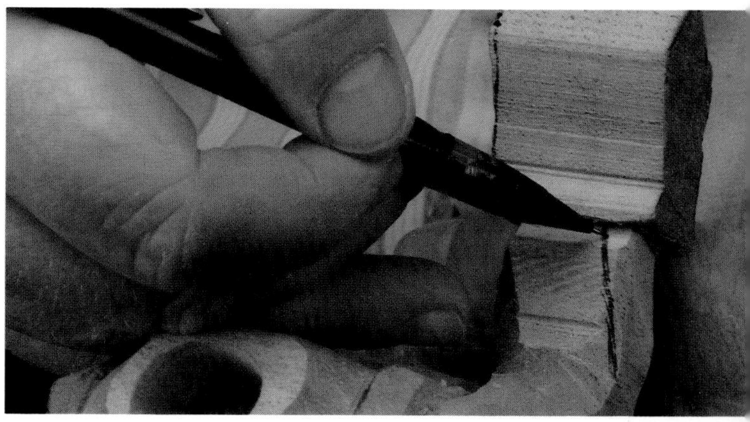

I want the forearm to come in a little bit. Make sure it is the same size as the other arm.

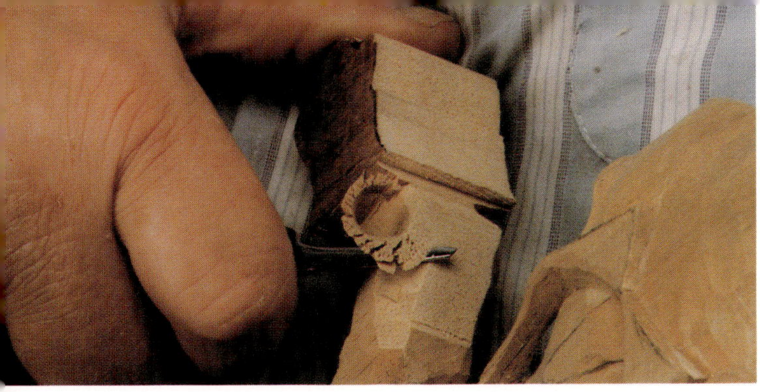

Trim the forearm.

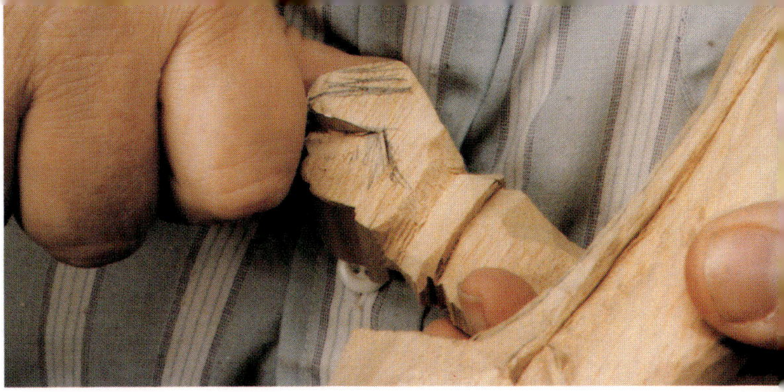

Make a stop cut on the lower line...

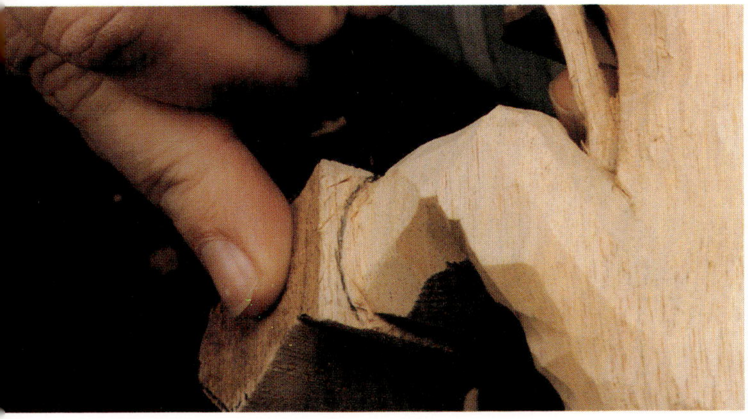

With the forearm trimmed, draw the edge of the cuff.

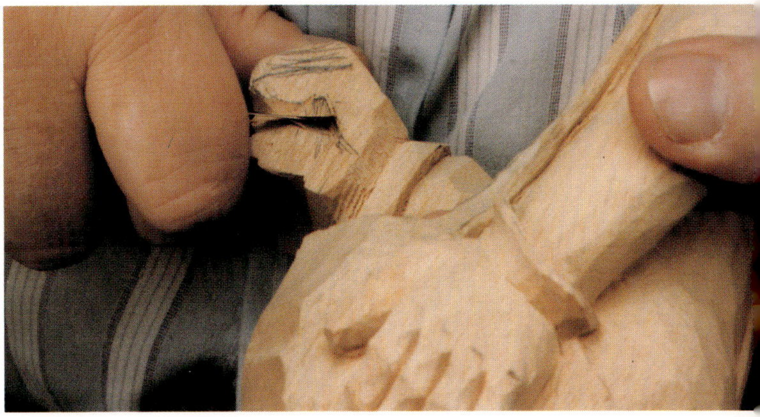

and trim back to it from the palm.

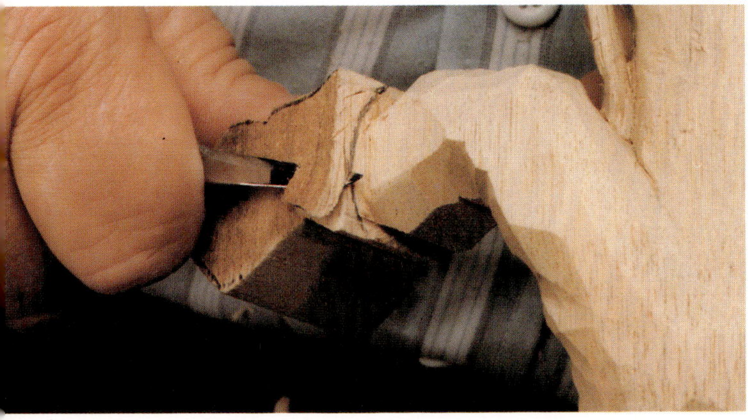

Cut the cuff down to the line.

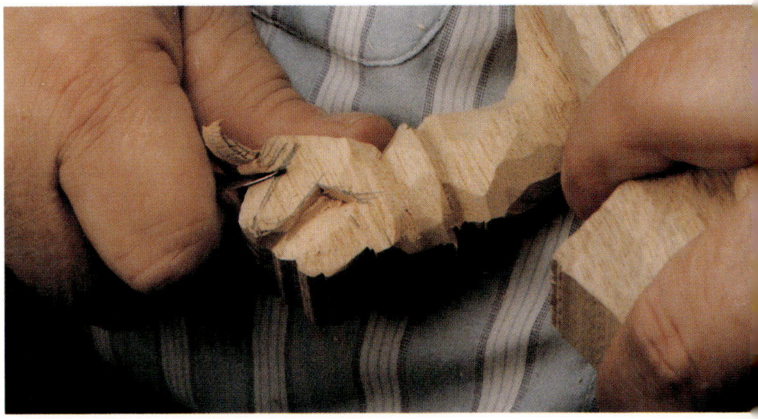

Remove the area above the thumb.

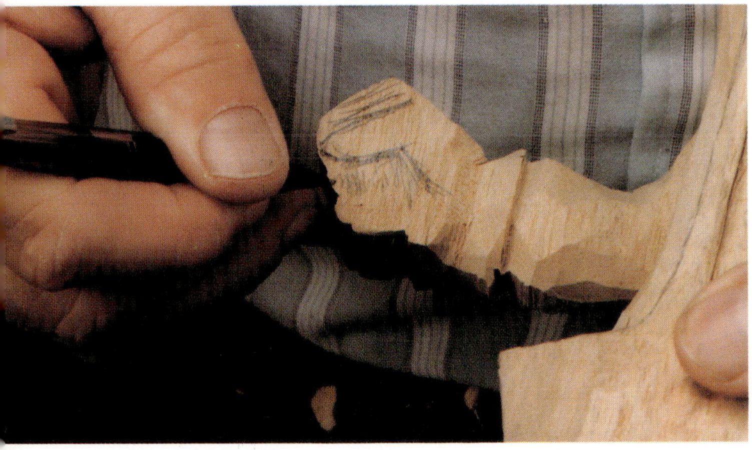

Draw in the thumb.

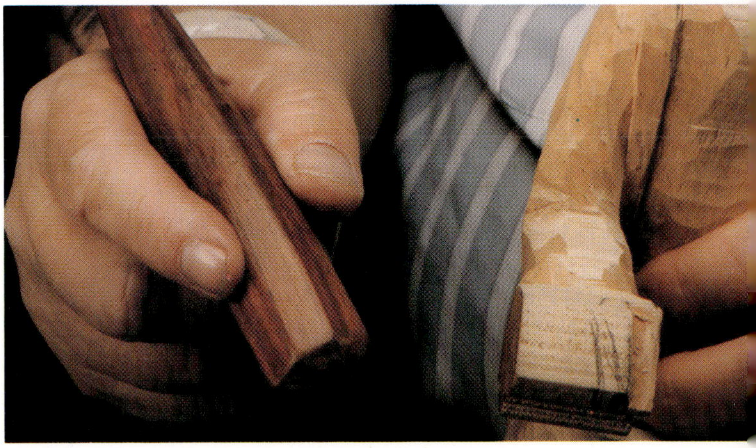

I want the clown to hold the cigar like you would a fat pencil.

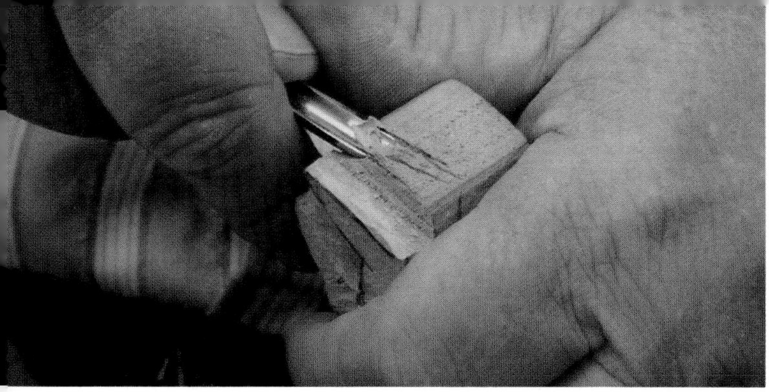

Create the gap for the cigar with a gouge. The gouge can easily slip and cut you, so I use the forefinger of the tool hand as a depth gauge and stop. At the same time I use the thumb of my other hand to provide a counterpressure for support.

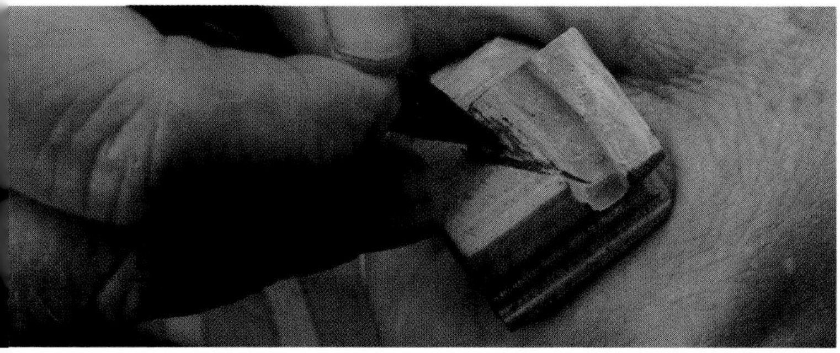

The forefinger will be crooked more than the others, so I need to take the darkened area out.

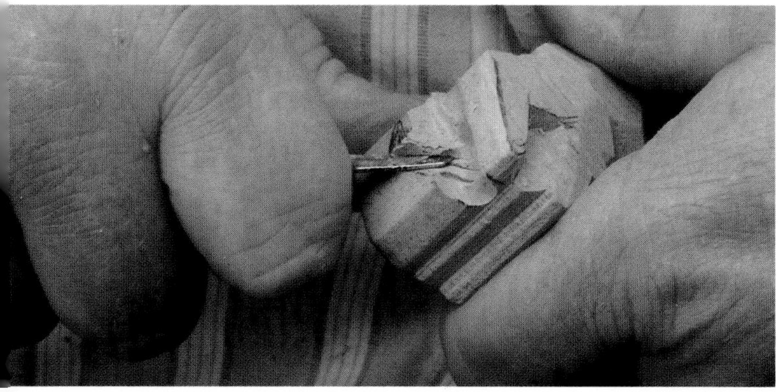

Carve it away with a knife.

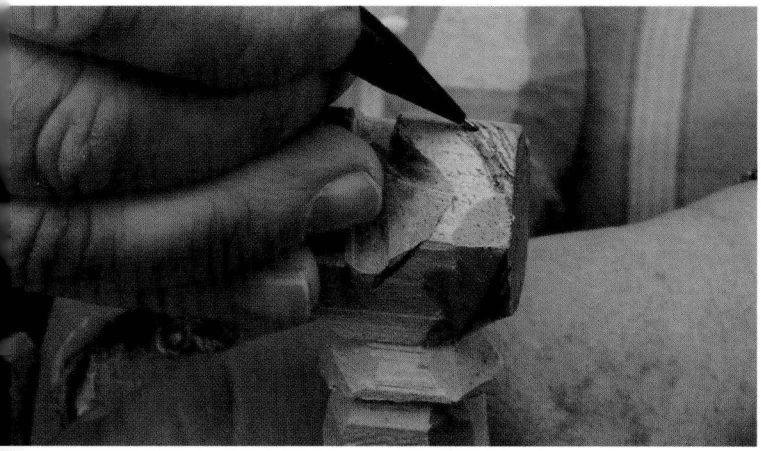

Mark the outside outline of the forefinger.

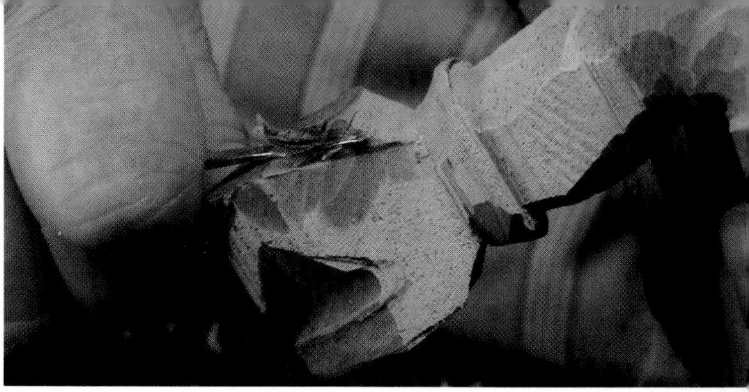

Pop off the back of the hand...

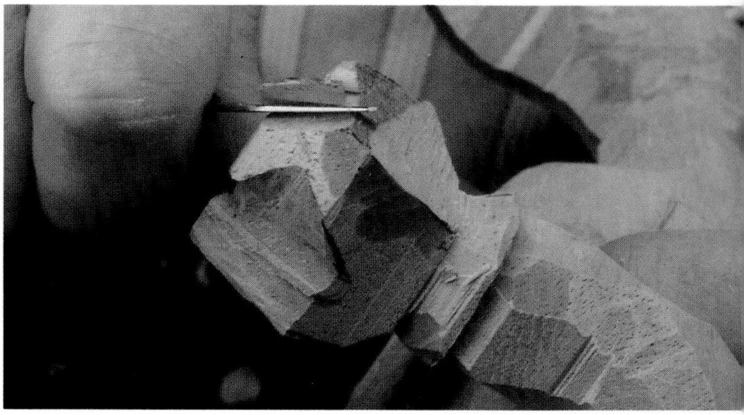

and the plane of the finger.

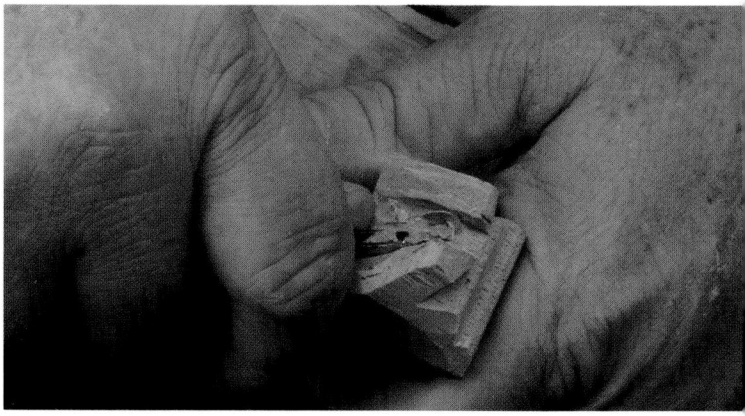

With a small gouge, open up the hand so you can see down into it. the cigar will cover most of this.

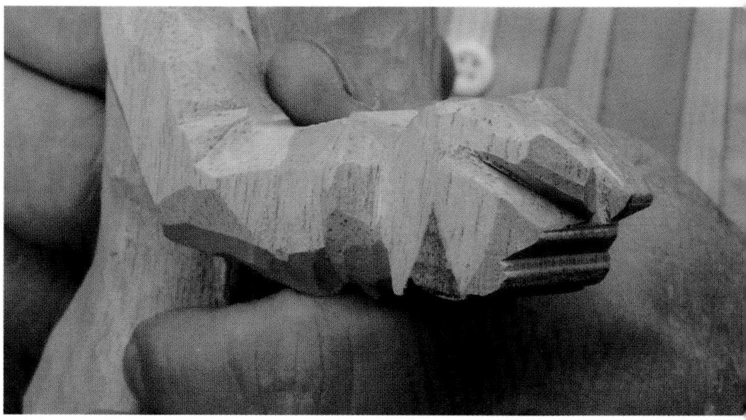

Progress.

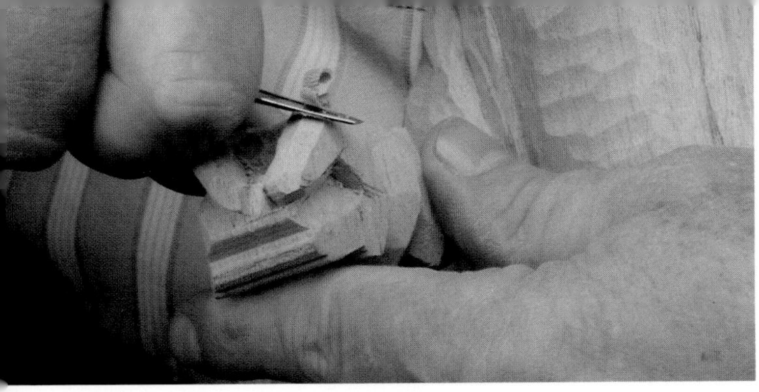

Round the thumb off while you're near it.

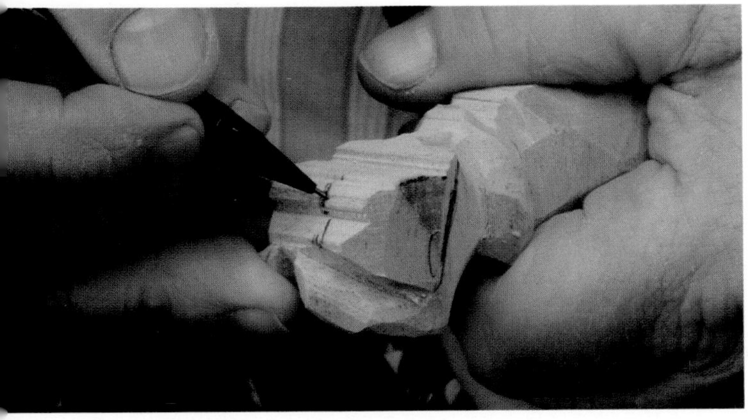

Mark the first two knuckles of the hand.

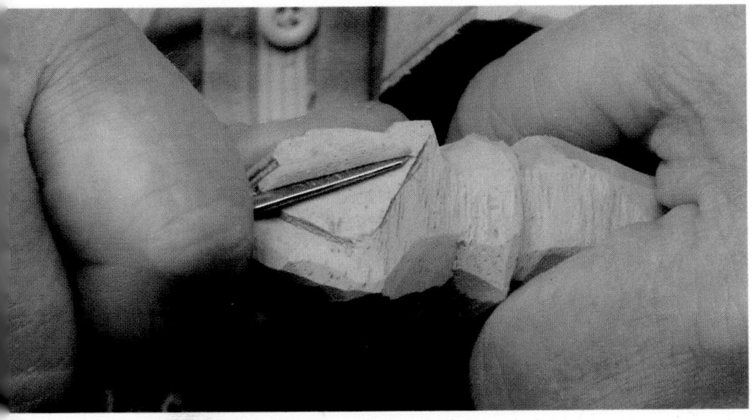

Carve the plane of the first finger segment.

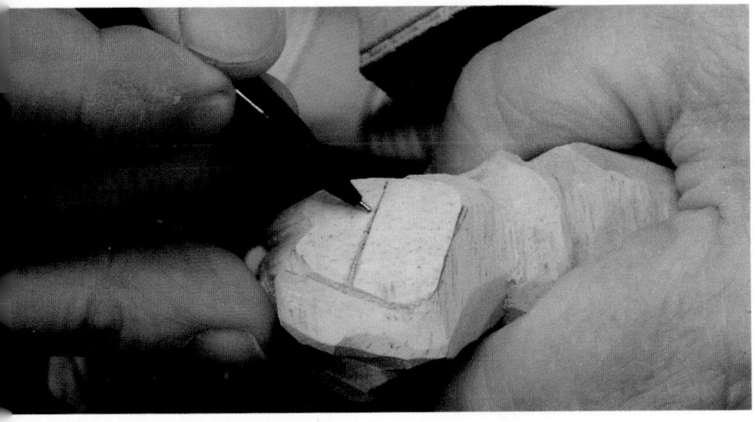

Draw the line of the second segment. This is for the three lower fingers where they come beneath the forefinger.

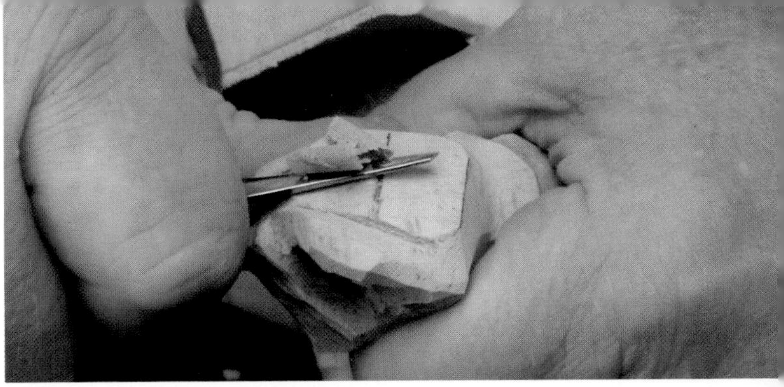

Start on the inside of forefinger, carve the plane.

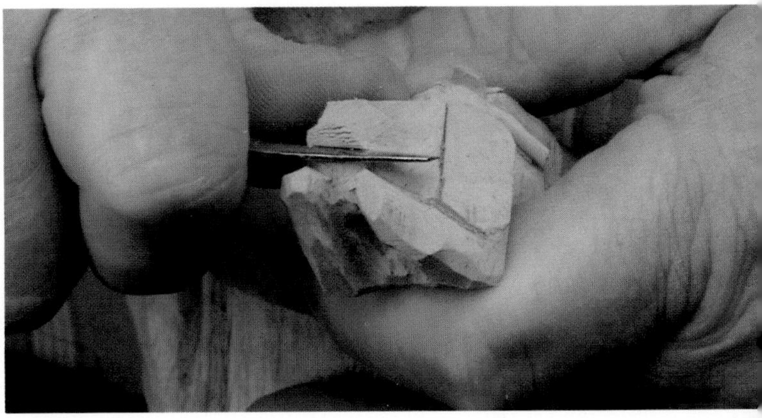

Remove the excess below the thumb and forefinger, carrying the plane all the way across.

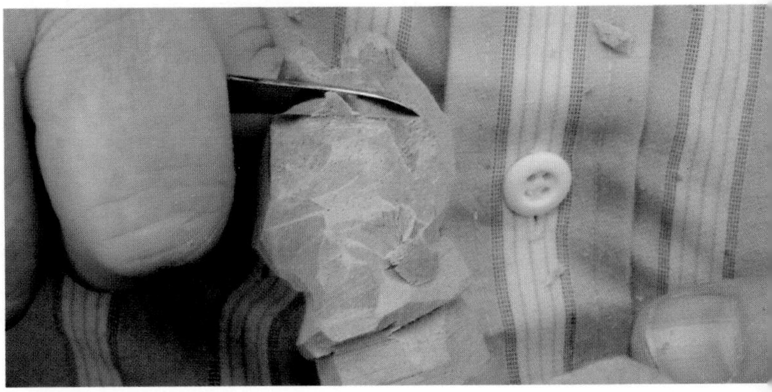

Working under the thumb is dangerous, so be careful.

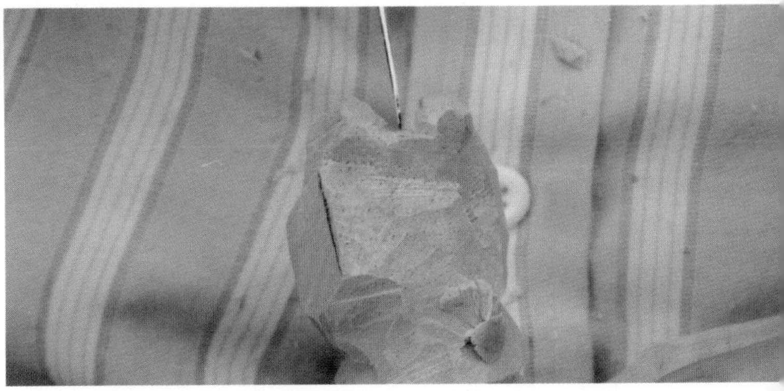

This little piece between the thumb and forefinger should come off for realism, but that would severely weaken the thumb. The cigar should hide it pretty well, though. Sometimes its a trade-off between accuracy and strength.

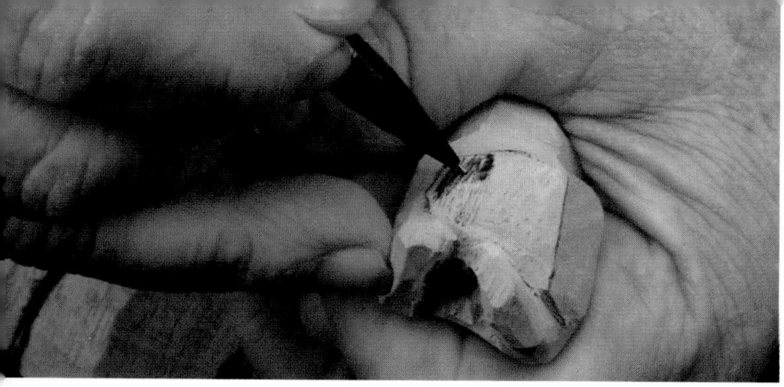

The last segment of the finger turns into the thumb. By removing the darkened area I leave the finger tips.

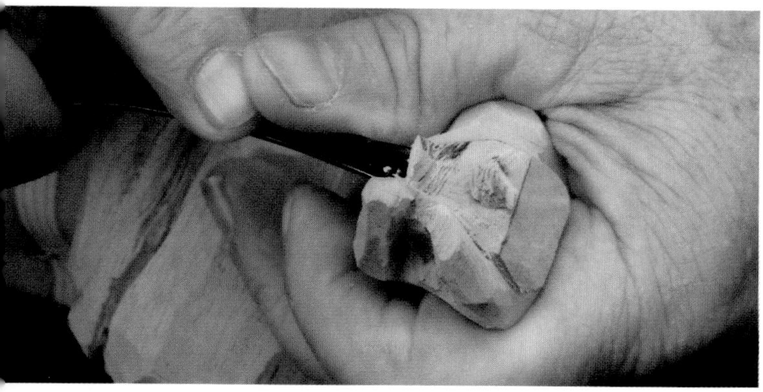

Come in with a gouge.

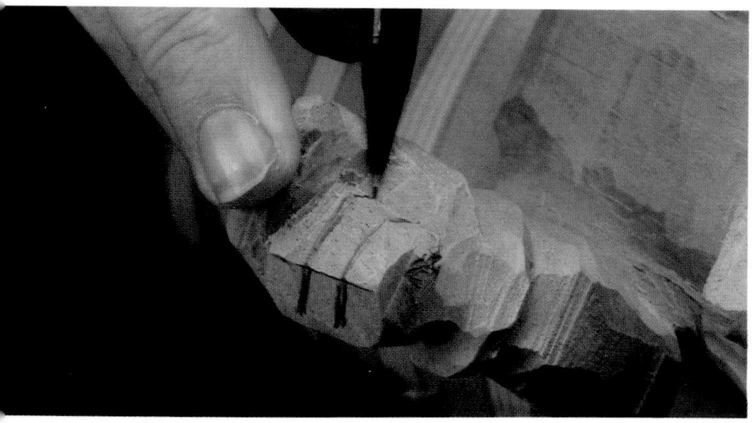

Draw in the lines of the lower three fingers.

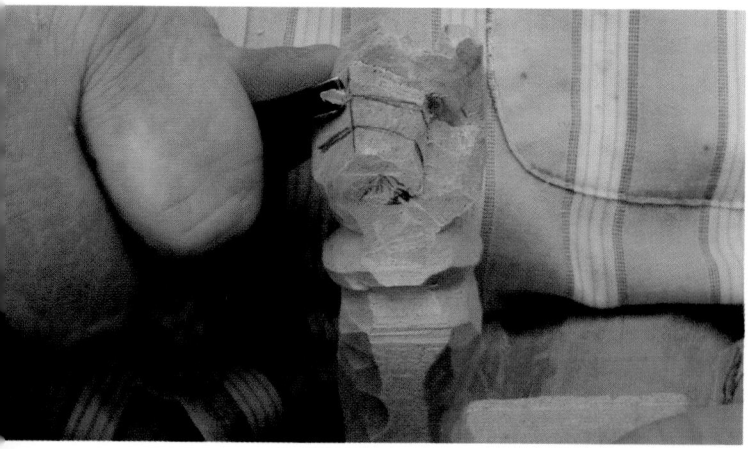

Run a v-tool between the fingers.

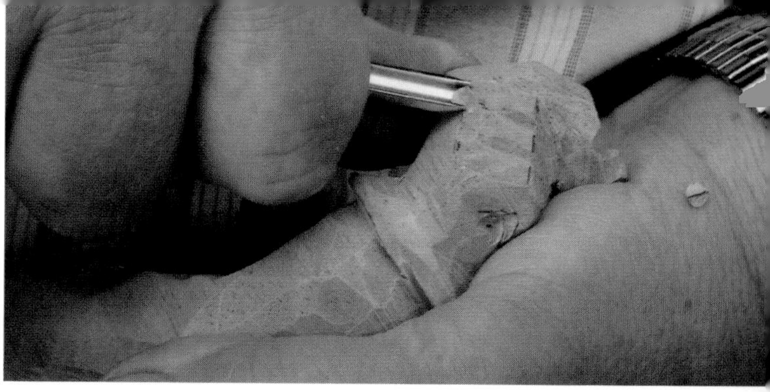

Gouge between the upper knuckles...

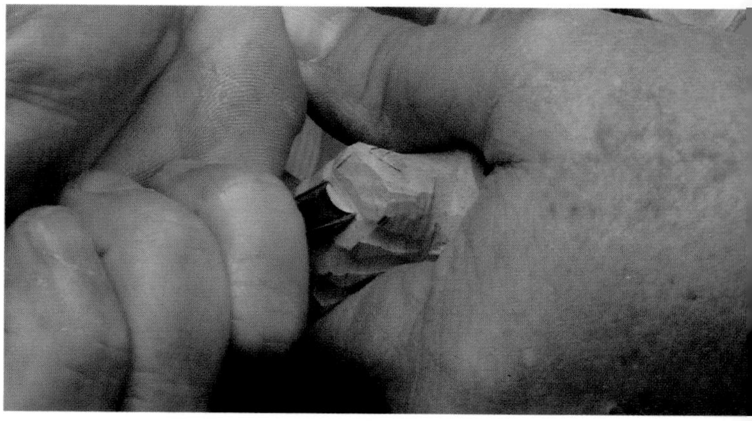

and shape the finger segments.

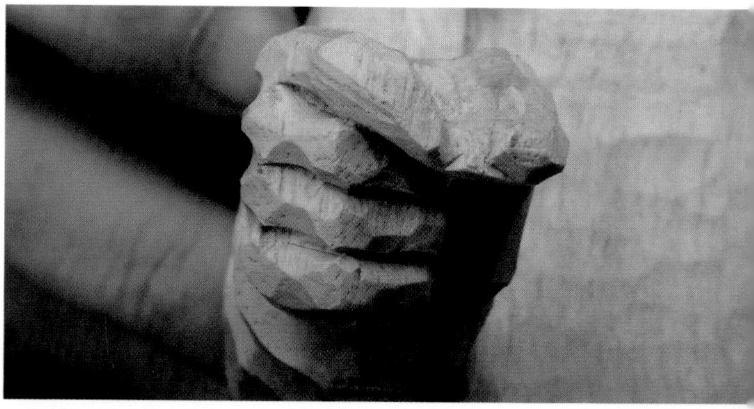

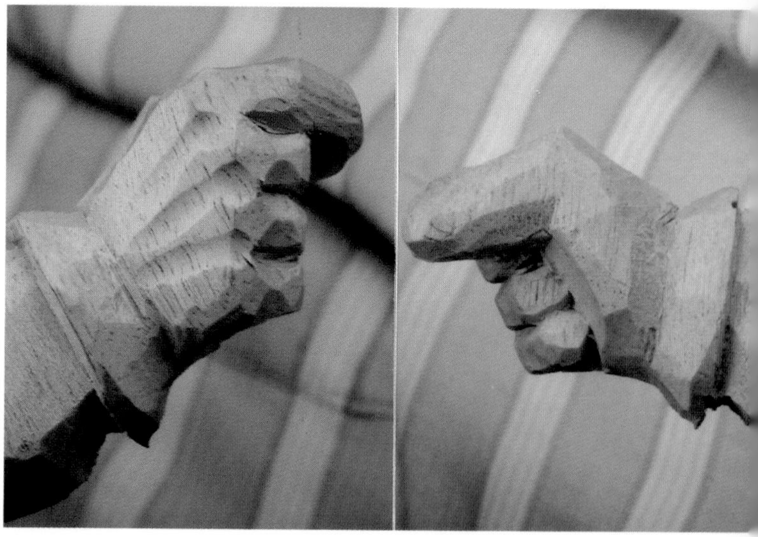

Progress.

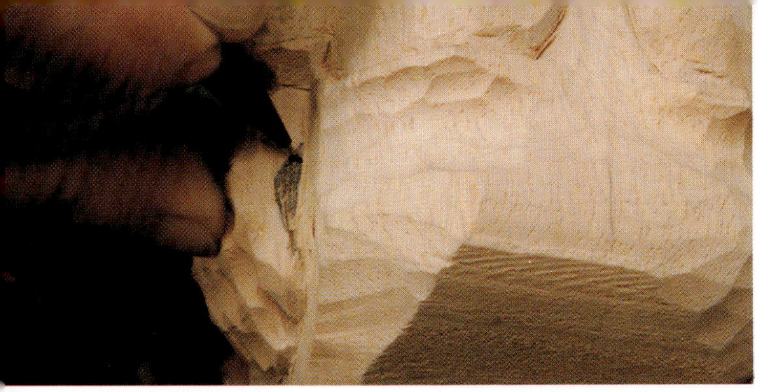

The left hand needs to be cupped away from the body.

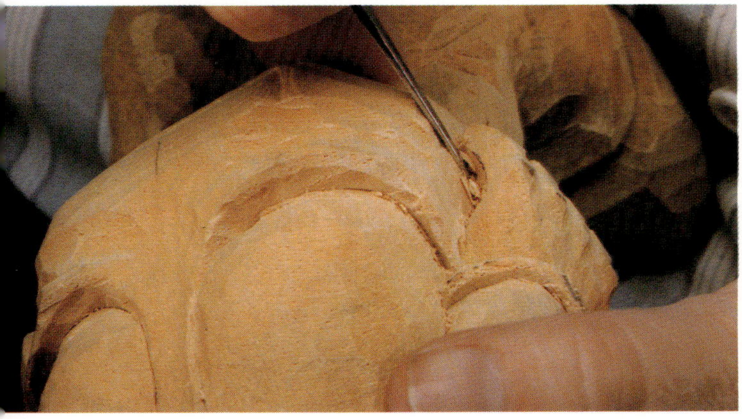

Clean it out with a knife. Undercutting like this makes the piece a lot more believable.

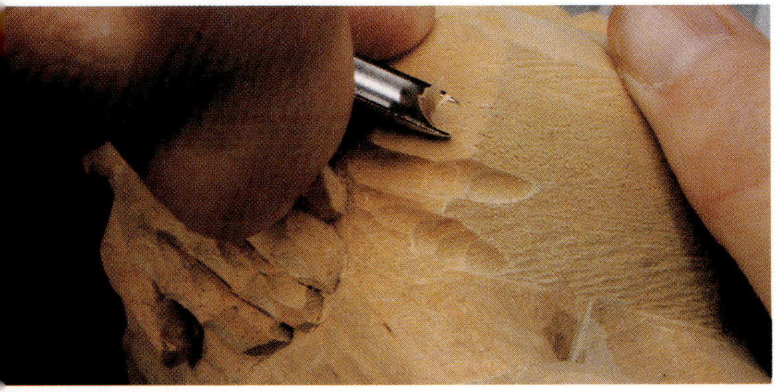

Gouge some folds in the seat of the britches to give them a baggier look.

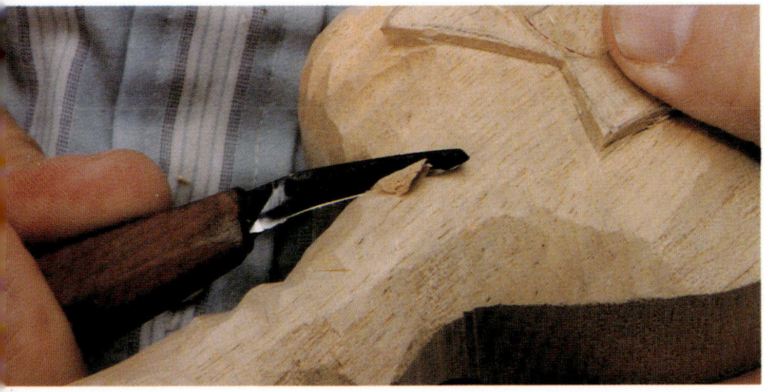

Go over the britches, smoothing things out and adding a wrinkle where it is needed.

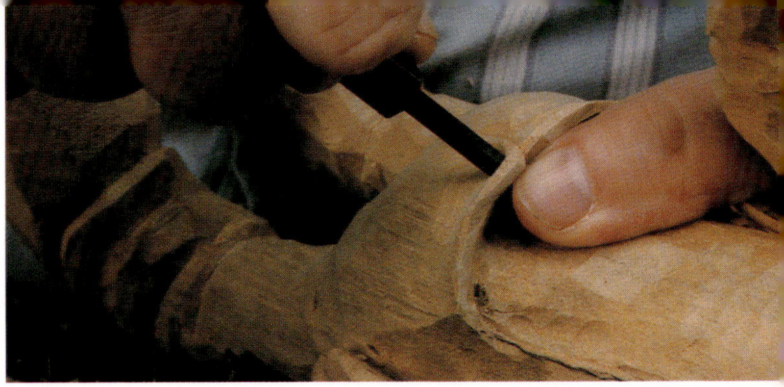

Use an eyepunch or nailset to add a button to the front of the pants.

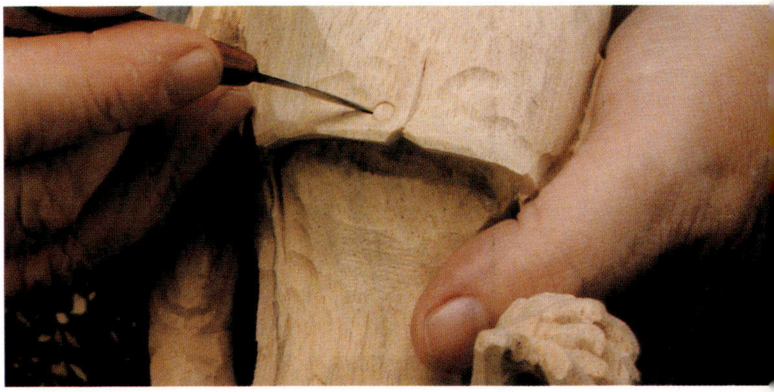

Carve a fly and a wedge to the side of the button for a button hole.

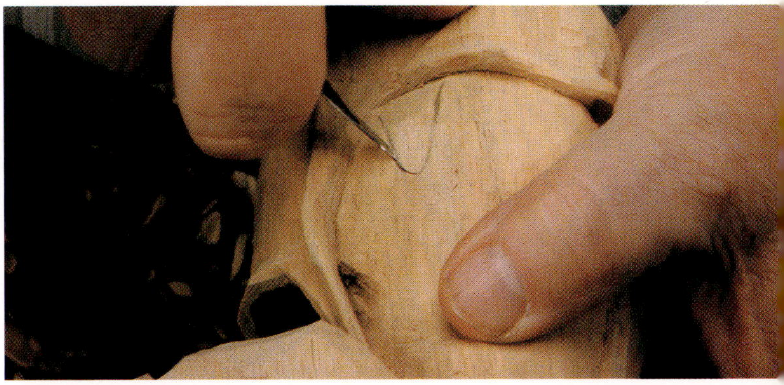

Cut around the opening in the side of the shirt to make a stop.

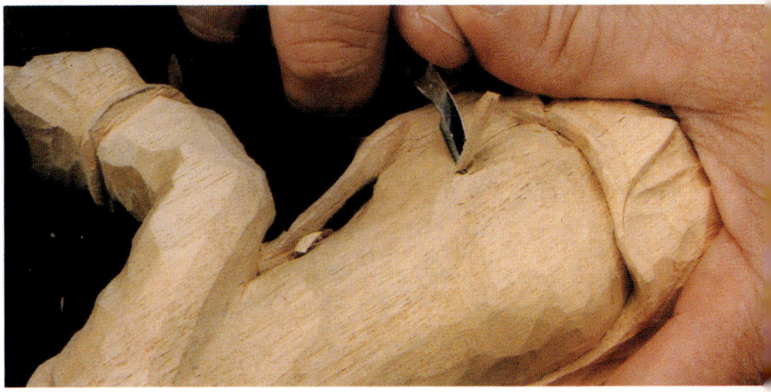

Cut back from the opening to clean it out, lowering the flesh beneath the shirt.

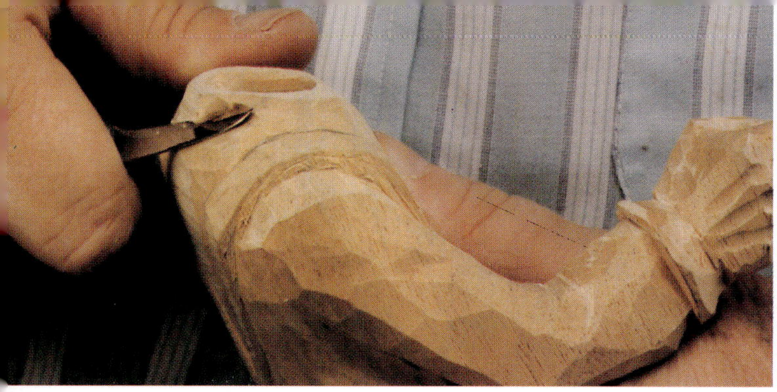

Go around the neck with a scooping cut to leave a little sweat shirt collar.

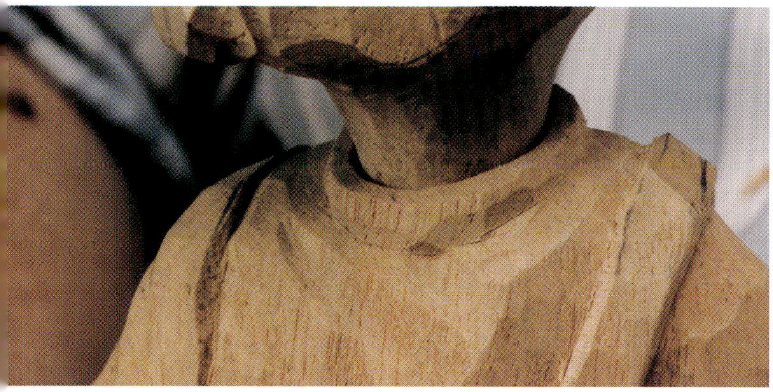

The result.

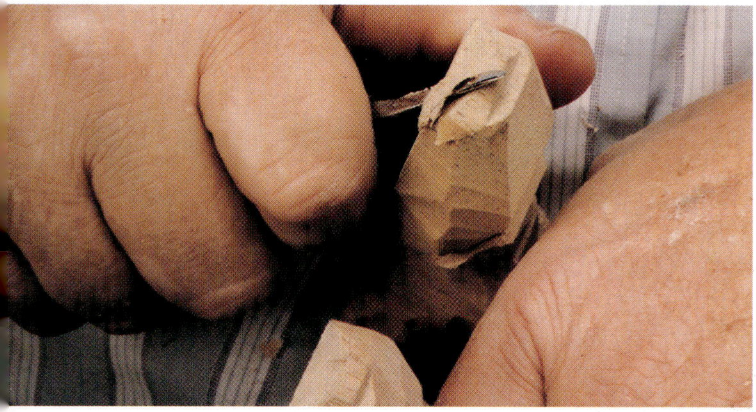

Smooth and round off the shoes.

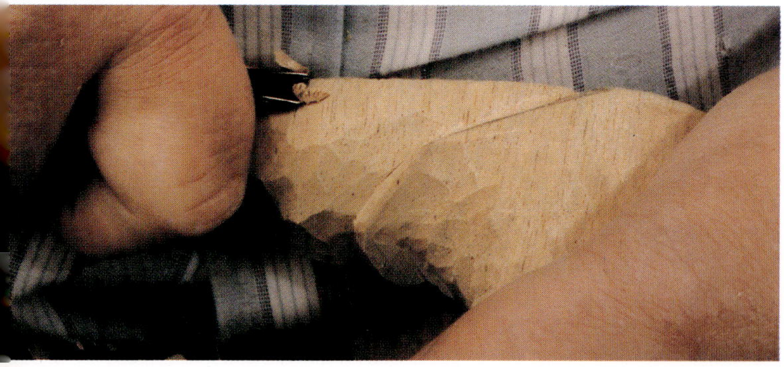

Establish the line of the sole. With this wood I can go all the way around with a v-tool. The alternative is to cut a stop and trim down to it from the shoe's upper. If you use a v-tool it has to be sharp.

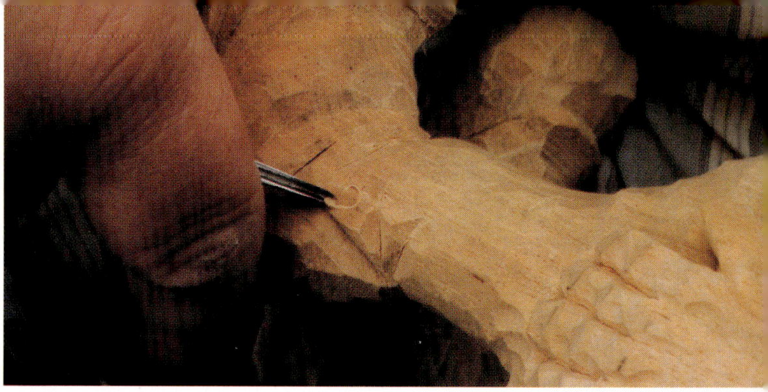

With a veiner run a seam up the outside of the britches.

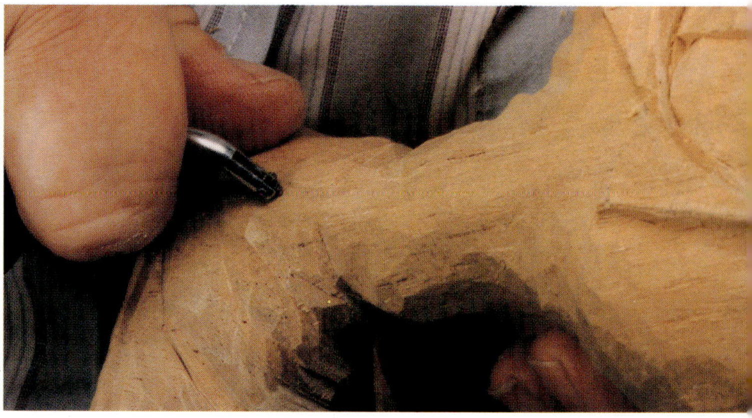

A tracing wheel run up beside the seam adds the detail of stitches.

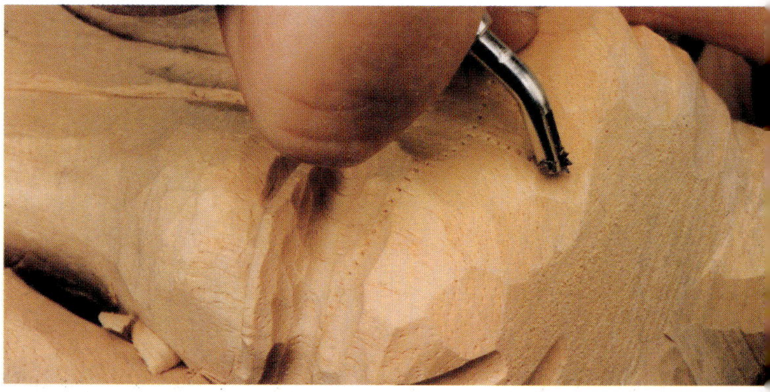

Add stitches on the saddle of the britches and down the crack, coming up beside the fly.

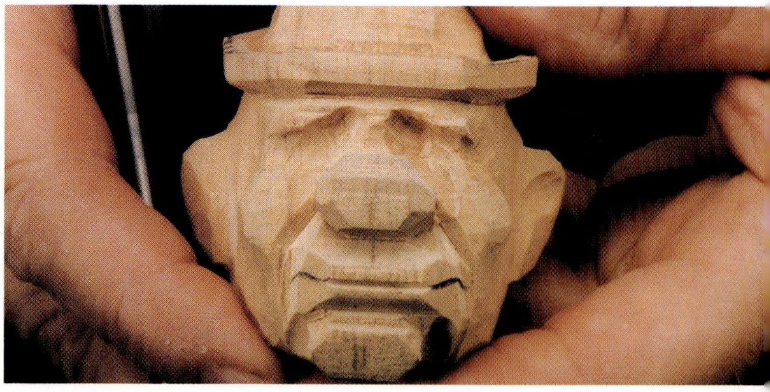

Mark the line of the mouth. I kind of want a smile and a frown at the same time, which is hard to do.

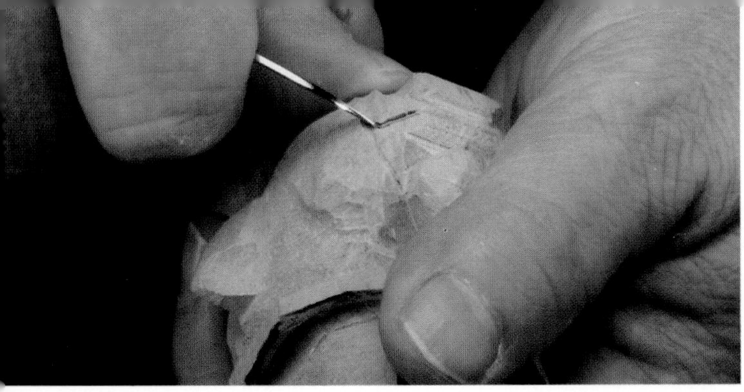

Make a stop under the upper lip...

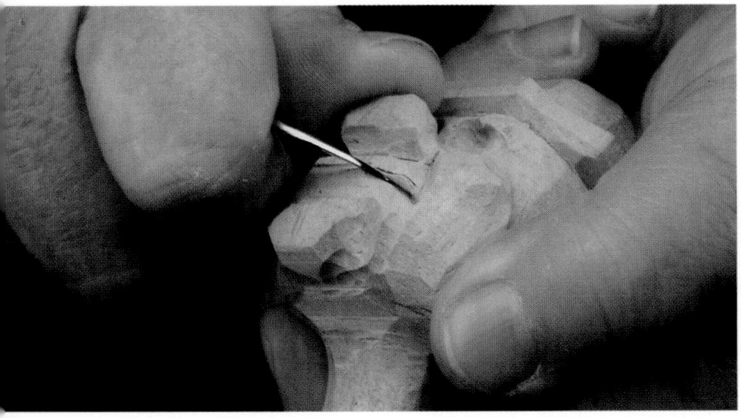

and from the bottom lip undercut it just a little bit.

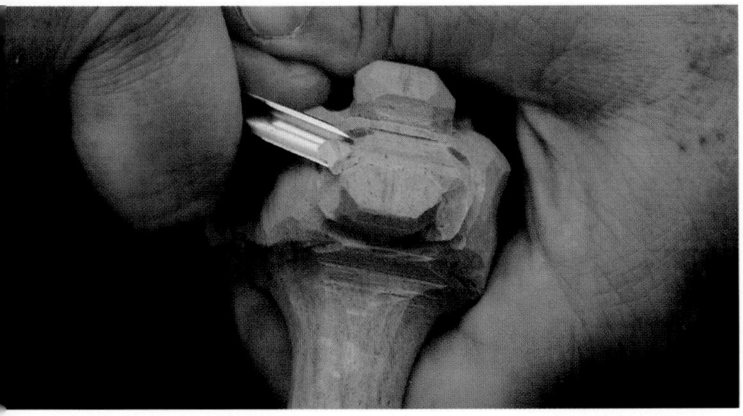

At the corners of the bottom lip come in with a gouge. This will make the lips look like the pooch out a little bit.

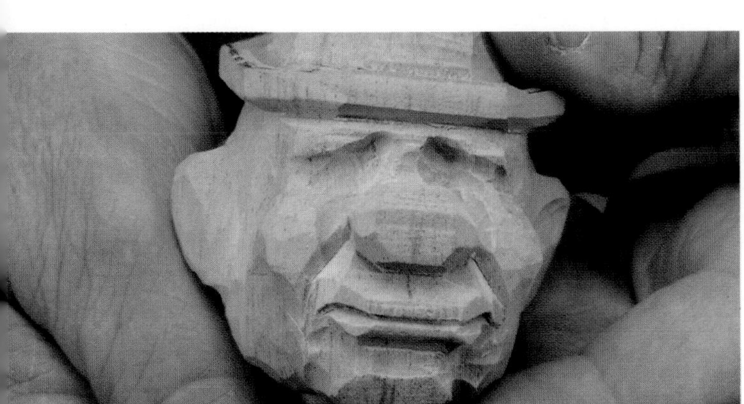

The result.

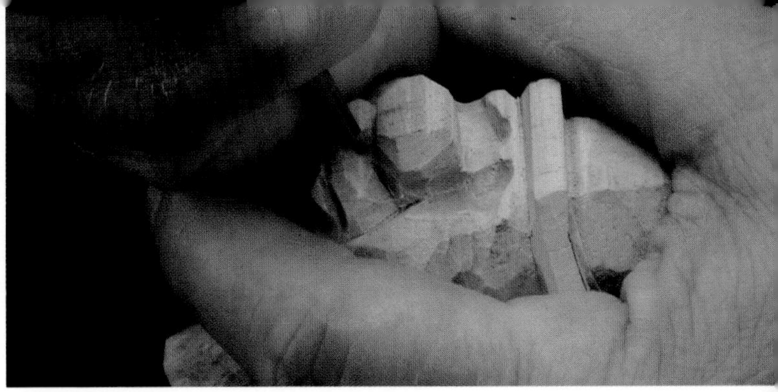

A little u-shaped gouge carves the philtrum.

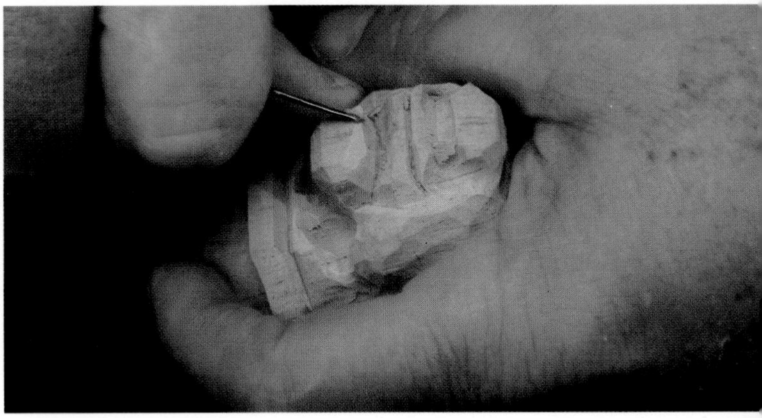

Refine the shape of the nose.

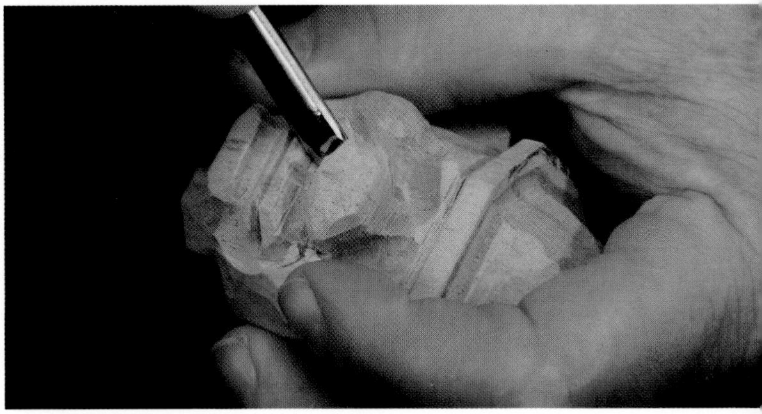

Create the nostrils by pushing straight in with a gouge.

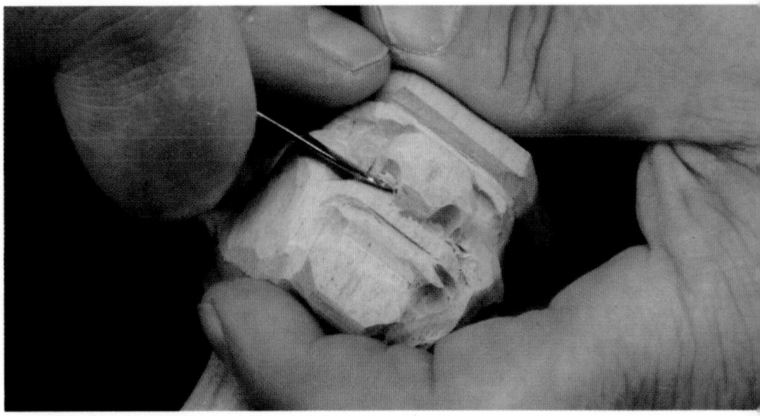

Trim it off with a knife. I'm keeping the nostrils pretty far apart to keep the bulbous look to the nose.

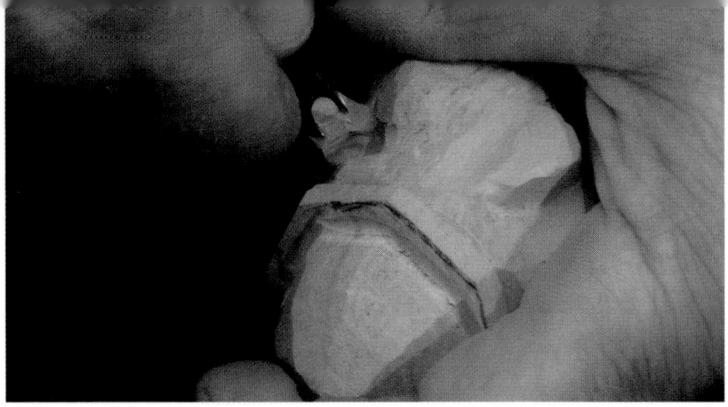

Come over the nostril flange with a gouge. Carry the cut up and around until it hits the up-and-down grain and breaks off.

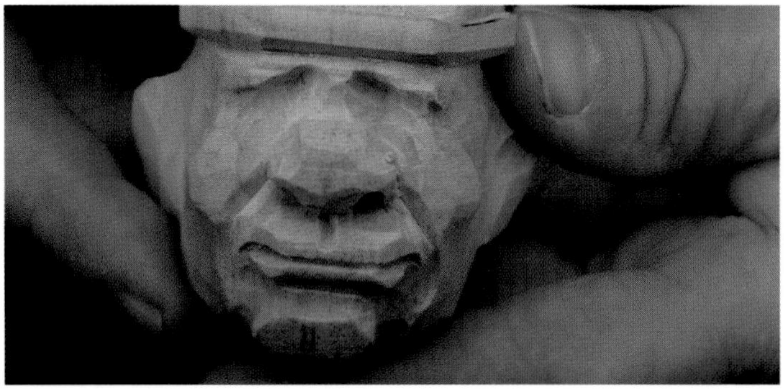

Progress on the nose and face.

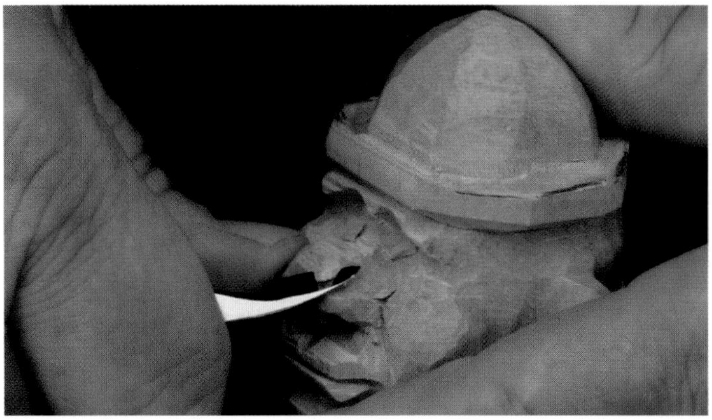

Go over the nose and face to clean everything up.

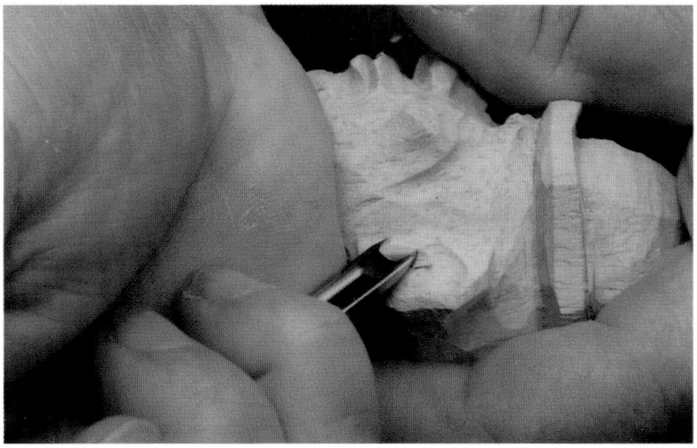

Hollow out the ear.

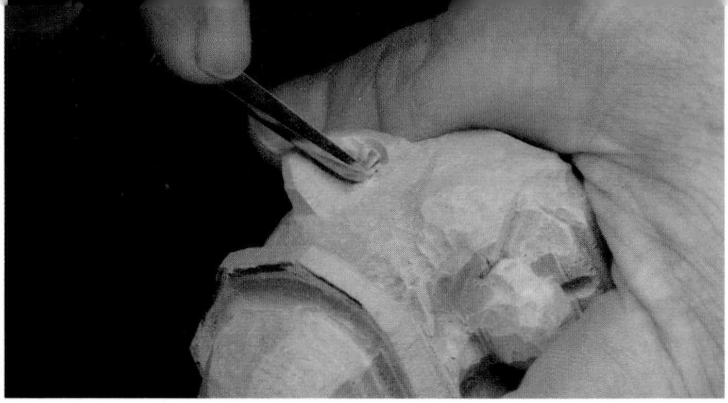

A small u-shaped gouge shapes the lower portion of the lobe ending in the ear hole...

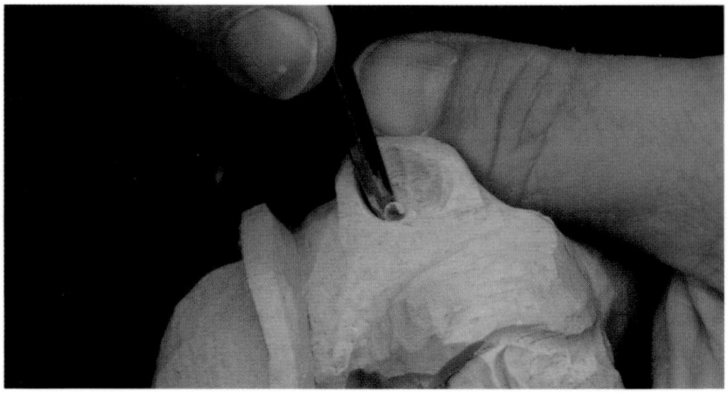

and the upper portion of the lobe.

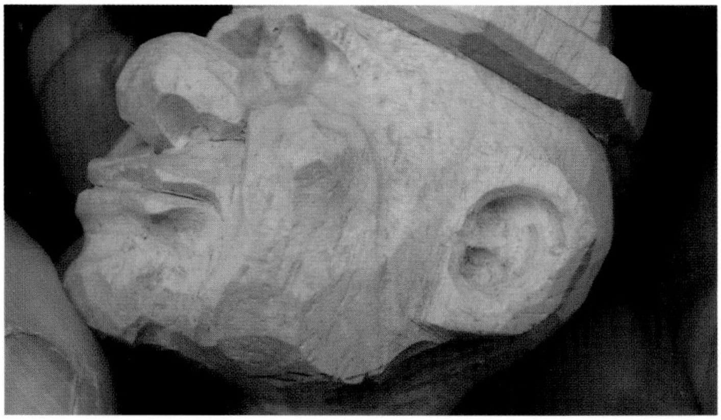

This is the result.

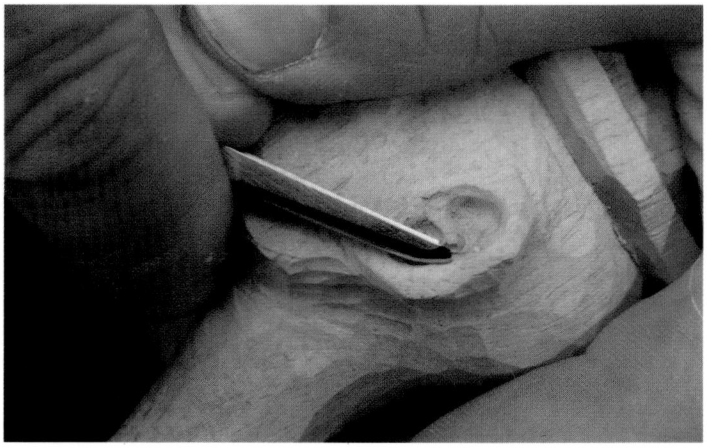

Cut a groove around the rim of the ear.

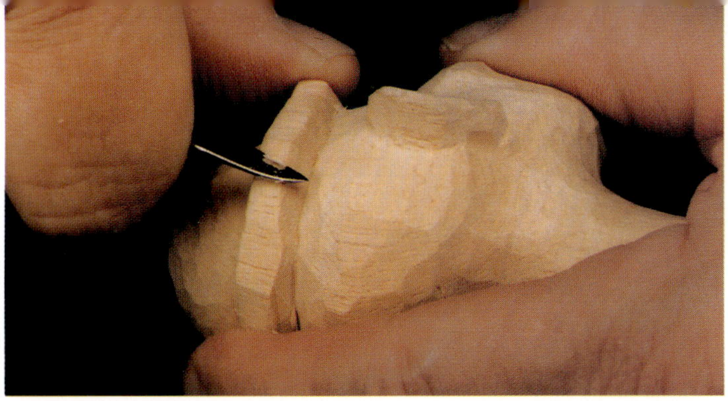

Round the brim of the hat.

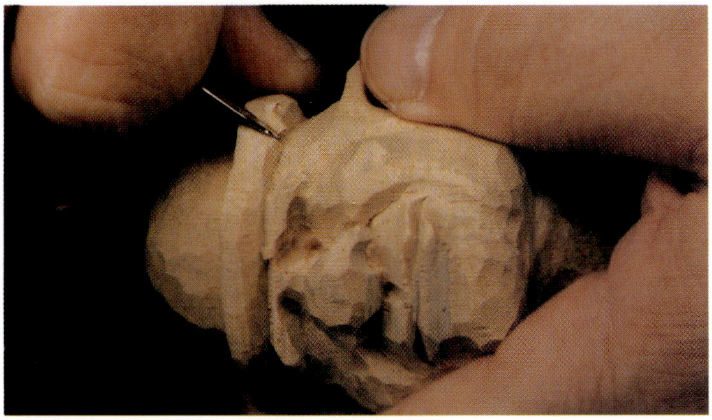

Round up the lower edge of the brim so it appears to turn up.

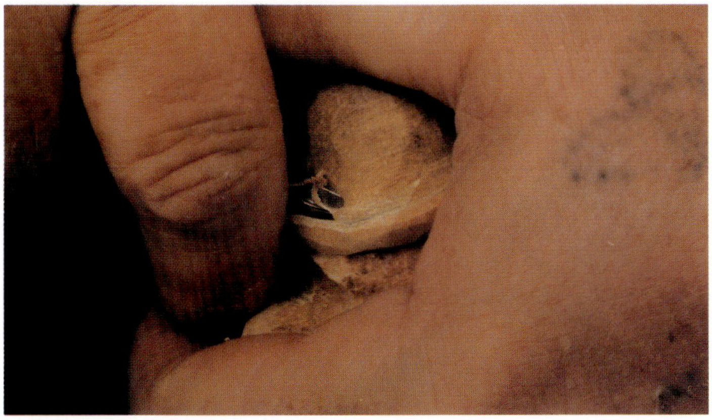

With a sharp veiner clean out the upper surface of the hat. This is fragile so use extra caution, supporting the underside of the brim with a finger.

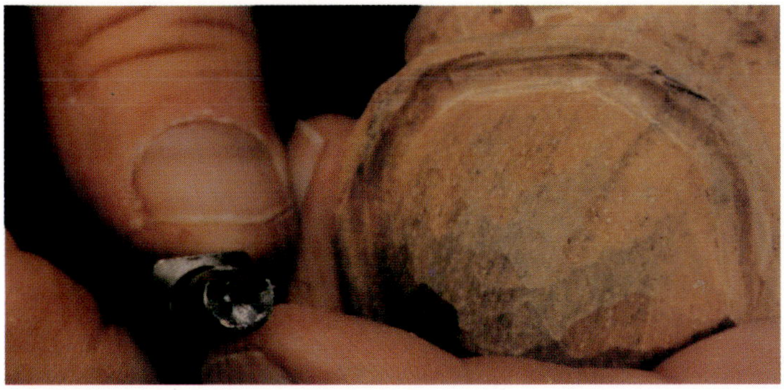

The eyepunch has about 1/4 of it ground off. This flat edge goes at the top.

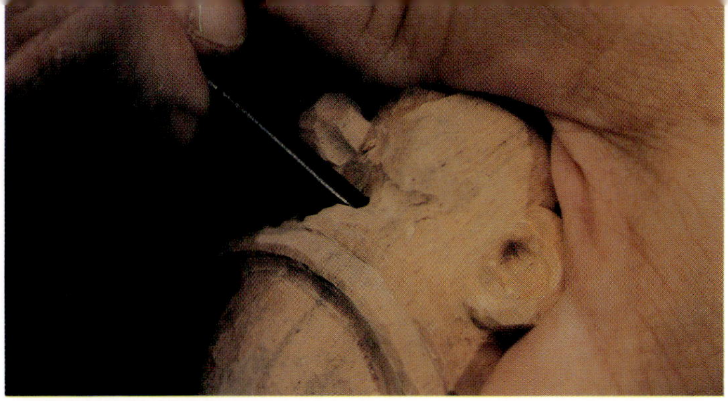

Push it in and rock it back and forth.

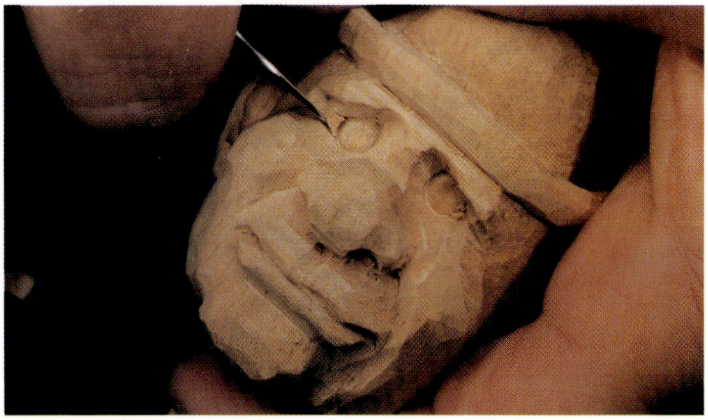

Cut a triangle at the outside corners of the eyes.

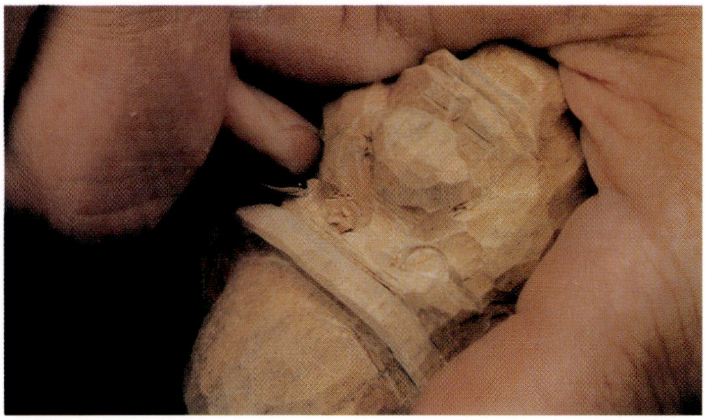

Carve the hair of the eyebrows with a veiner.

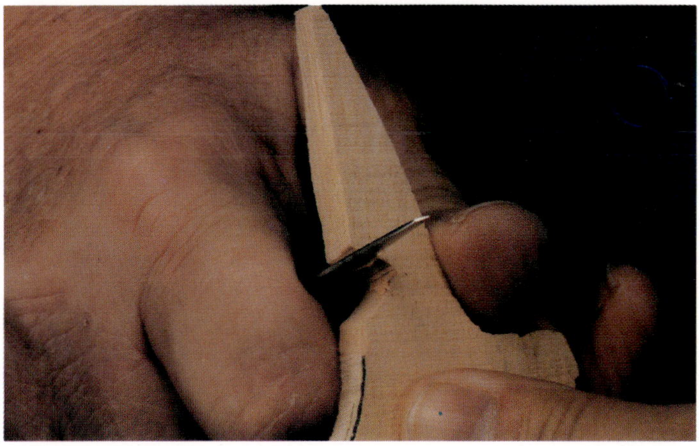

From a piece of scrap, rough out a cigar.

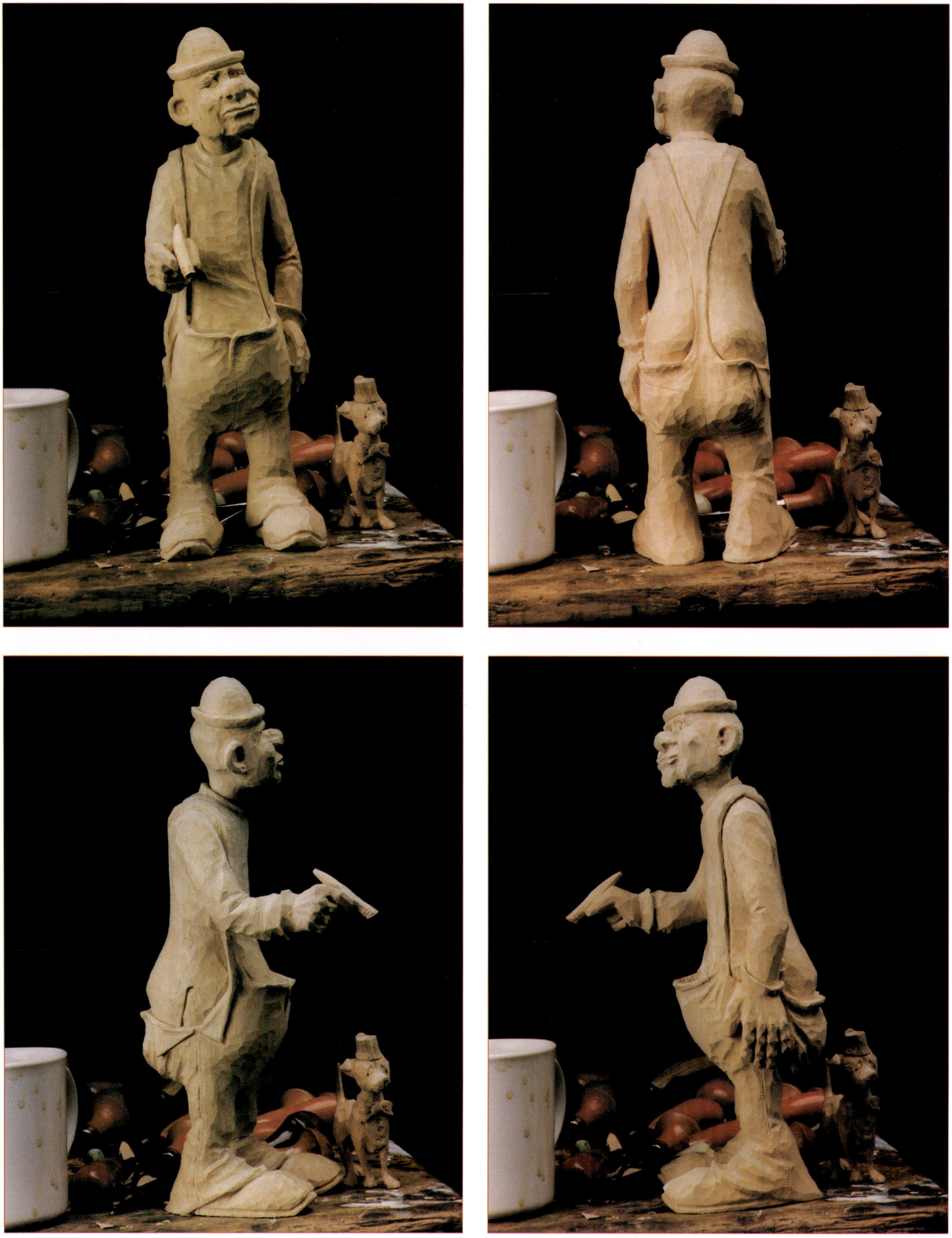

Ready for painting.

PAINTING THE CLOWN

For wood carving I use Winsor and Newton Alkyd tube paints. For most coats the paints are thinned with pure turpentine to a consistency that soaks into the carving, giving subtle colors. What I look for is a watery mixture, almost like a wash. In this way the turpentine will carry the pigment into the wood, giving the stained look I like. It has always been my theory that if you are going to cover the wood, why use wood in the first place. It should be noted that with white, the concentration of the pigment should be a little stronger. I use some pigments right from the tube to add some dry brushed highlight colors.

I mix my paints in juice bottles, putting in a bit of paint and adding turpentine. I don't use exact measurements. Instead I use trial and error, adding a bit of paint or a bit of turpentine until I get the thickness I want.

The juice bottles are handy for holding your paints. They are reclosable, easy to shake, and have the added advantage of leaving a concentrated amount of color on the inside of the lid and the sides of the bottle which can be used when more intense color is needed.

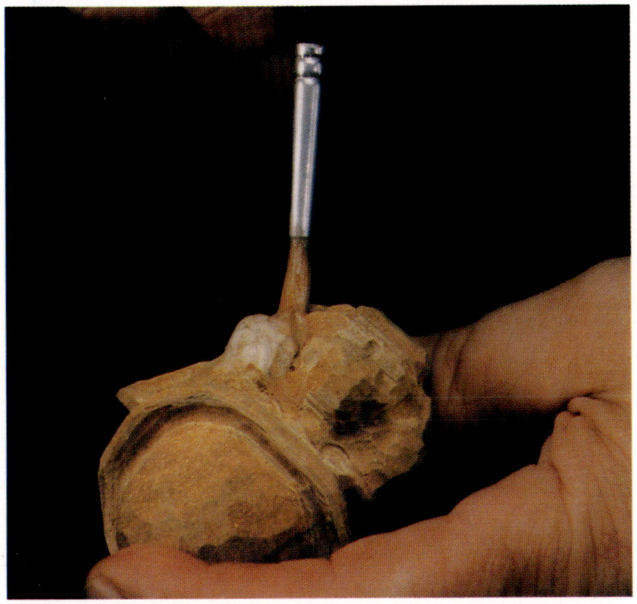

Apply an under coat of flesh tone to the skin areas and eyes. This is a mixture of white, raw sienna and a touch of pink. This doesn't cover the wood much, but gives a lively base from which to work.

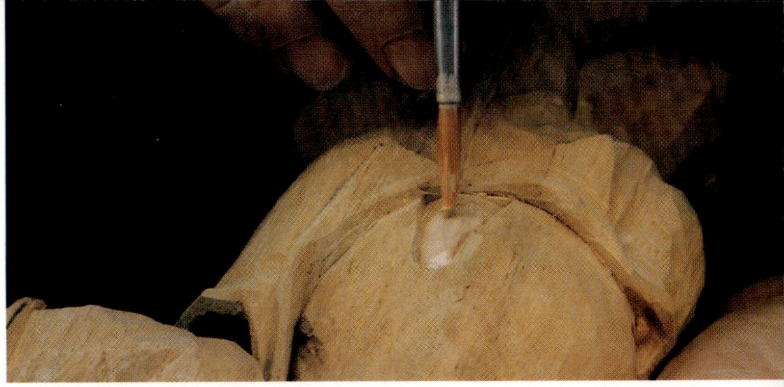

Don't forget the patch at the hip.

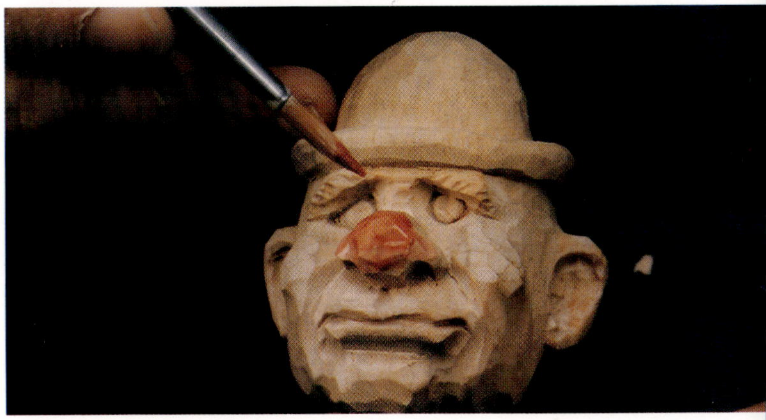

Apply red to the nose.

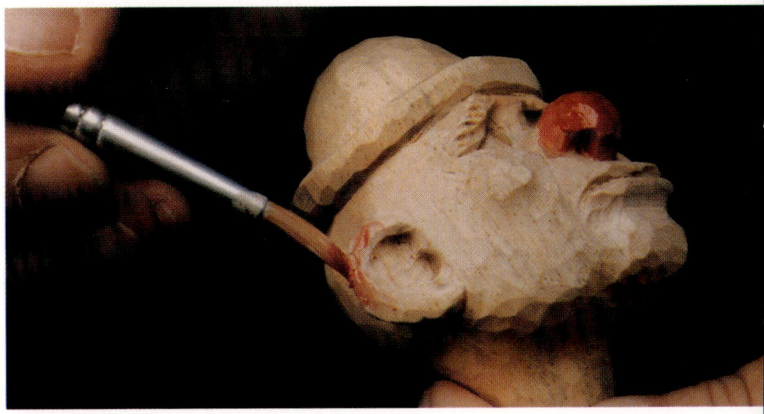

Add a red blush to the tips of the ears...

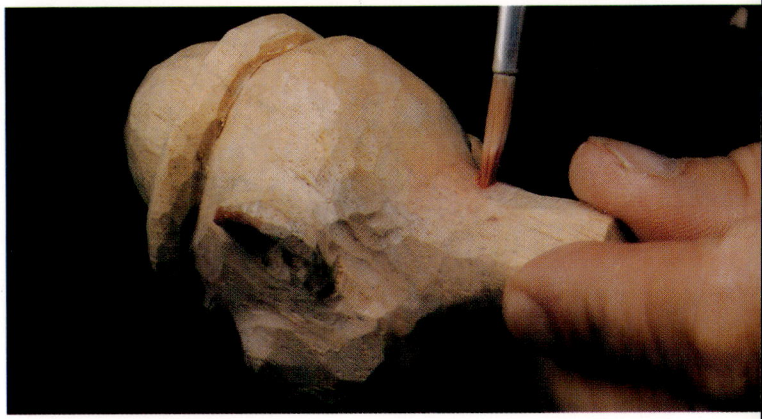

the back of the neck...

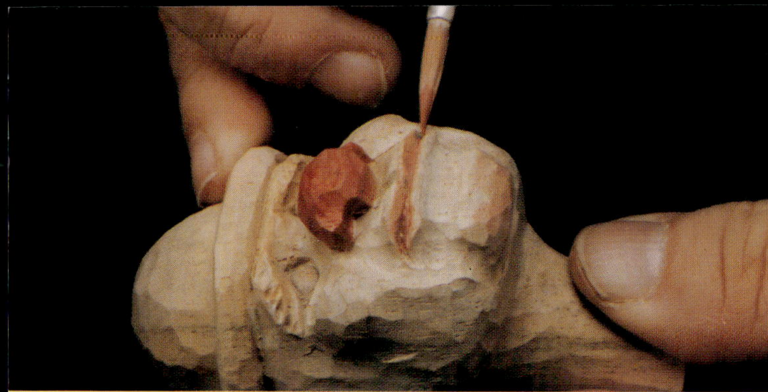

the chin and the lips...

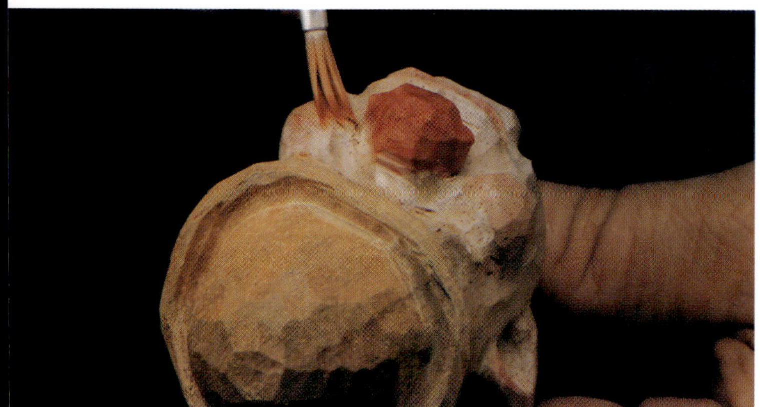

the cheeks...

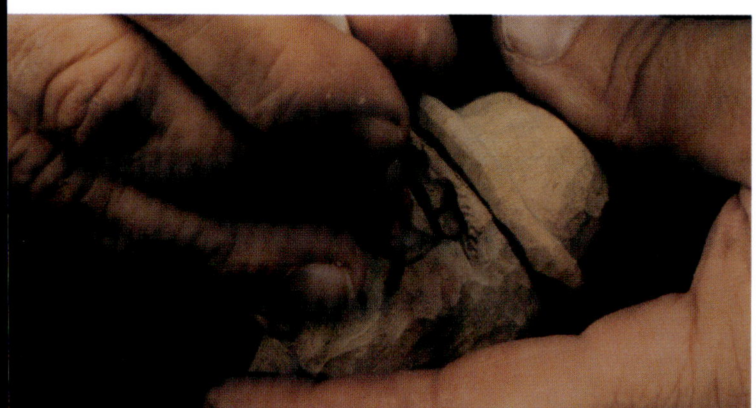

and around the eyes.

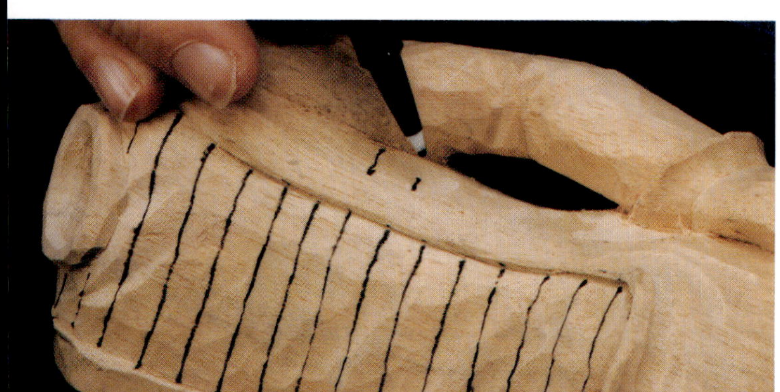

With ink that isn't soluble by your paint, draw in the stripes of the shirt. With my turpentine based paints I use a Flair™ pen with a white tip. With water-based paints, this would be a disaster, running into a black blob.

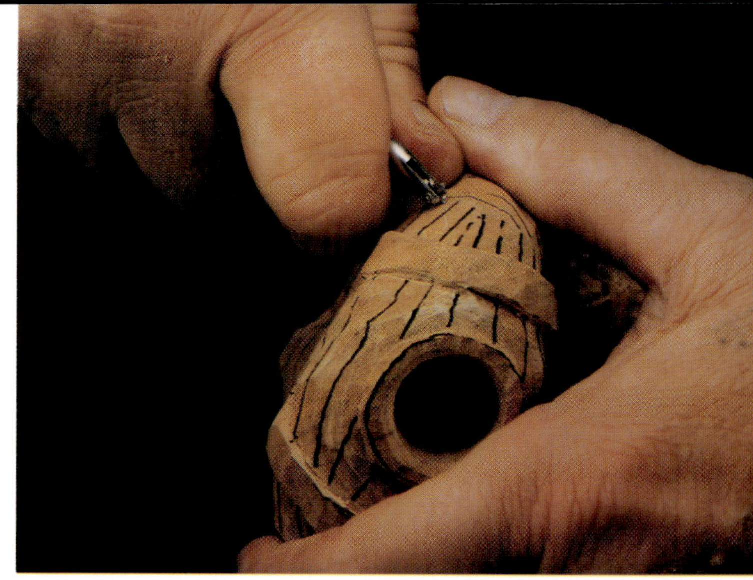

Go over the seams of the shirt with the pattern wheel.

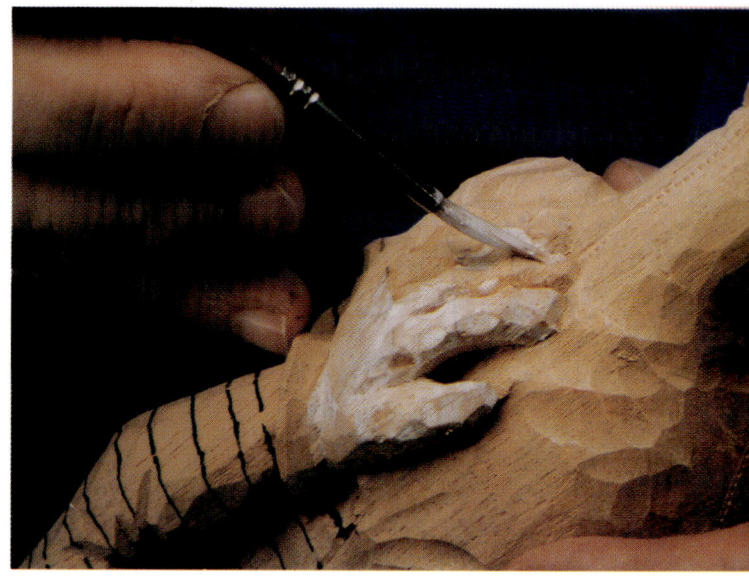

Paint the gloves white. White doesn't look like much until it dries. When it does all the spots will show up like a sore thumb...or in this case, like a white glove.

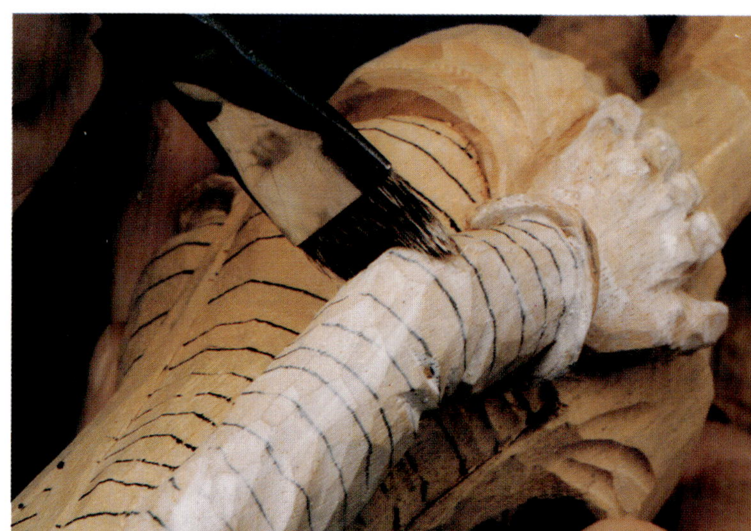

Switch to a bigger brush and go over the shirt with white too.

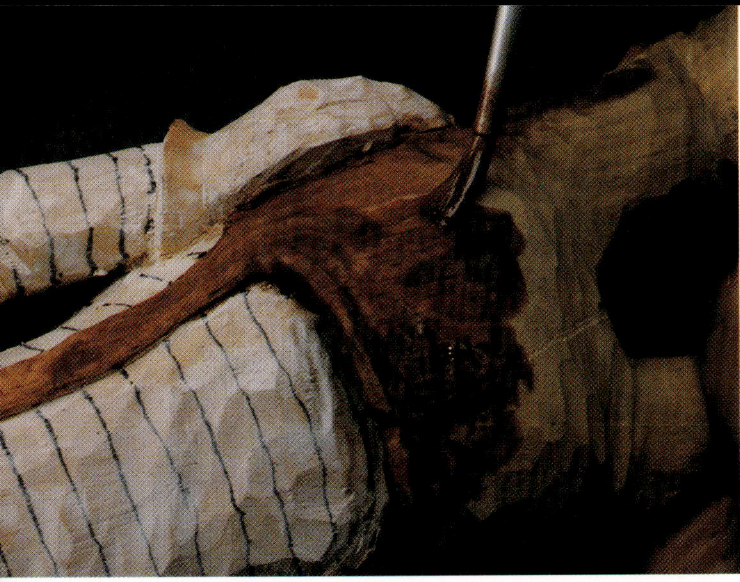

The pants are brown.

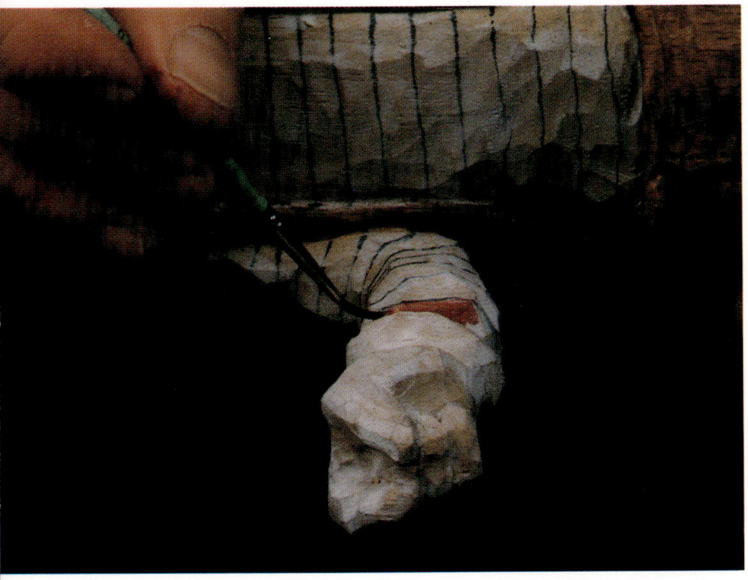

When the white of the shirt has dried sufficiently you can paint the stripes. I have chosen an Alizarin crimson to alternate with the white. Starting above the cuff helps define where the sleeve ends and the glove begins.

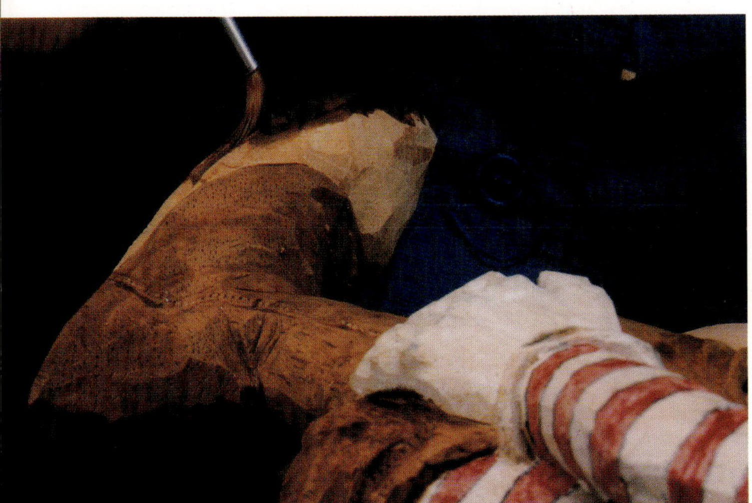

Paint the shoes with burnt umber.

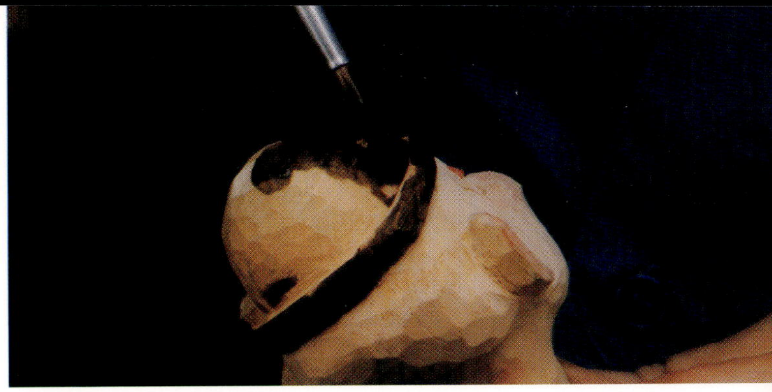

Continue with the burnt umber on the hat.

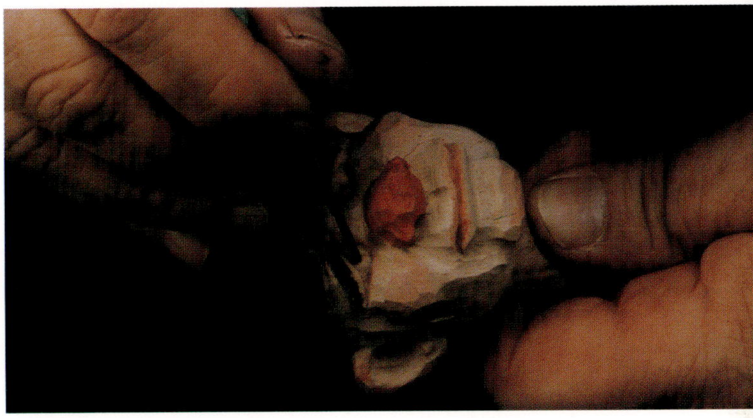

Paint the eyebrows black, to give them a theatrical look. Take some thicker burnt umber from the cap and apply it to the iris.

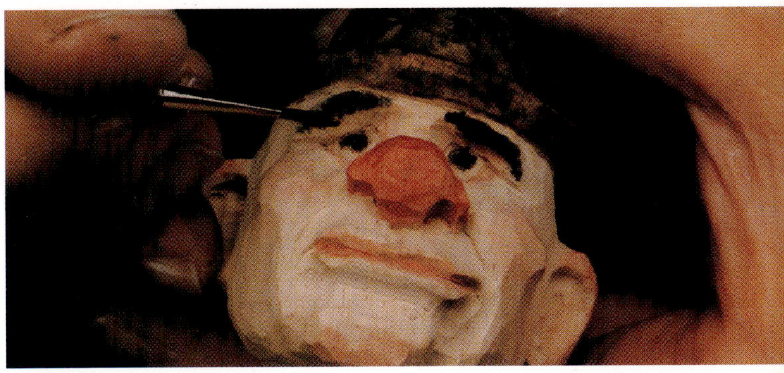

Add a little black to darken it up.

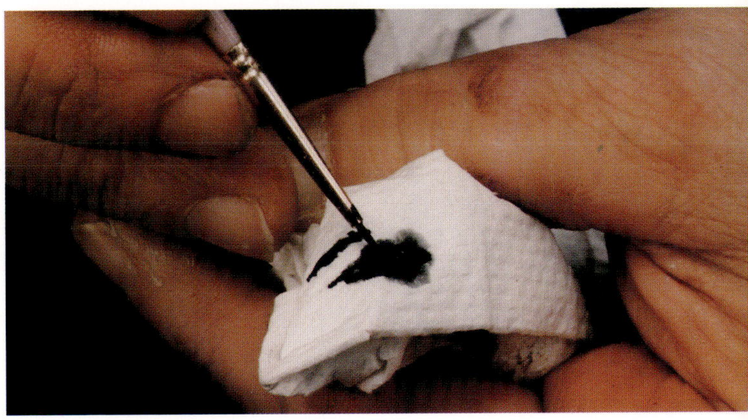

Use a paper towel as a palette for the pupil black. this takes almost all the turpentine out of the paint.

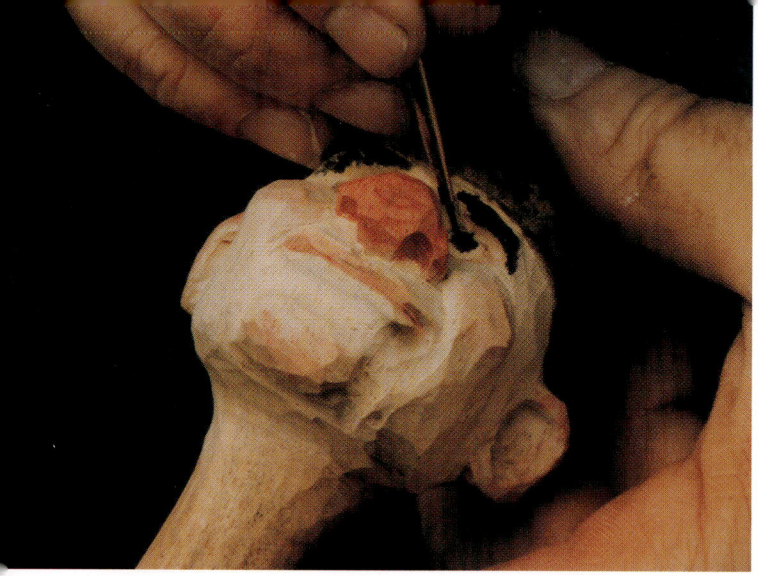

Paint the iris.

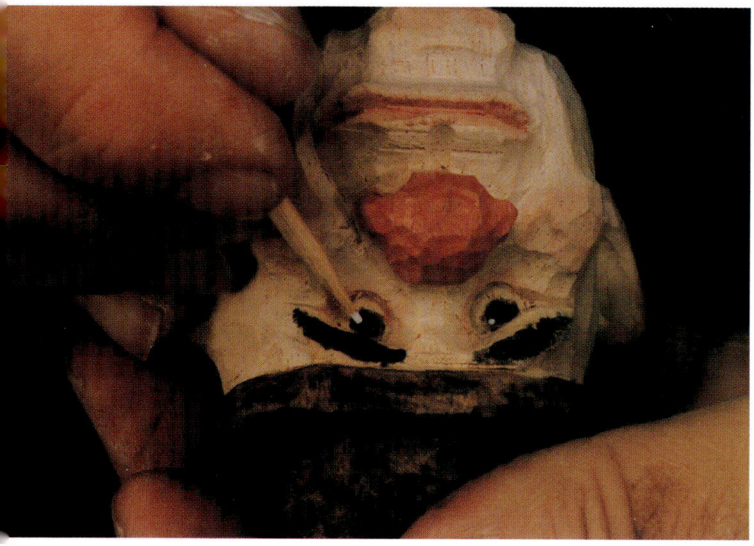

Add glints of white to the eyes. To do this I use the point of a bamboo skewer.

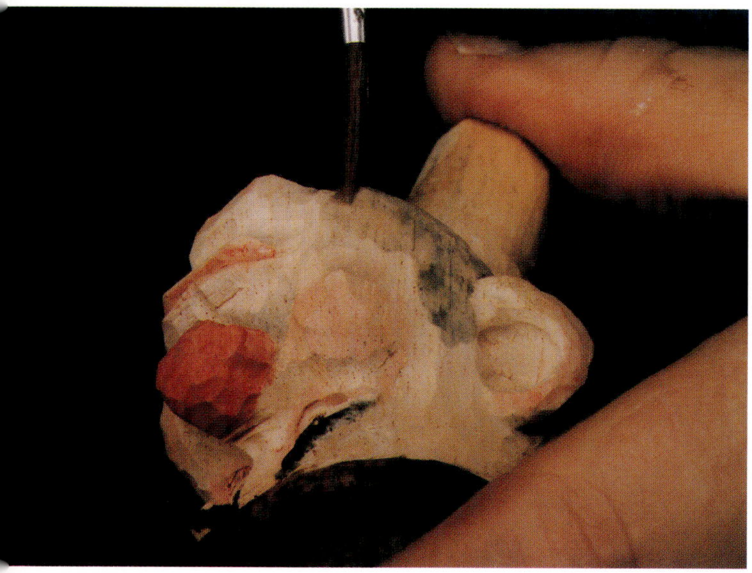

I use the pigment from my slag bottle to create a beard shadow.

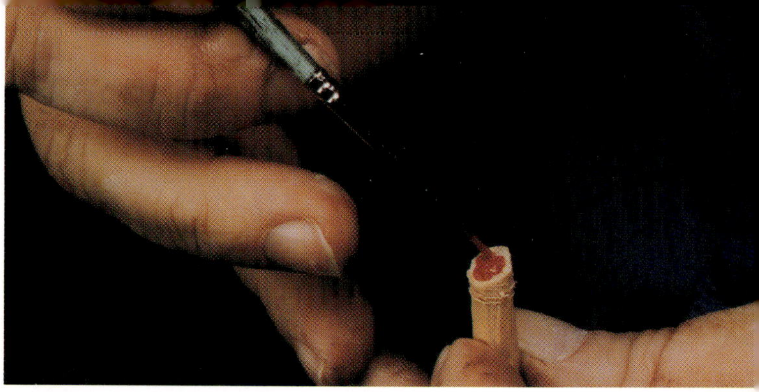

Paint the end of the cigar a bright red.

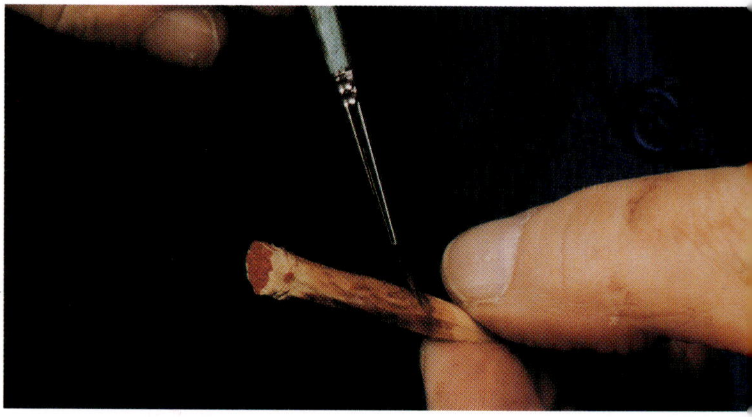

The cigar itself is burnt sienna.

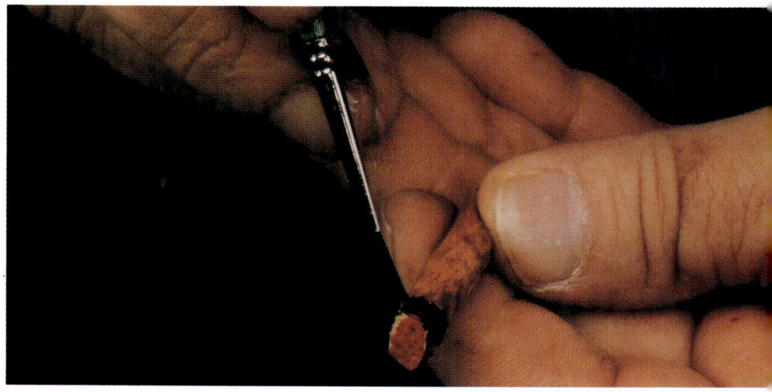

Black with a little red peeking through creates the base color for the ash.

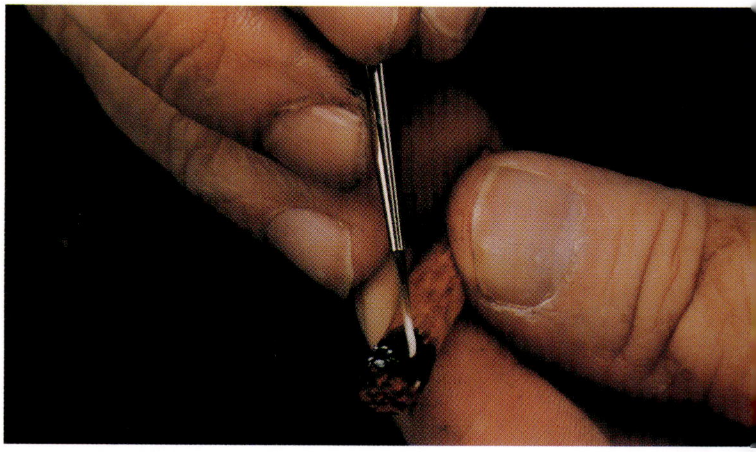

Add some white dots to complete the ash.

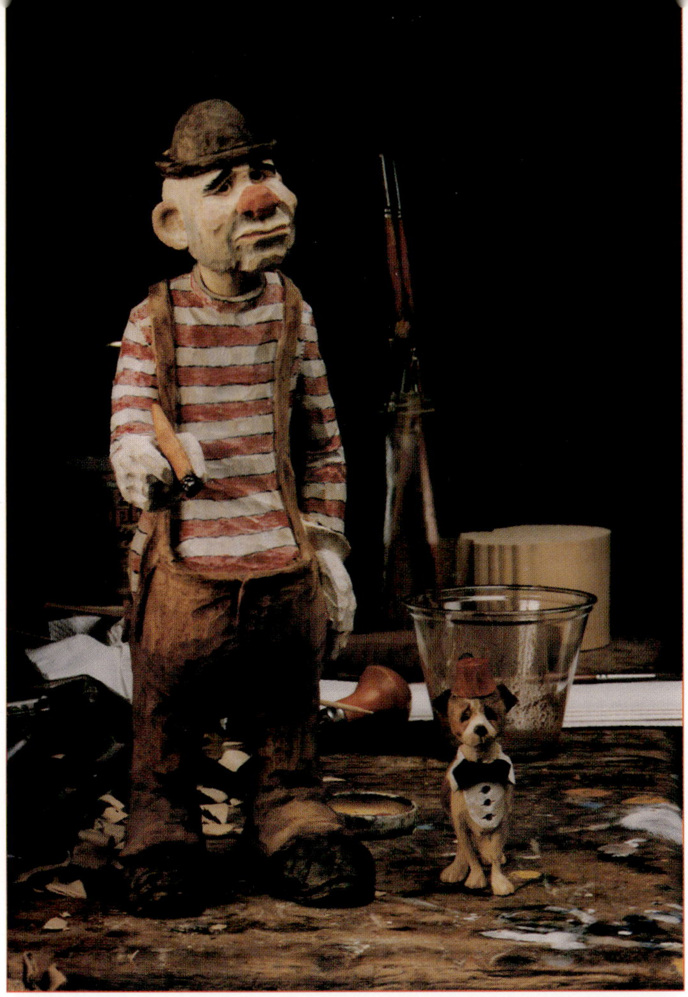
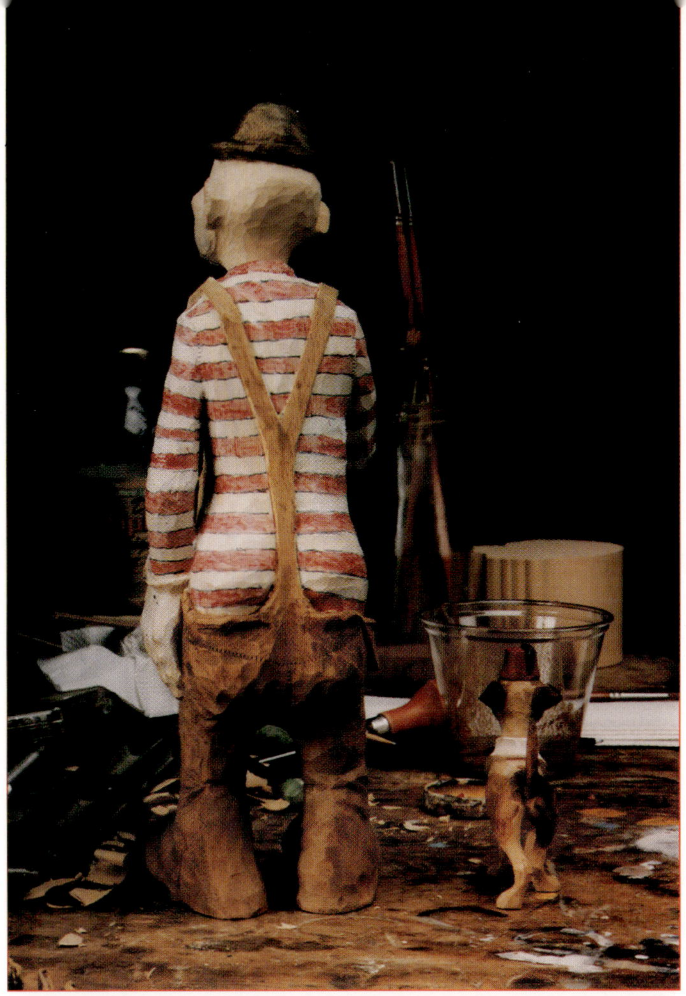
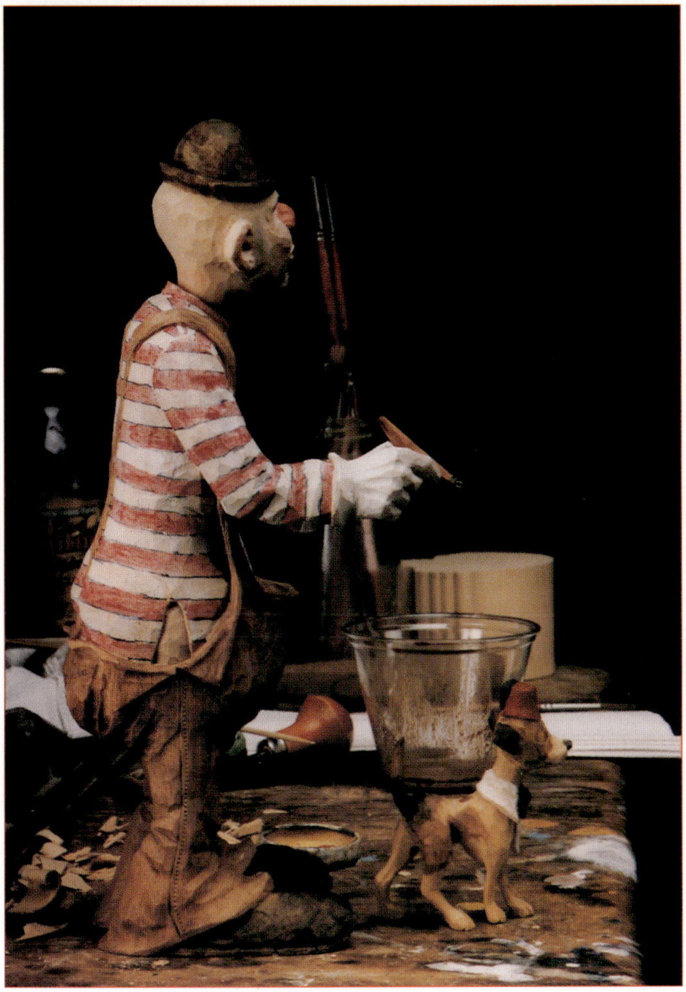
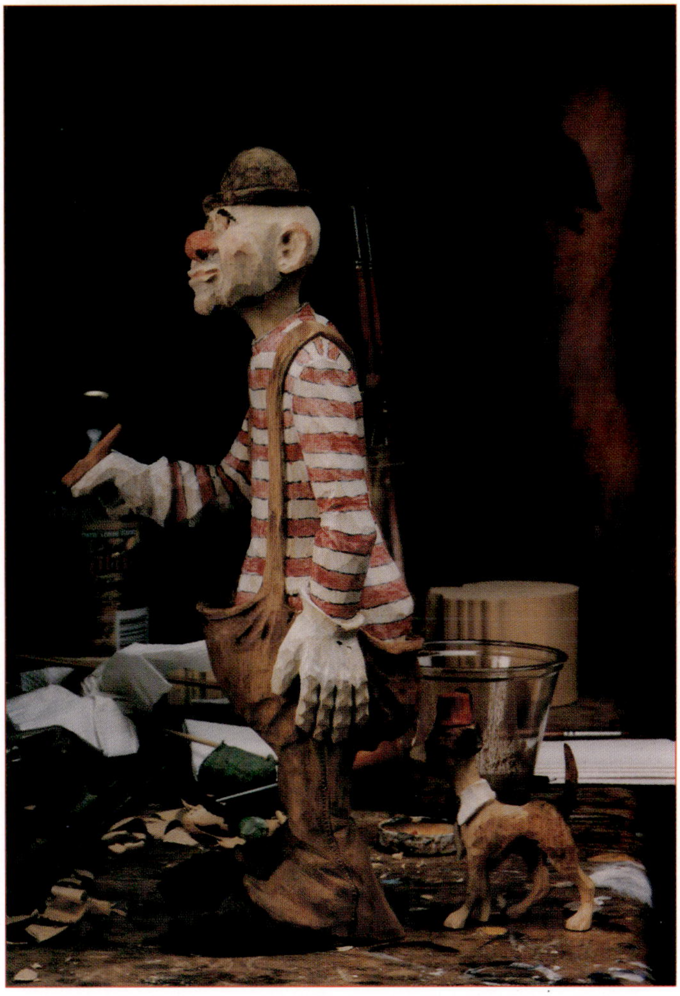

A QUICK LESSON IN LETTERING

Old English script may be pretty, but it is hard to read and harder to carve. This is a script that gives the same feel, but is easier to use.

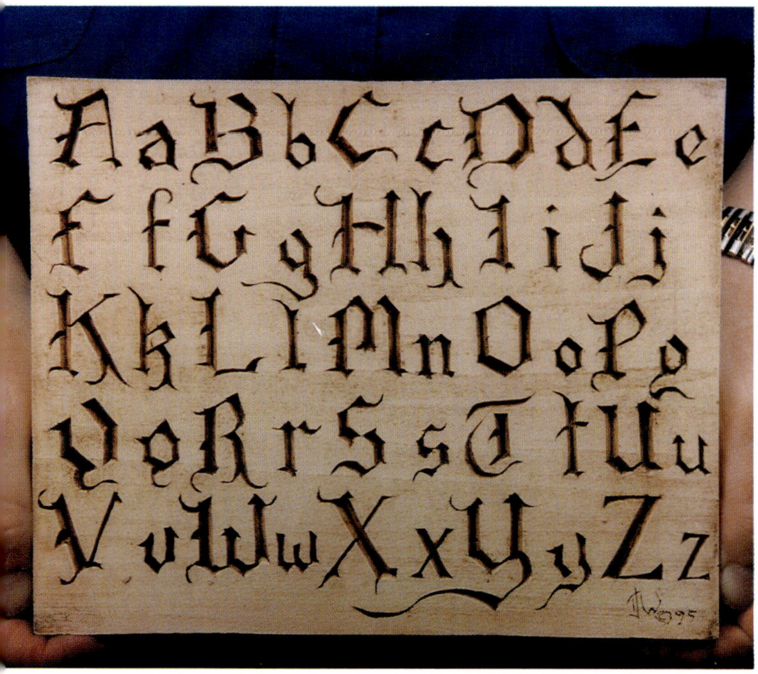

This is a cast study piece that will be available to carvers. You can contact me for information.

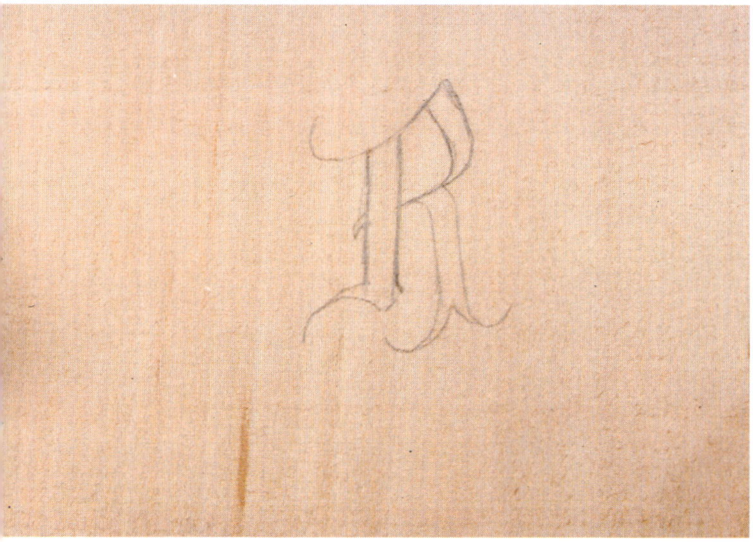

This R should provide help teach some techniques. Copy the letter onto a board.

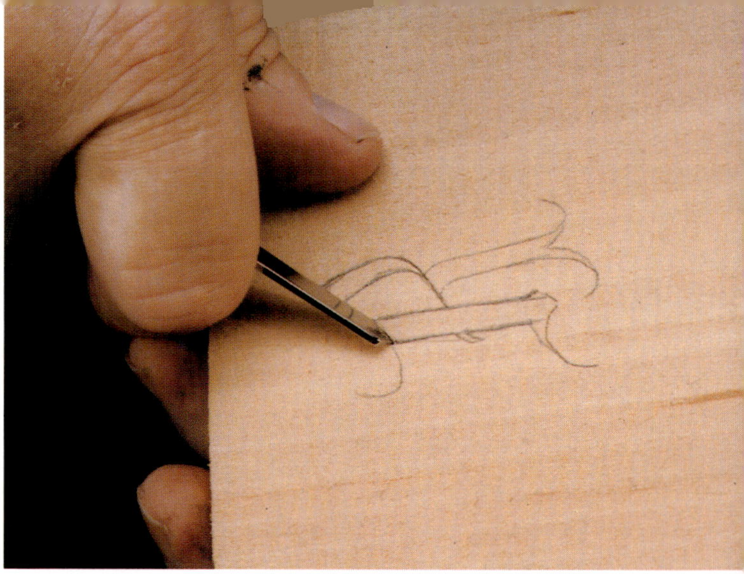

Cut in at an angle on the top of the vertical member.

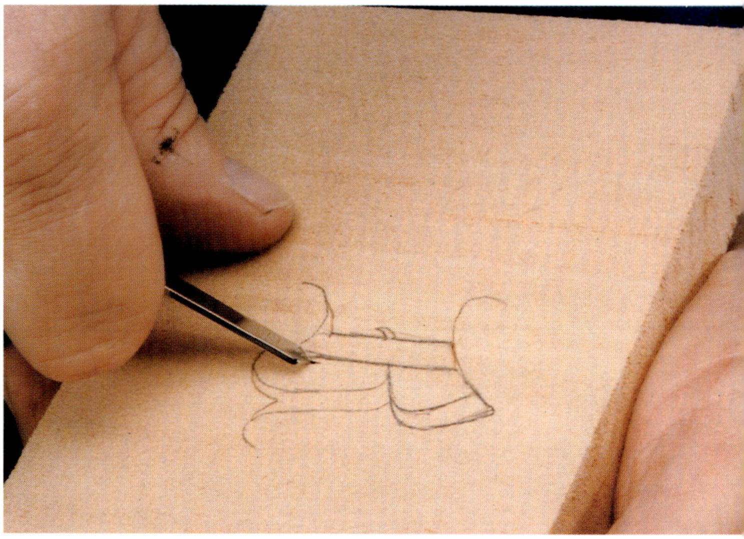

In the same way, cut in at the short side of the curved triangle that is at the base of the vertical member.

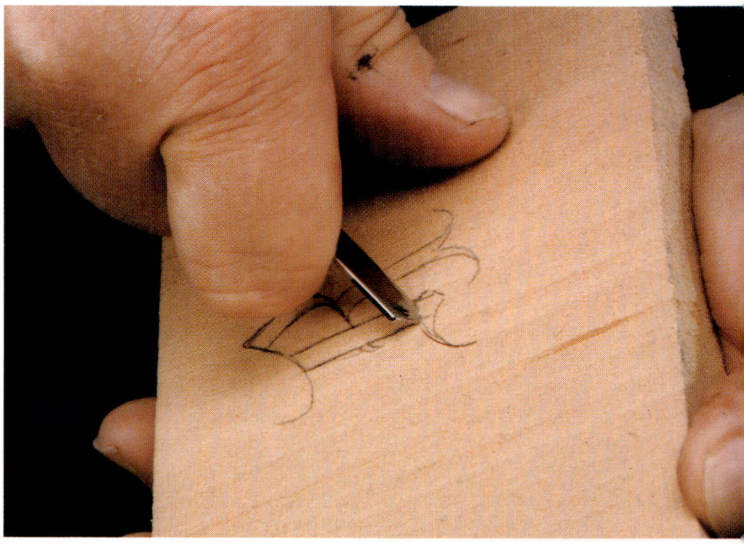

With the knife angled, start at the point of the triangle and follow the upper line to the side you just cut.

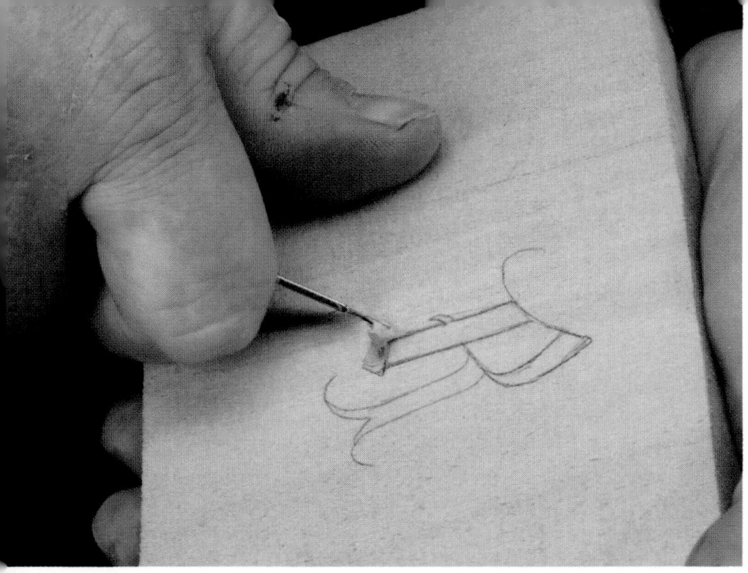

Begin at the short side and follow the bottom curve back to the point. Again, have your knife at an angle so trough pops out of the serif.

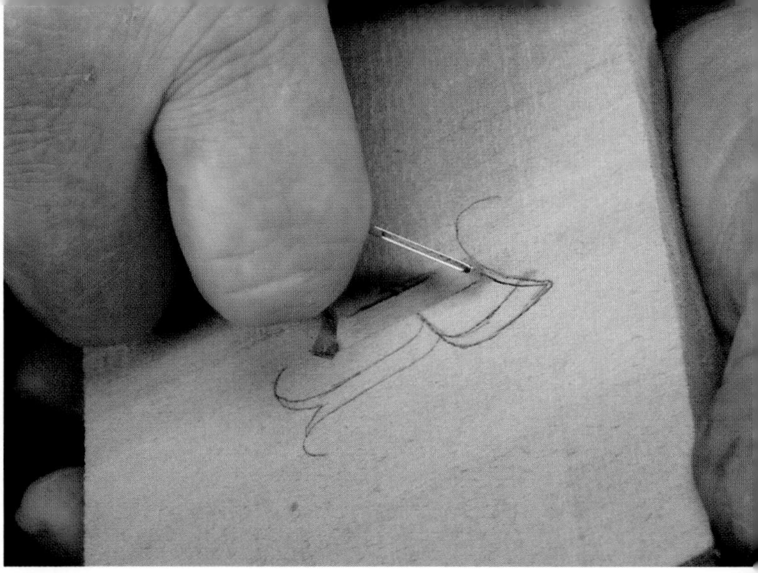

Starting at the top right corner, lean your knife over and cut the curve...

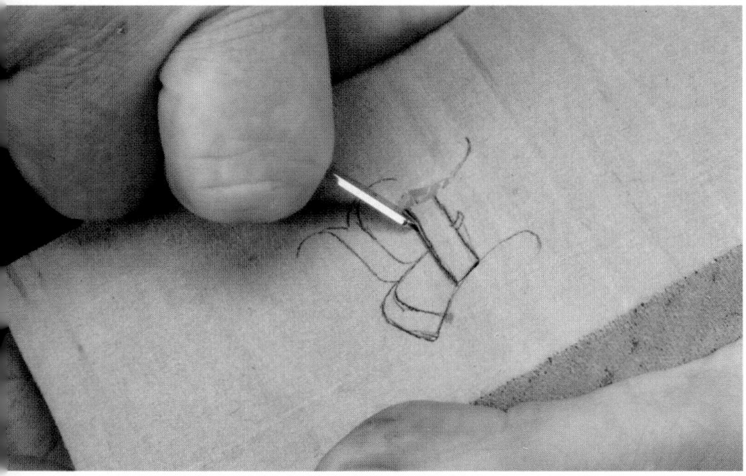

Cut down one side of the vertical member...

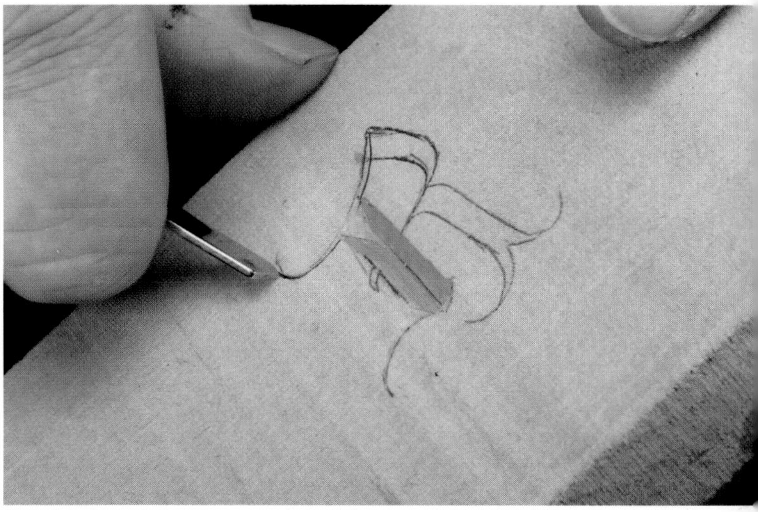

up to the top left corner.

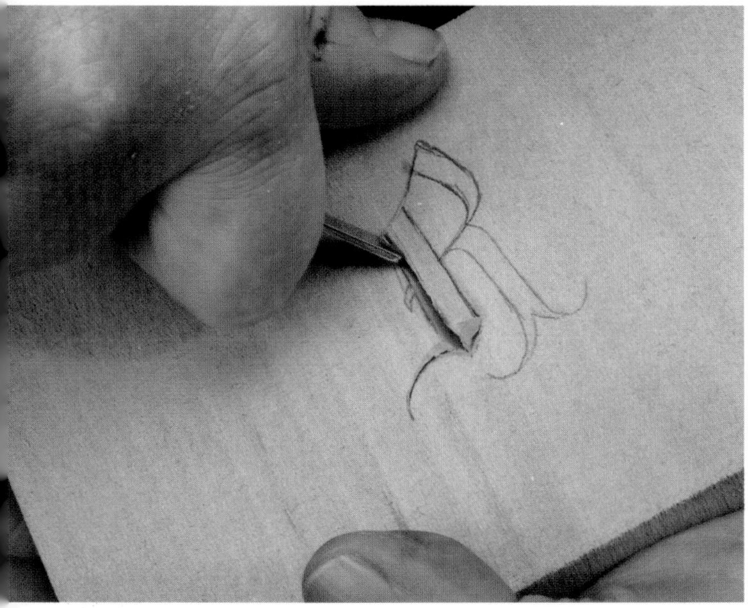

and up the other to pop out the vertical member.

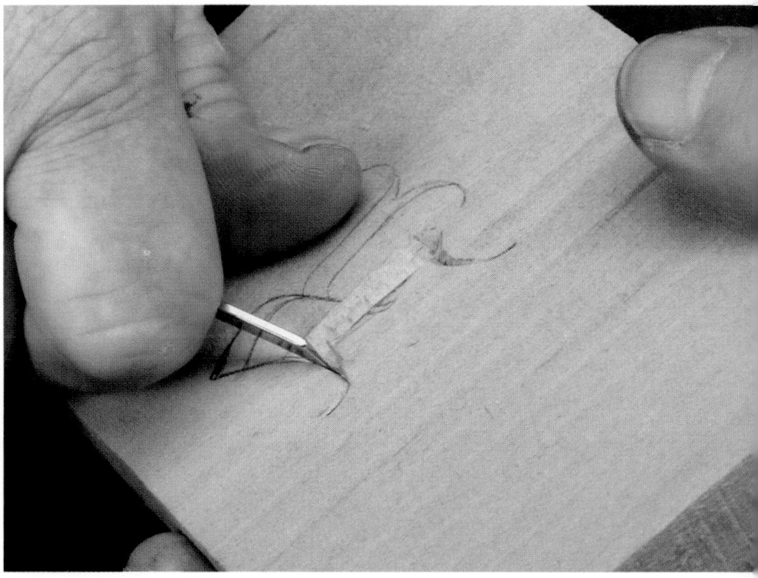

Straighten you knife and follow the line back to pop out a nice thin running wedge.

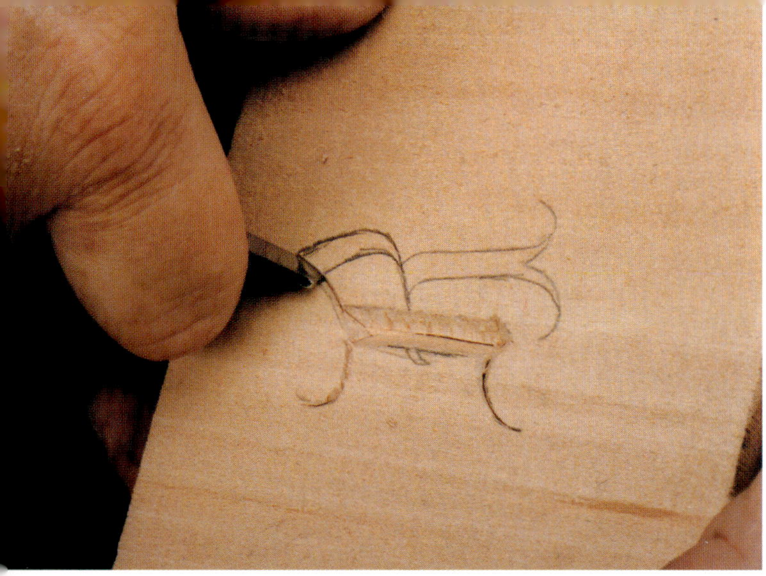

At the top of the curved element on the right, Make a deep angled cut.

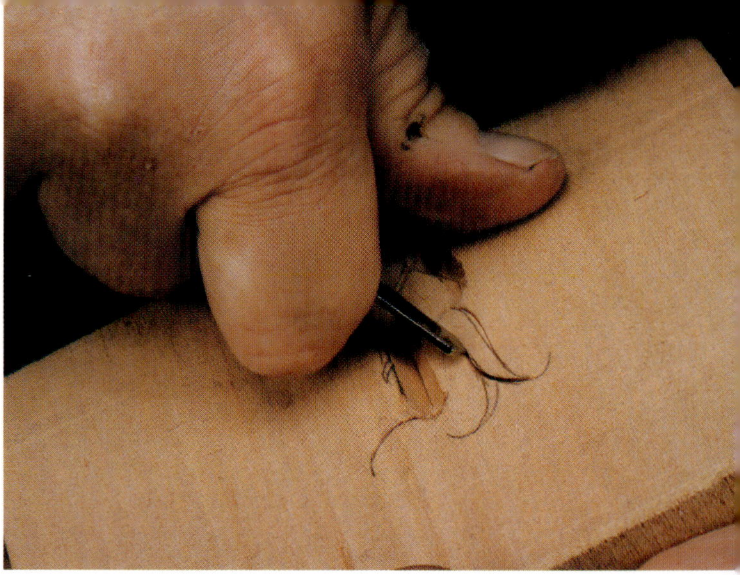

Starting straight and shallow cut back on the other side, deepening and increasing the angle of the knife as you go.

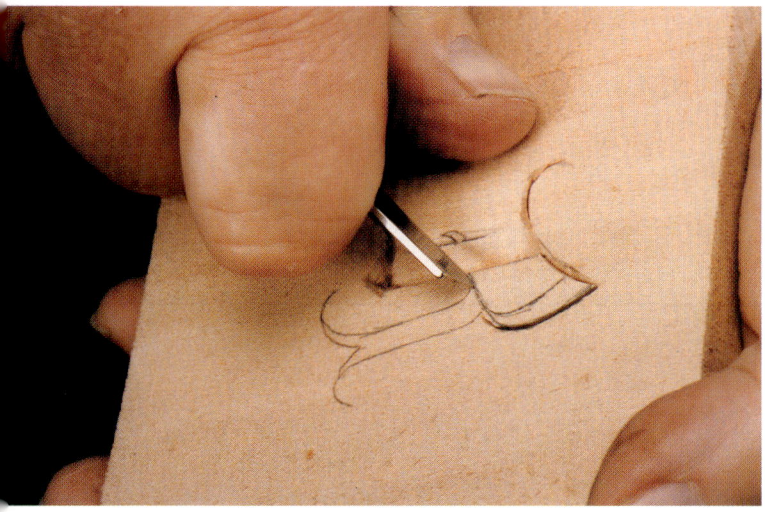

Lean your knife over and follow the outside line from the corner to the vertical member. Come back on the other line to pop out the running wedge.

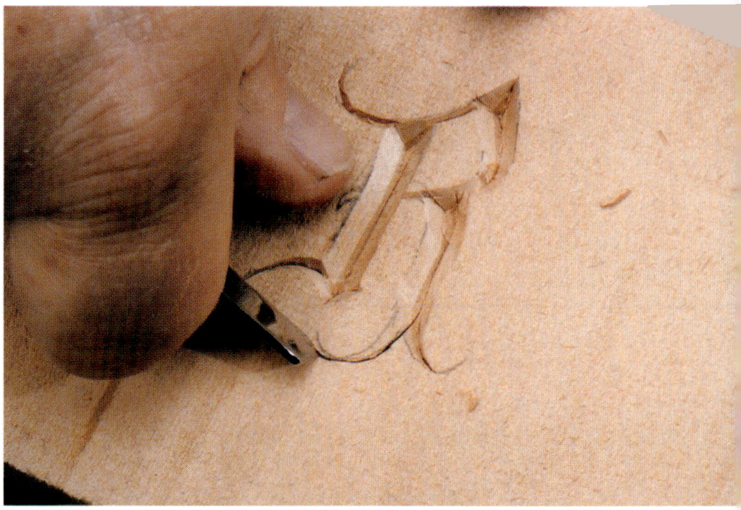

Where the tail divides cut out to the end...

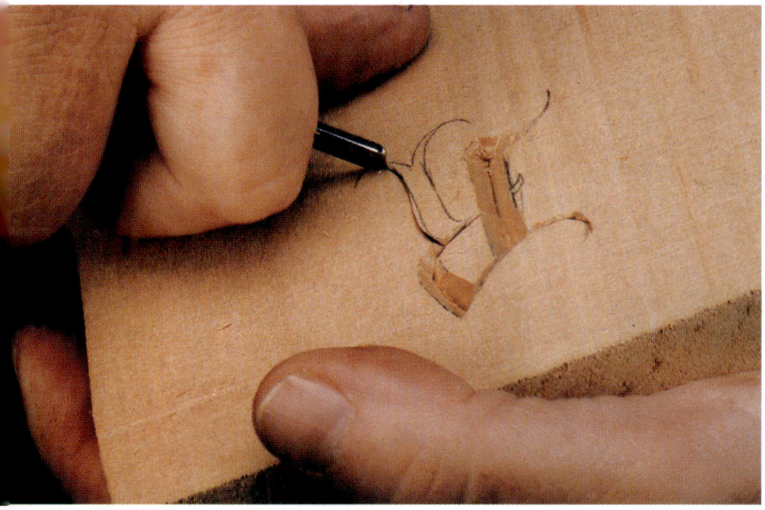

On the tail of the R, start at the top and cut to the end. Start with you knife leaning over and deep, and end with it straight up and shallow.

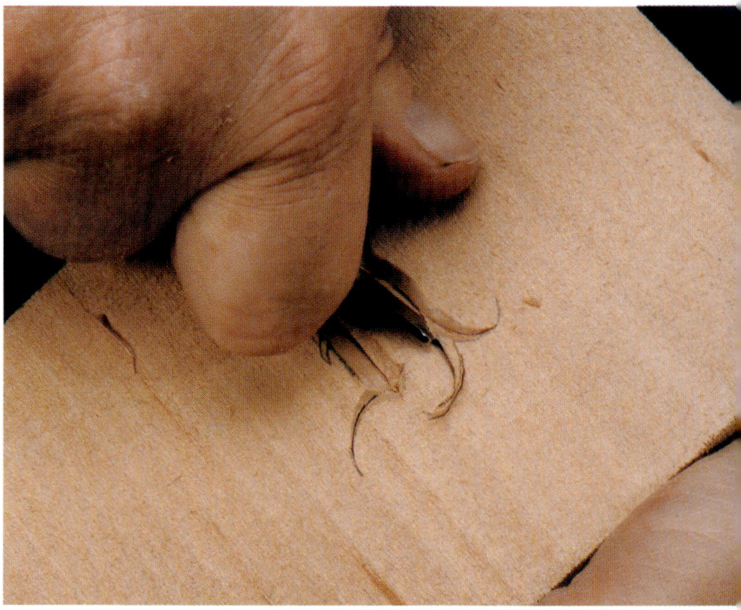

and come back on the other line.

THE GALLERY AND PATTERNS

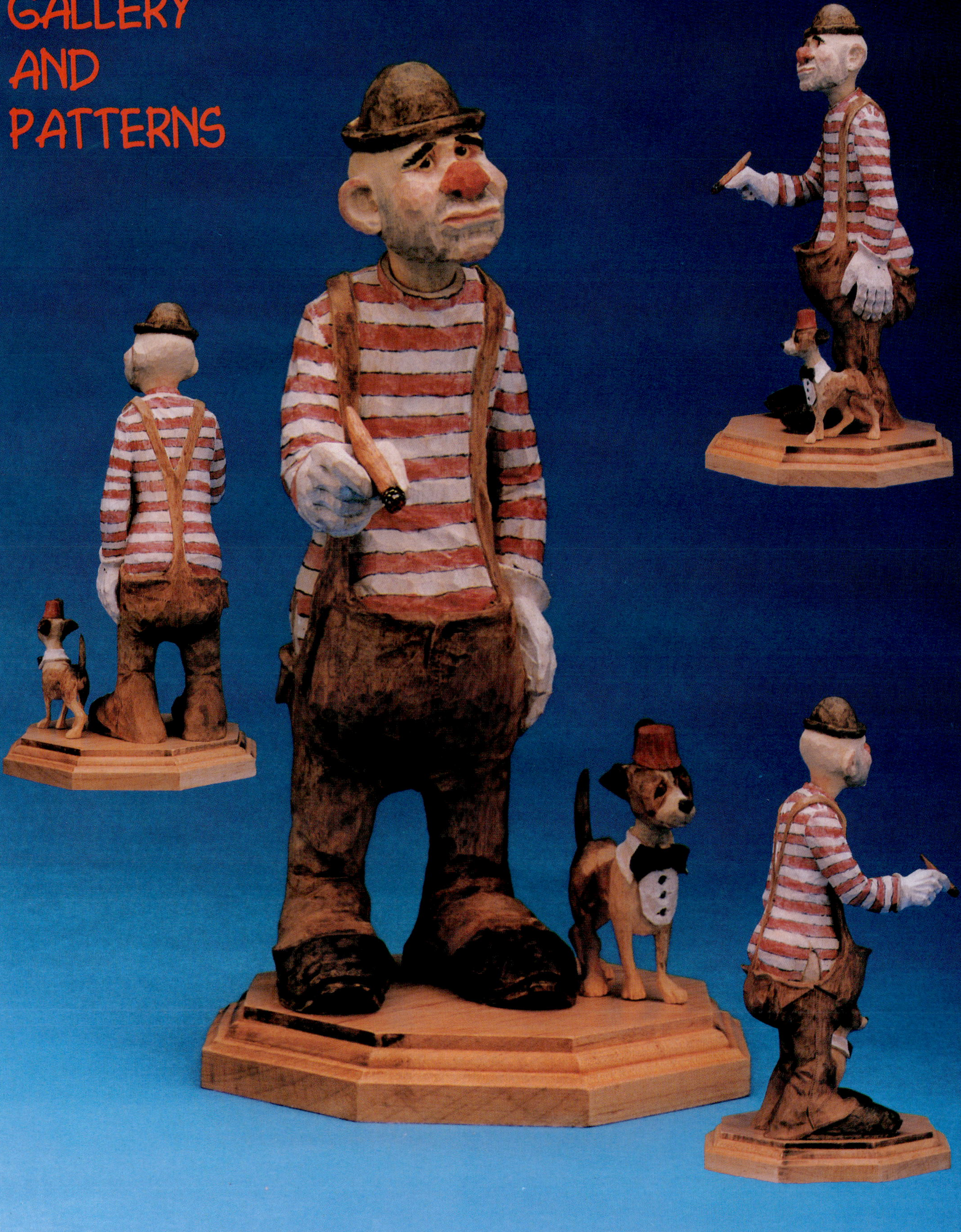

FIXIN' BROKEN ♥S

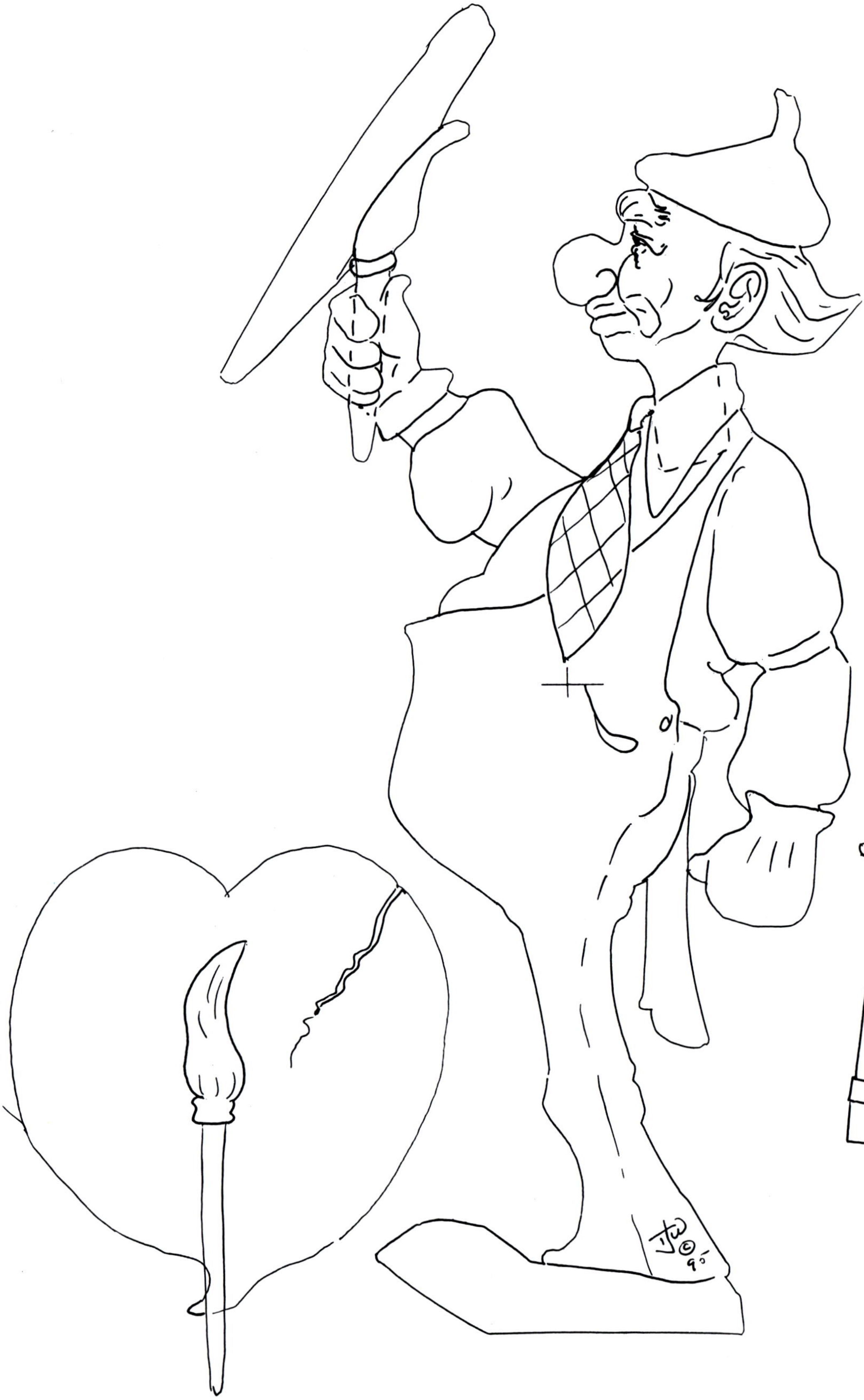

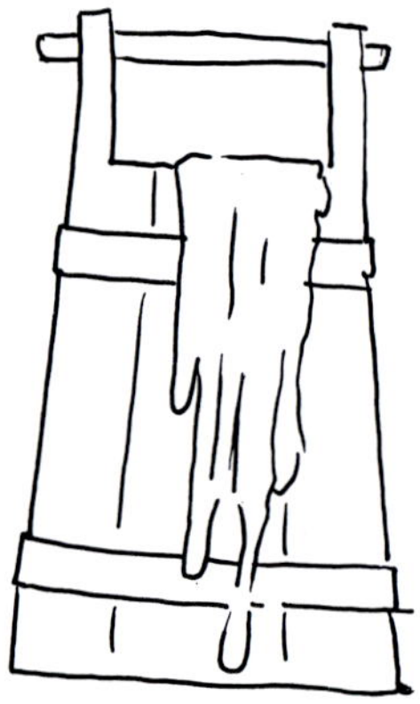

THESE PATTERNS ARE 70% OF ORIGINAL SIZE.

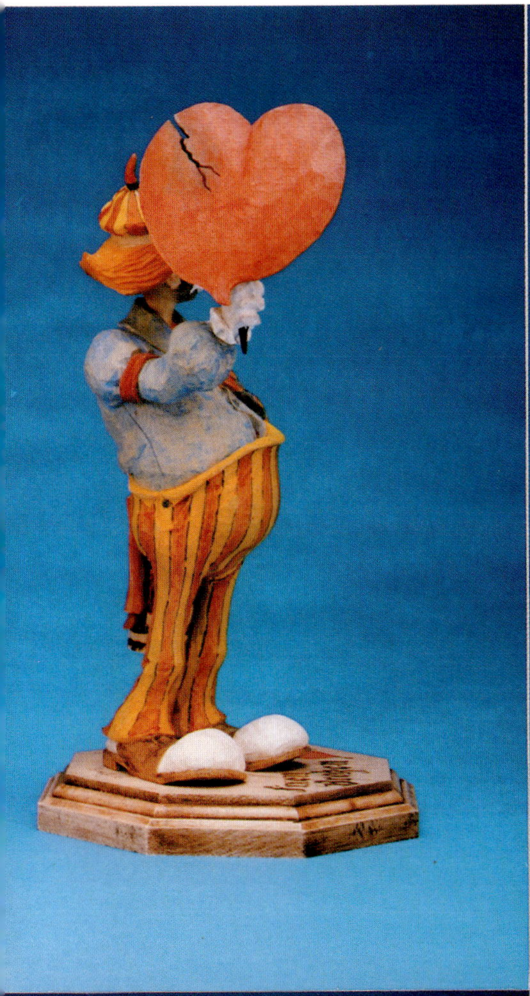

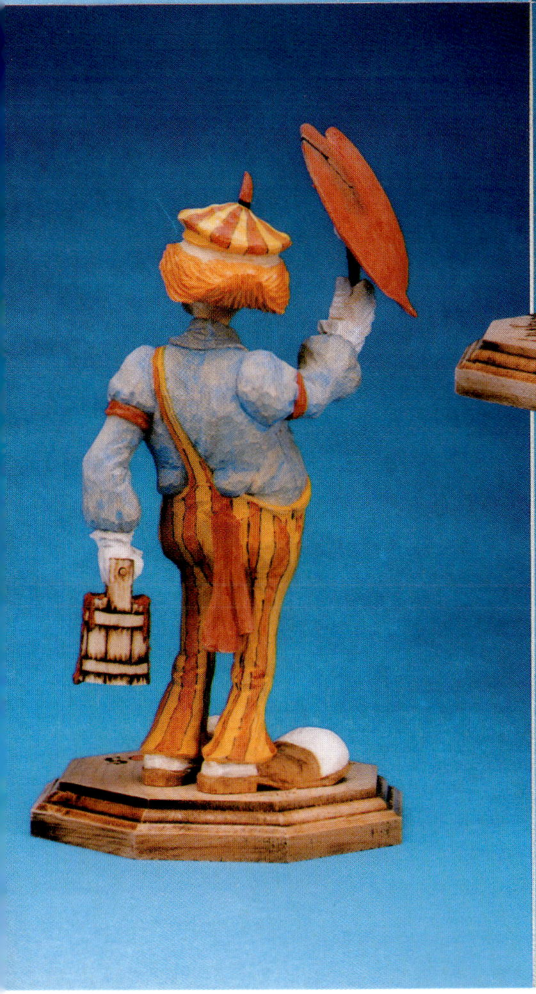

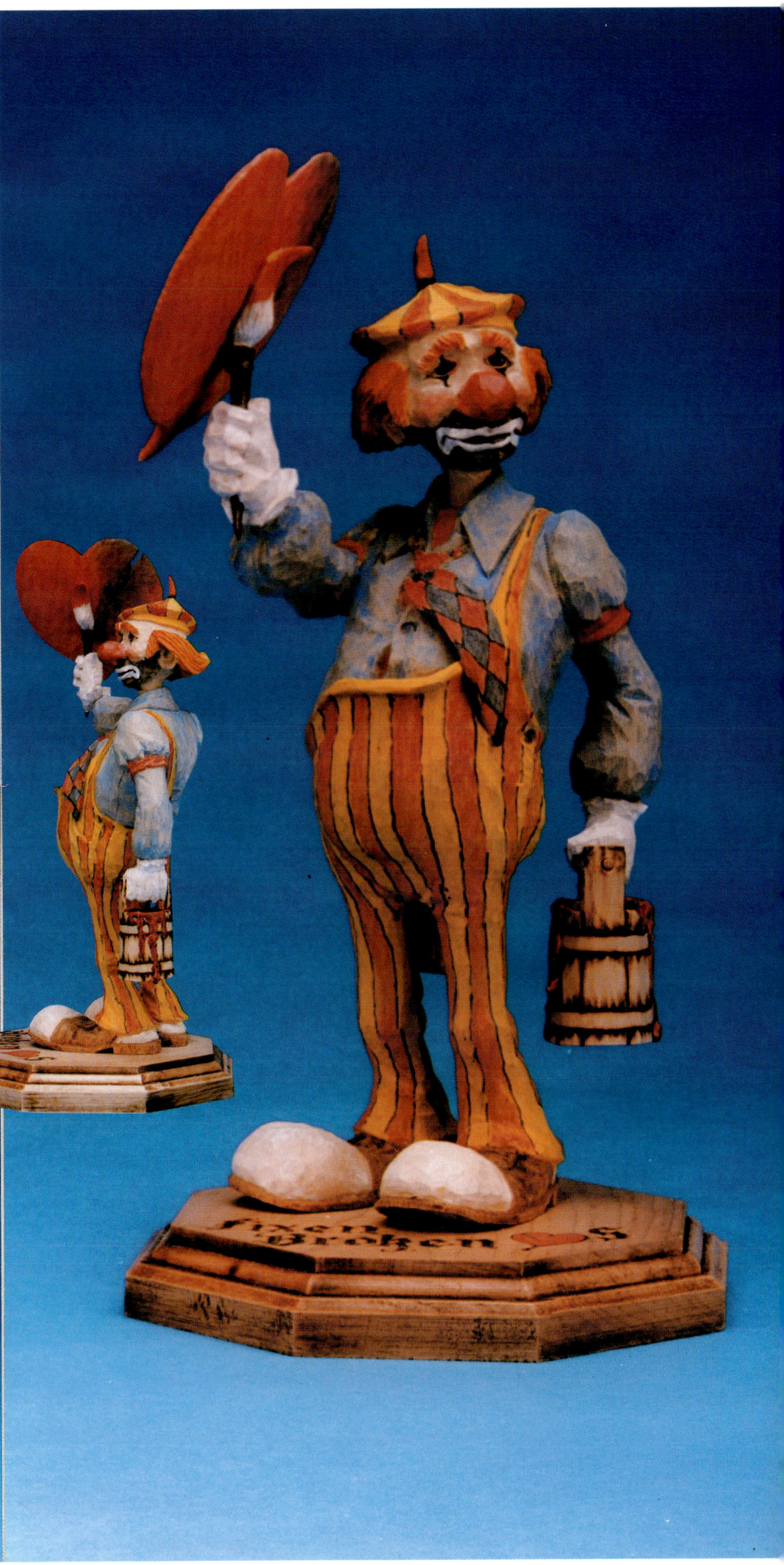
fixen
Broken

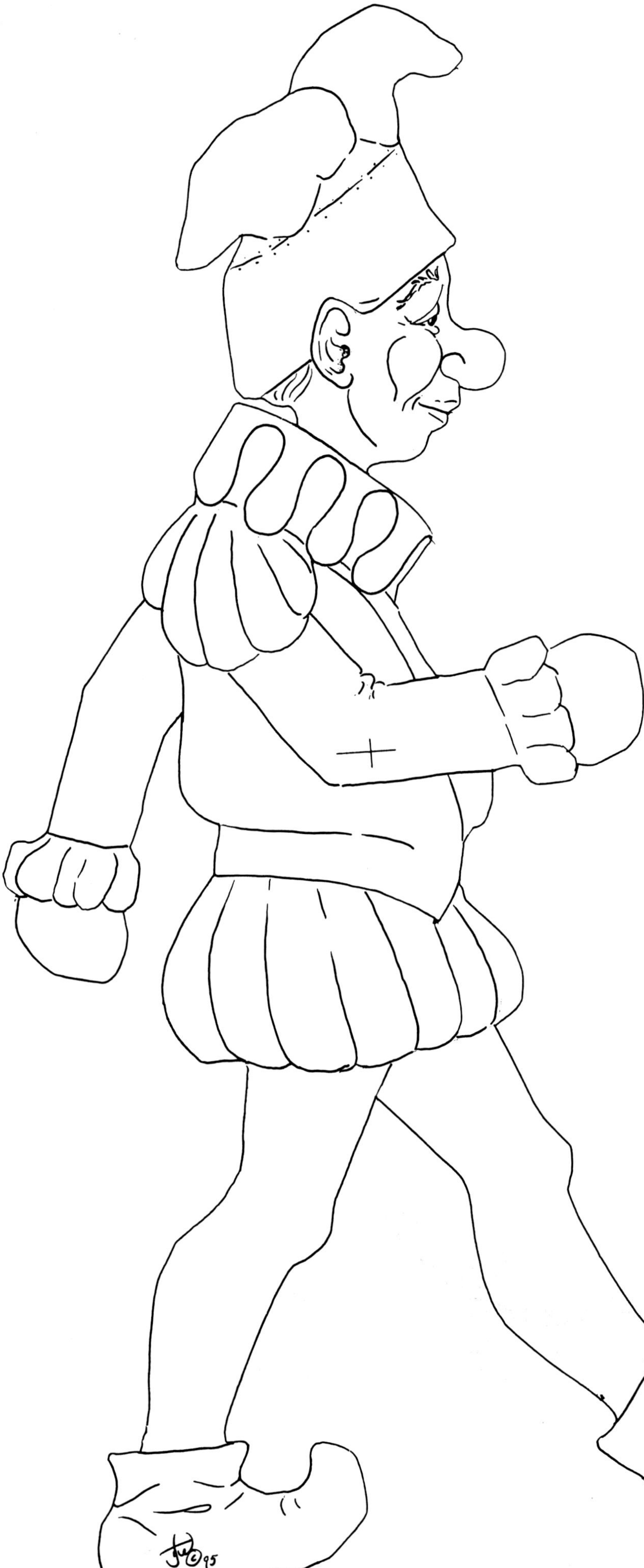

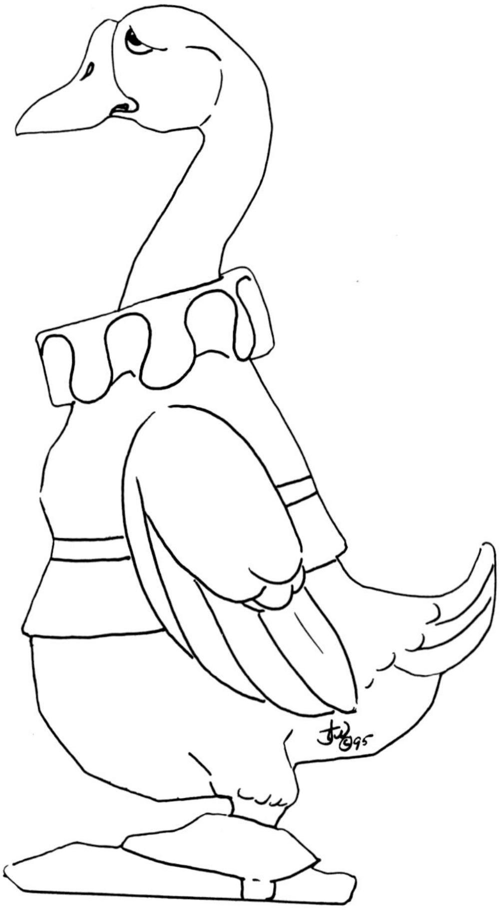

THESE PATTERNS ARE 70% OF ORIGINAL SIZE.

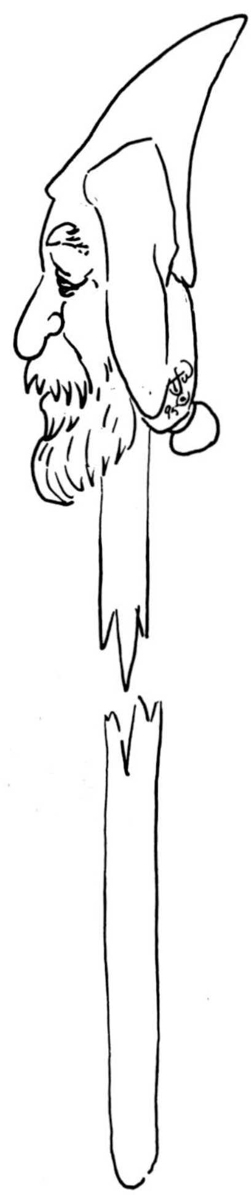

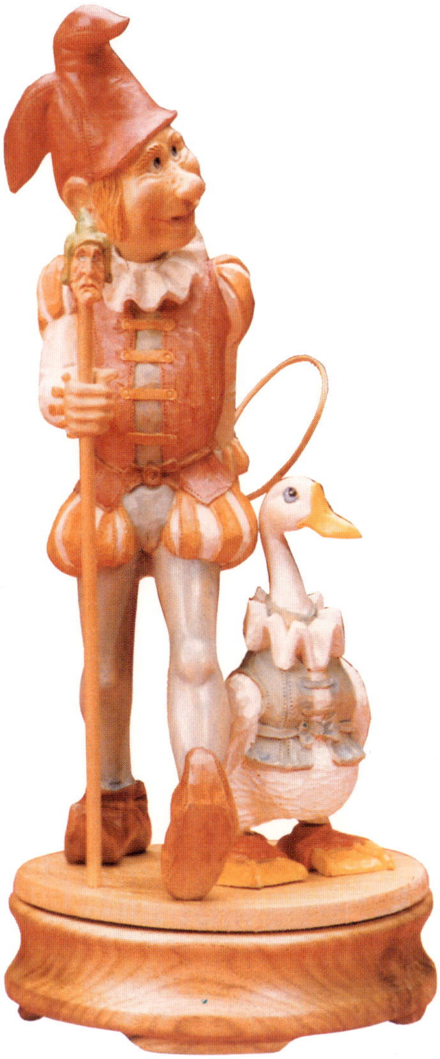

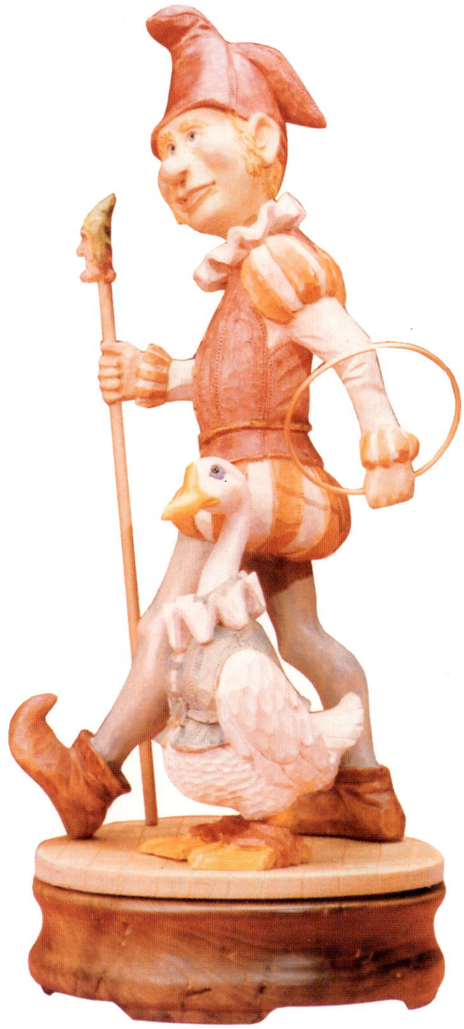

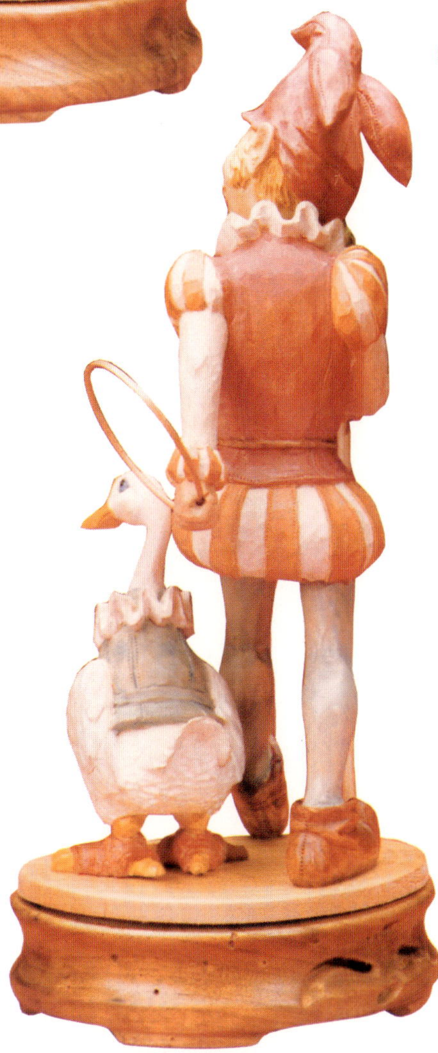

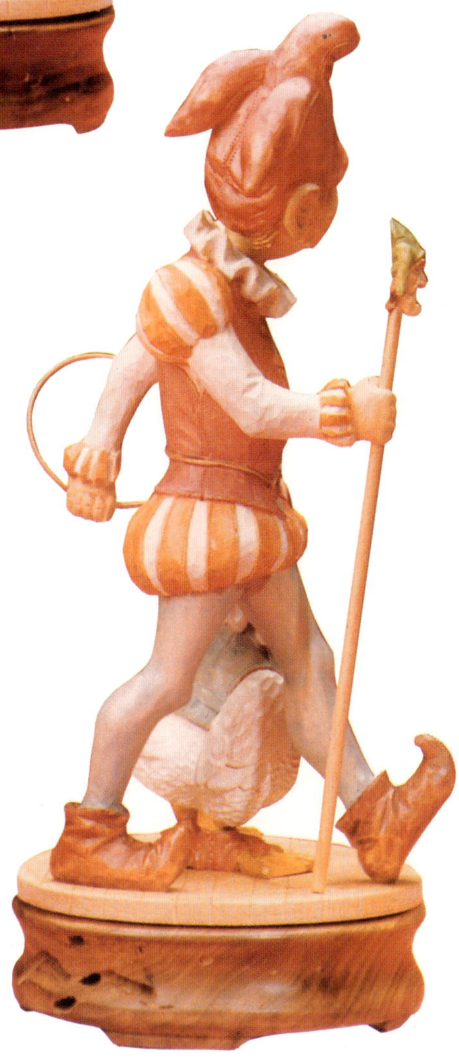

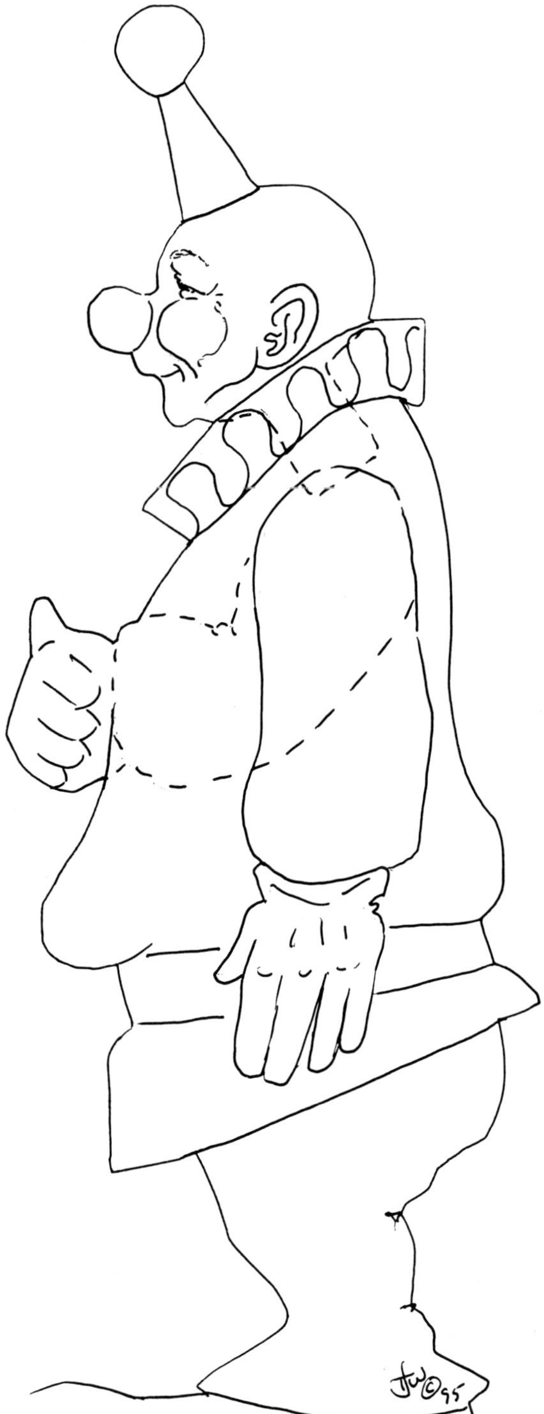

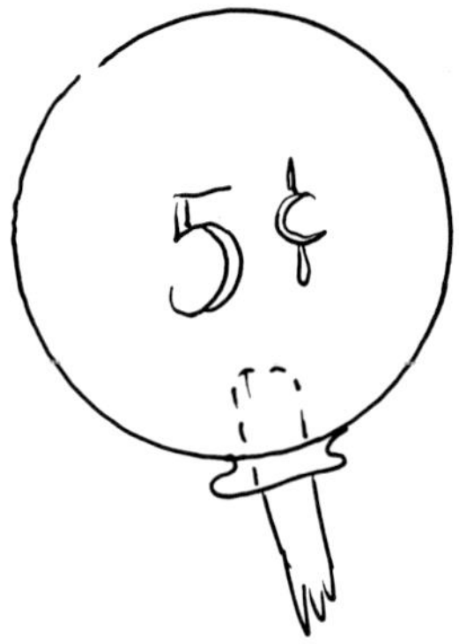

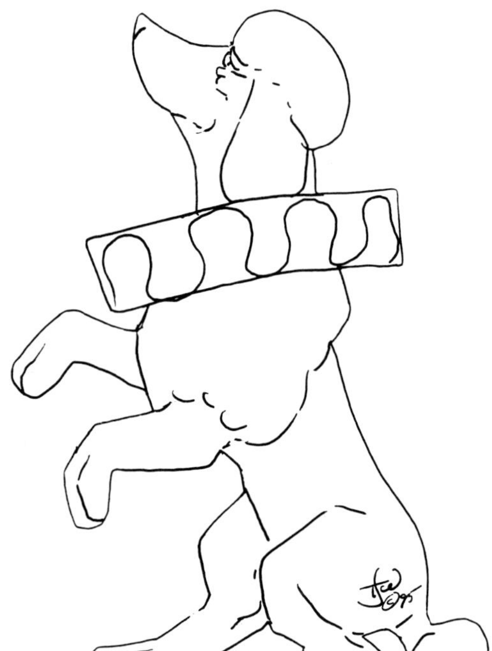

THESE PATTERNS ARE 70% OF ORIGINAL SIZE.

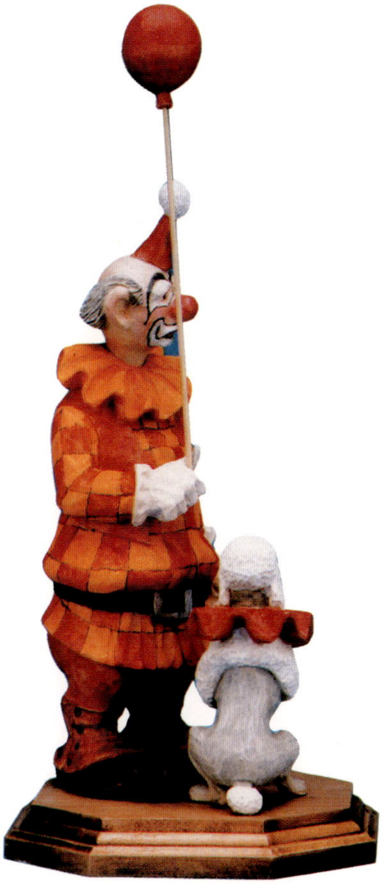

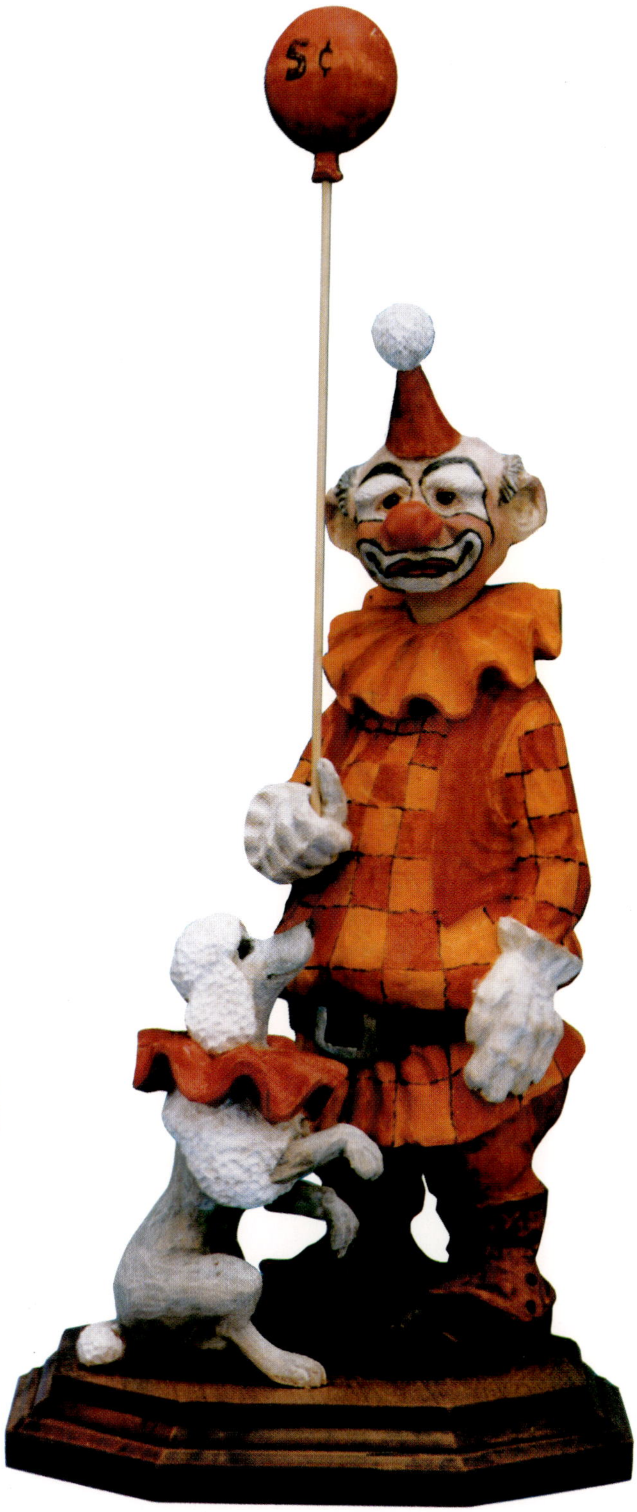
5¢

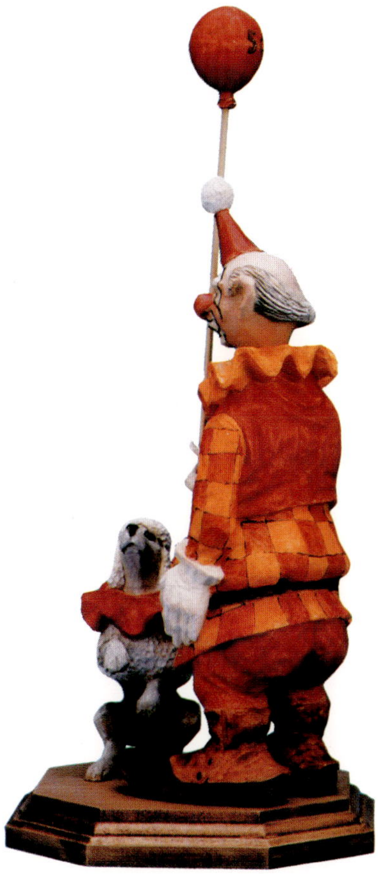

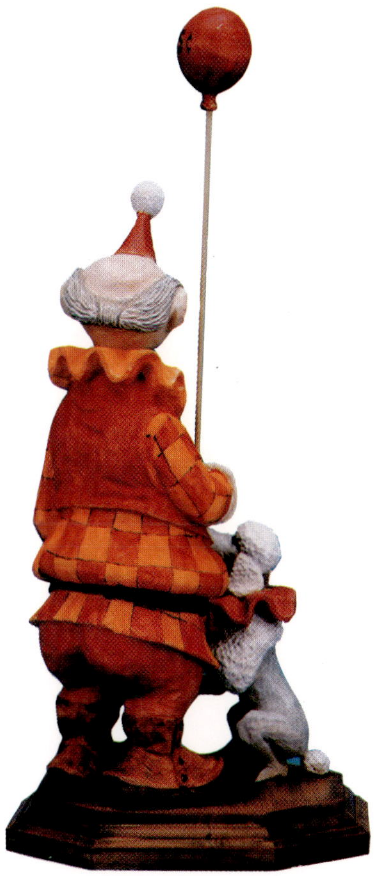

I SAID "WATER"

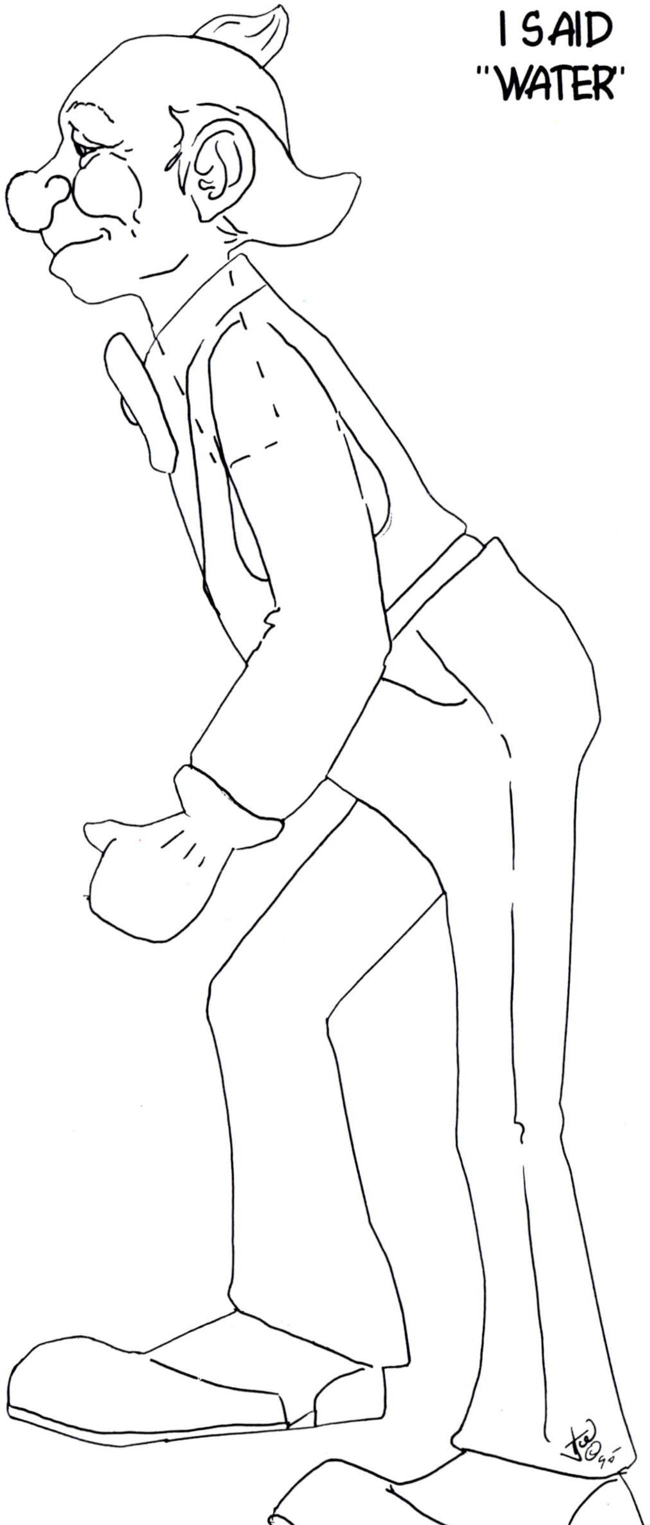

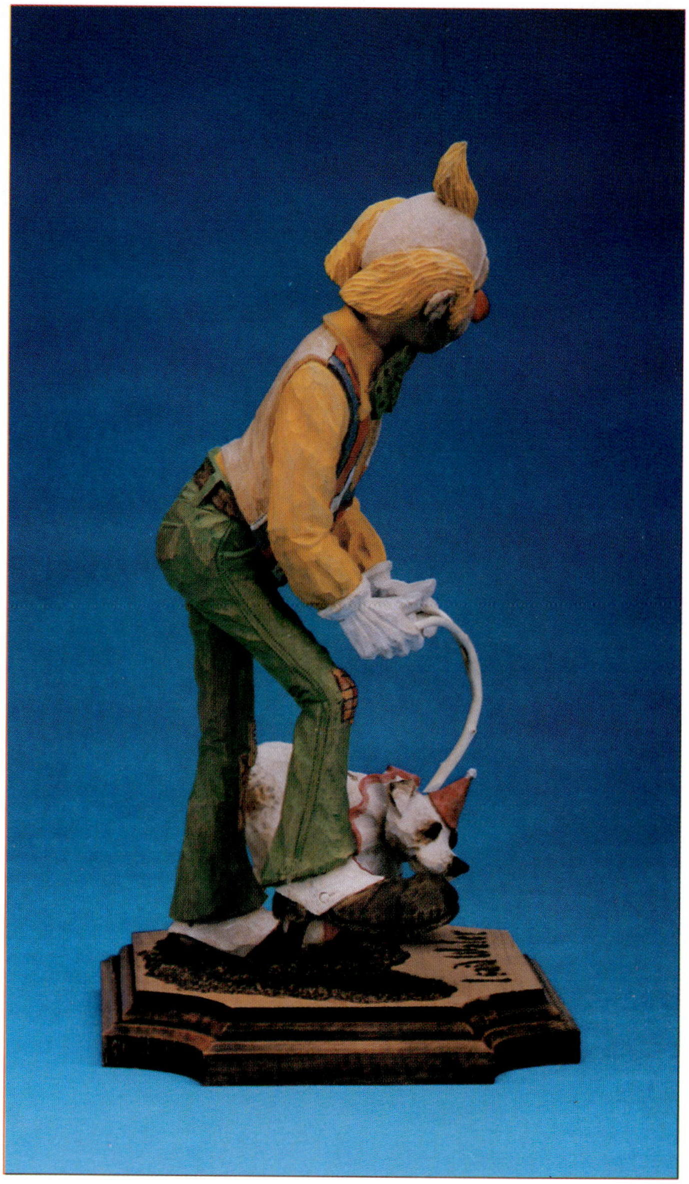

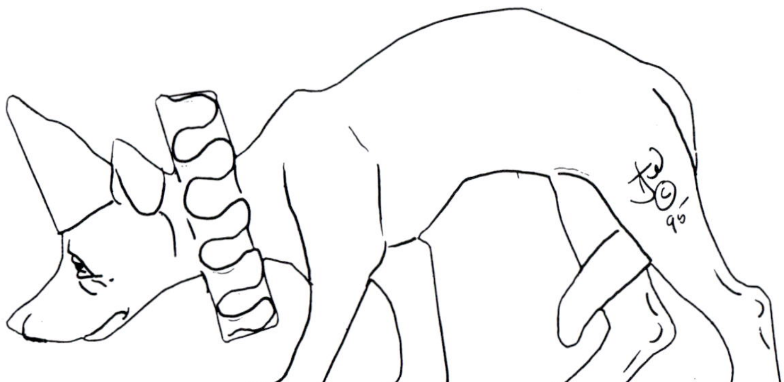

THESE PATTERNS ARE 70% OF ORIGINAL SIZE.

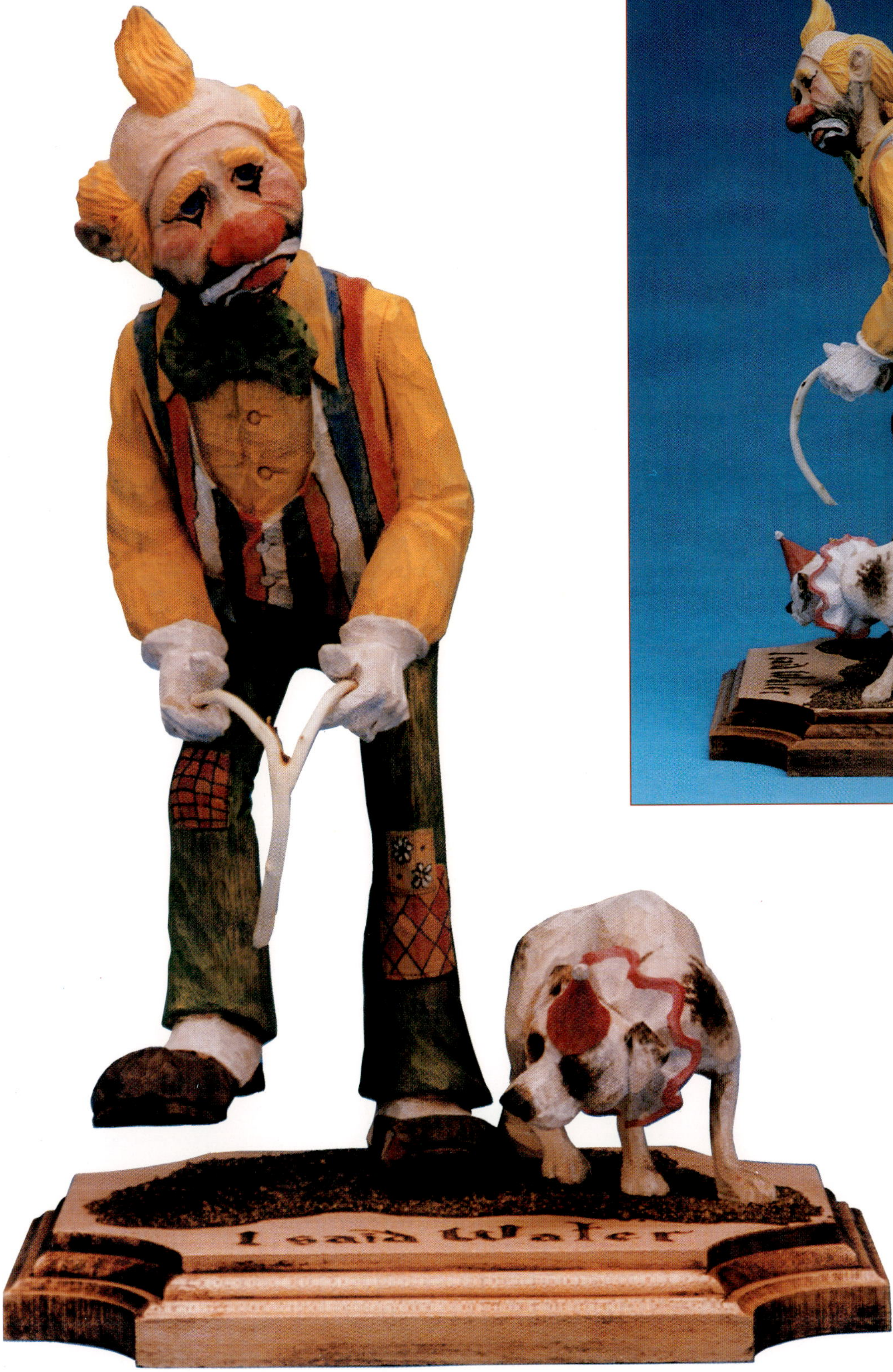
I said Water

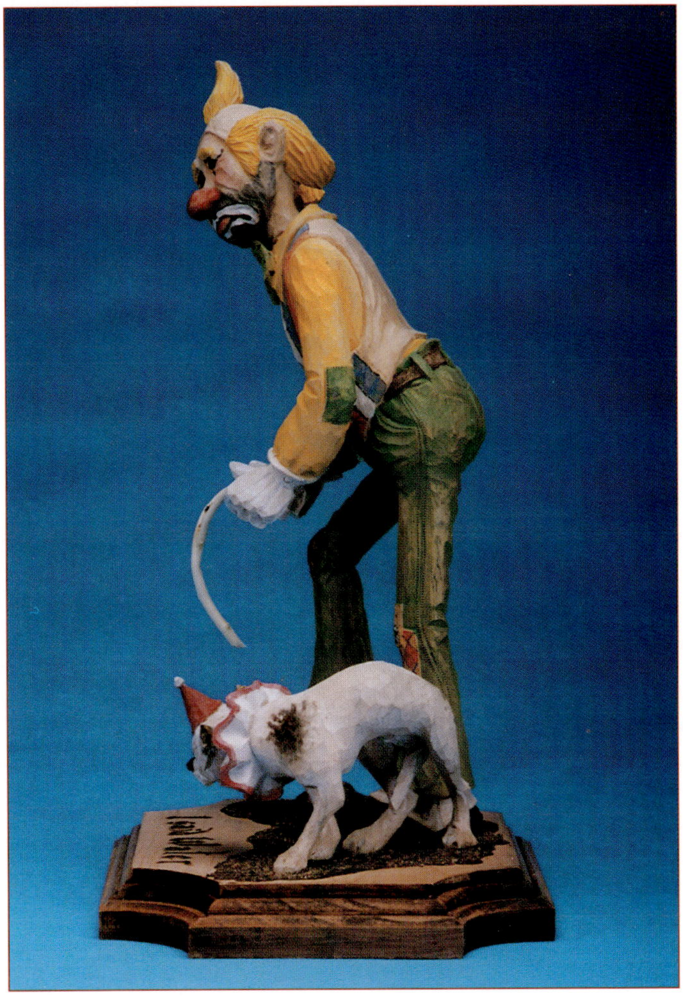

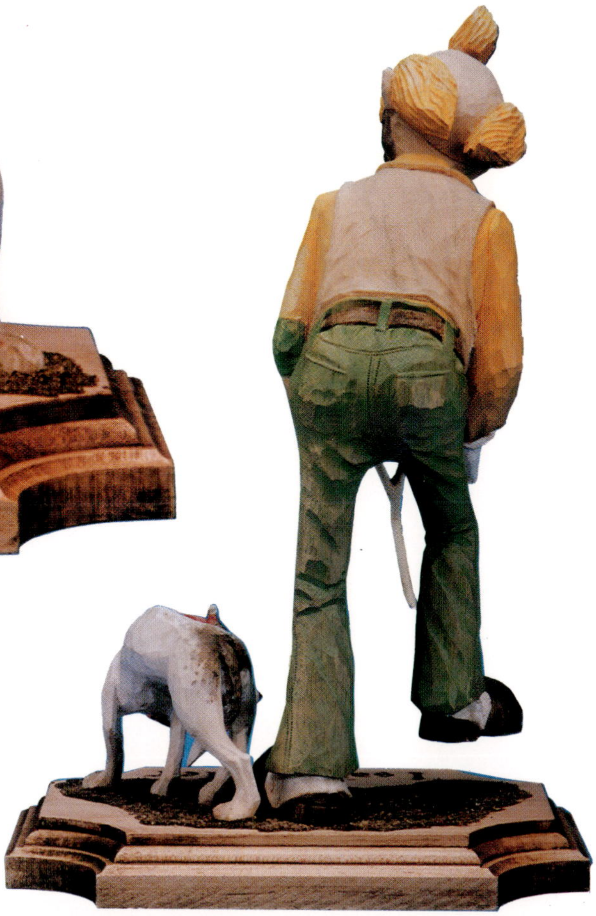

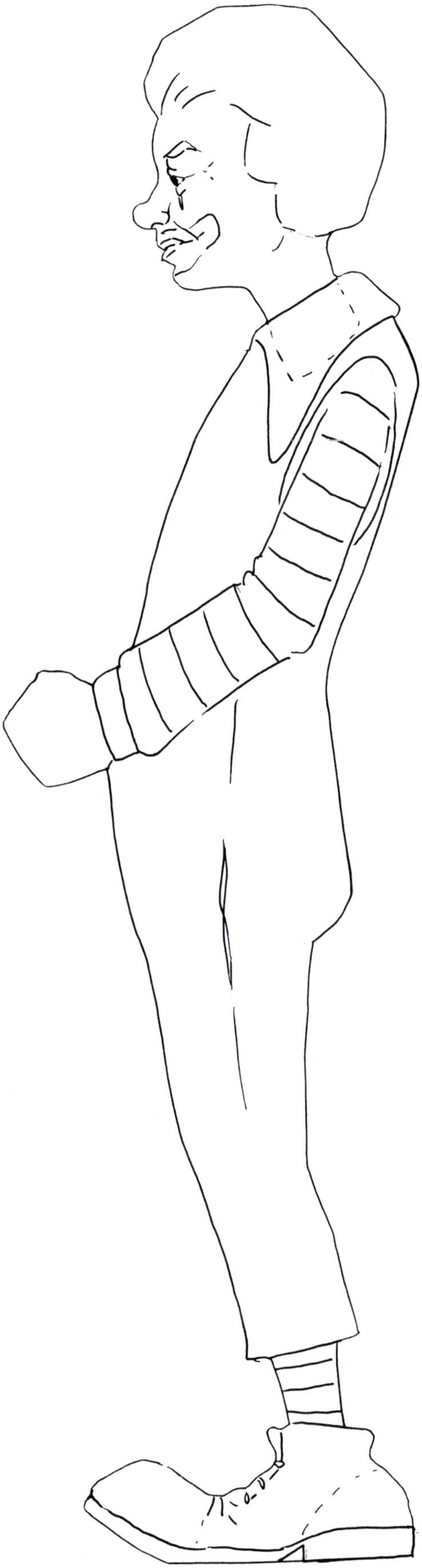

PATTERN IS 70% OF ORIGINAL SIZE.

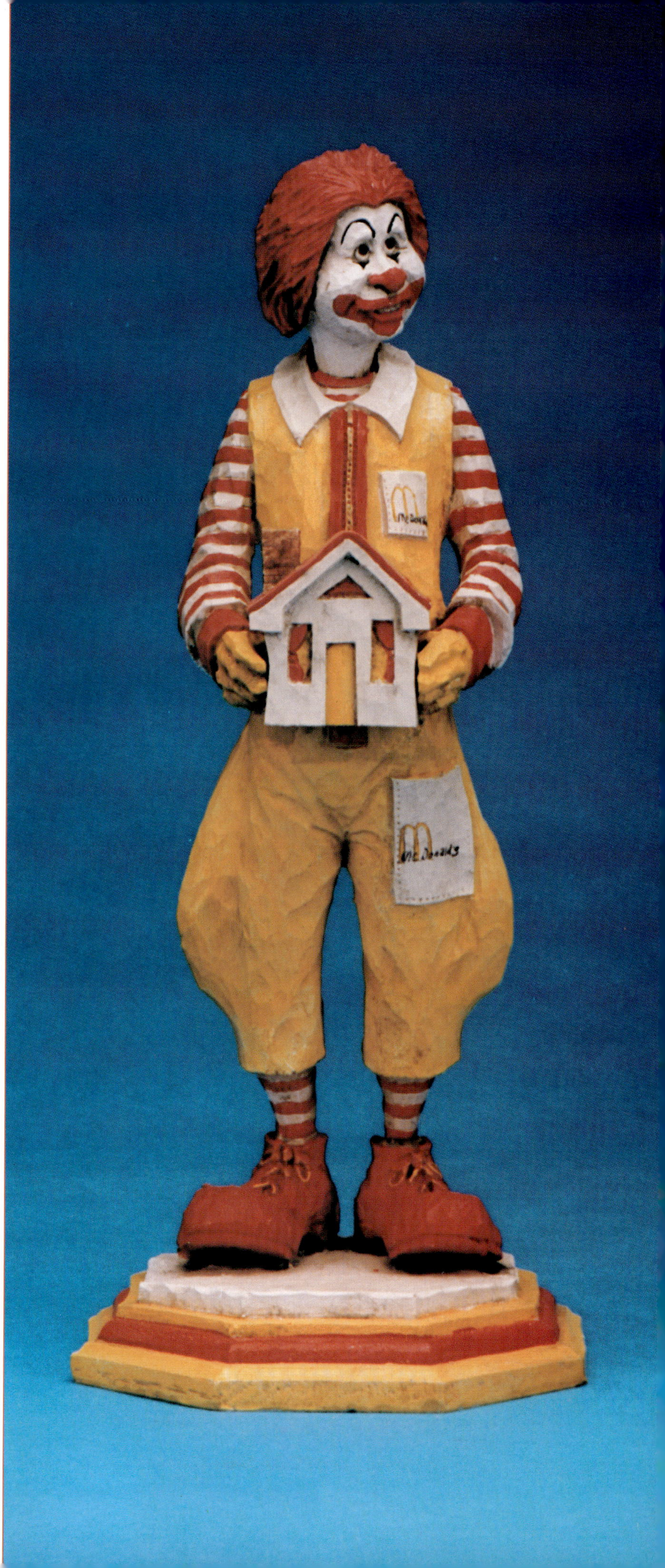

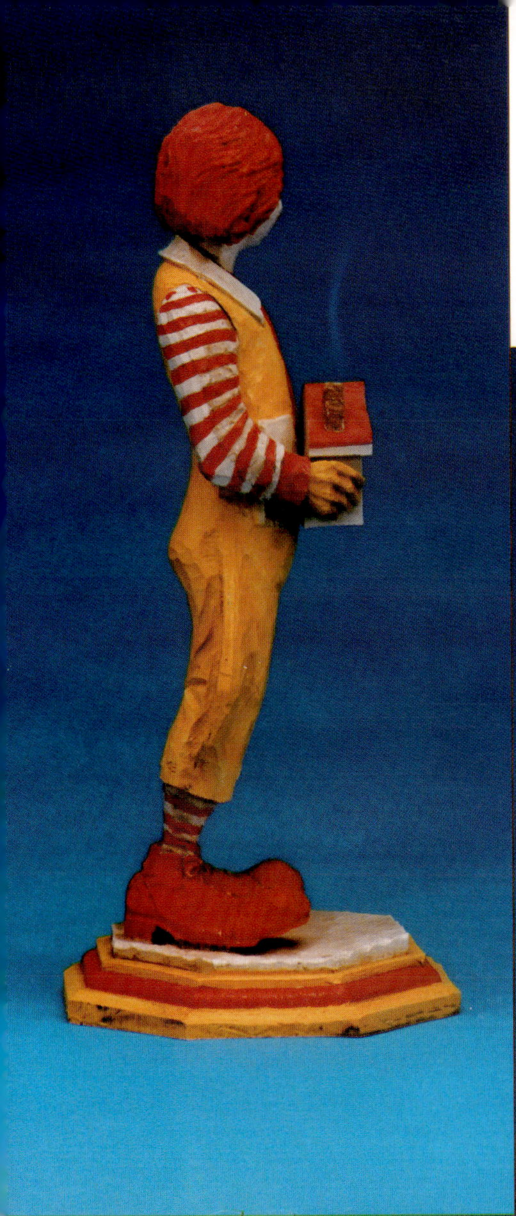

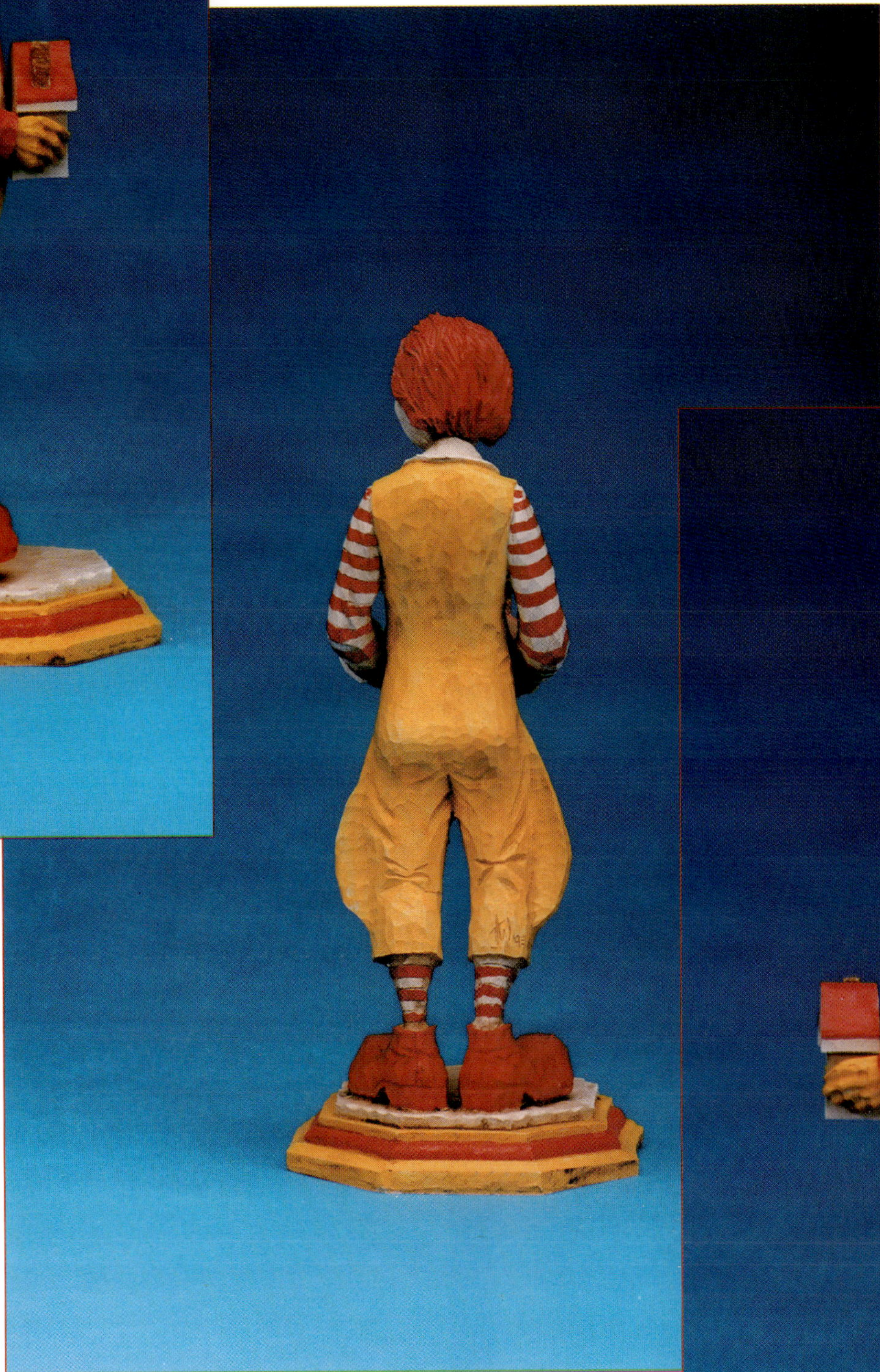

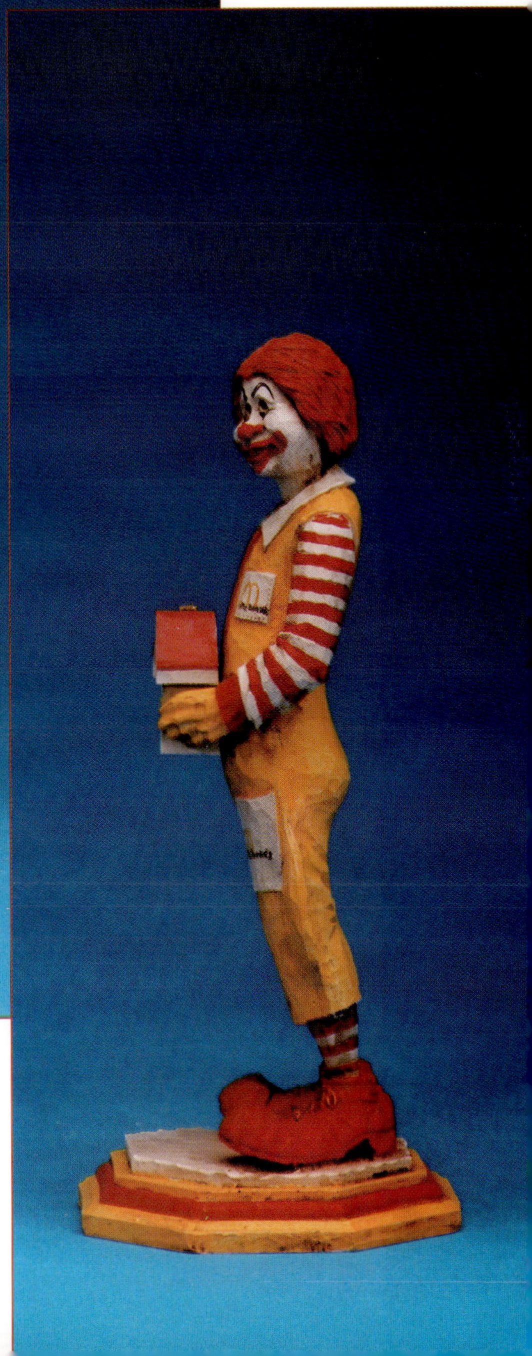

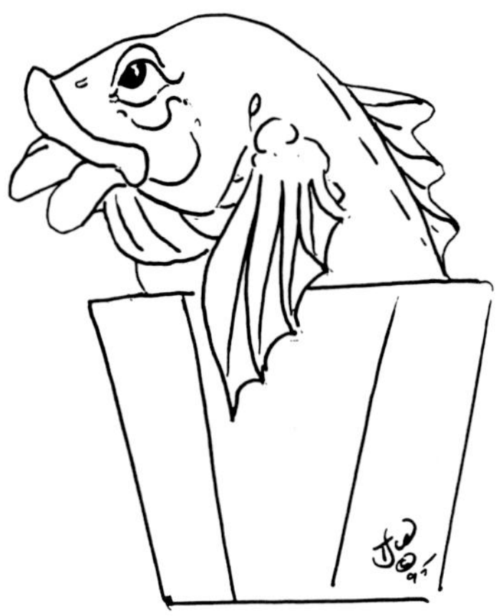

BIG FISH
CAN'T JUMP

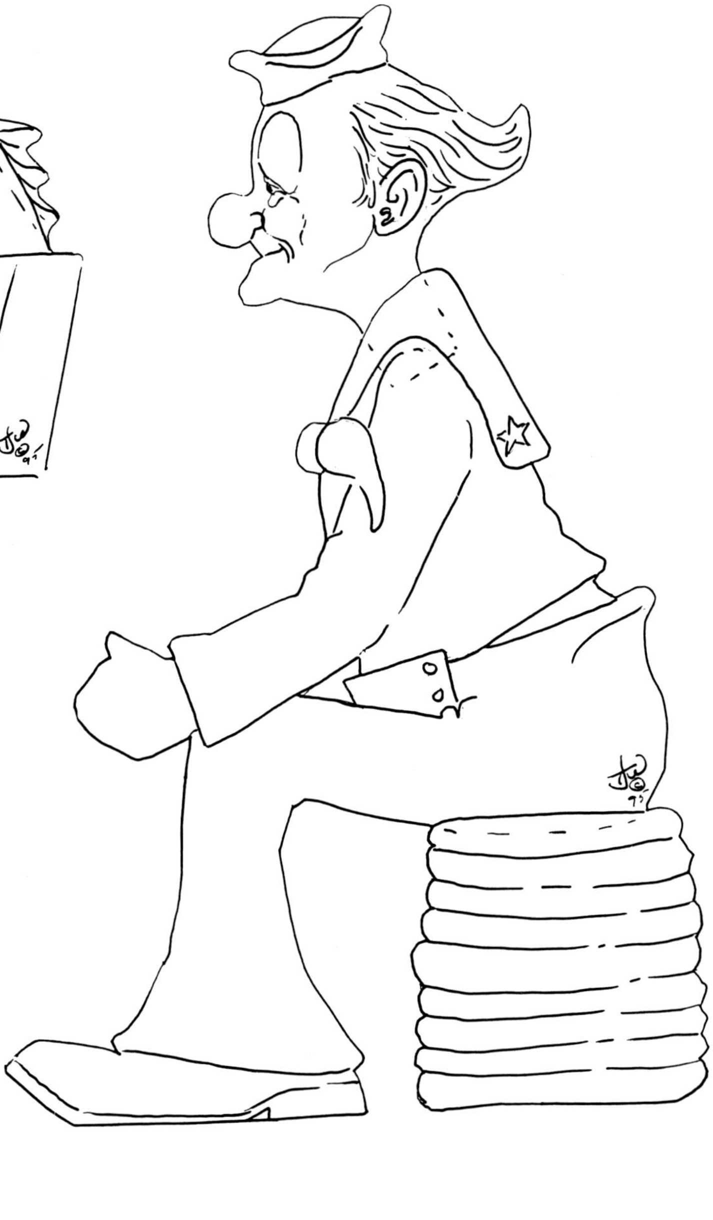

THESE PATTERNS ARE 70% OF ORIGINAL SIZE.

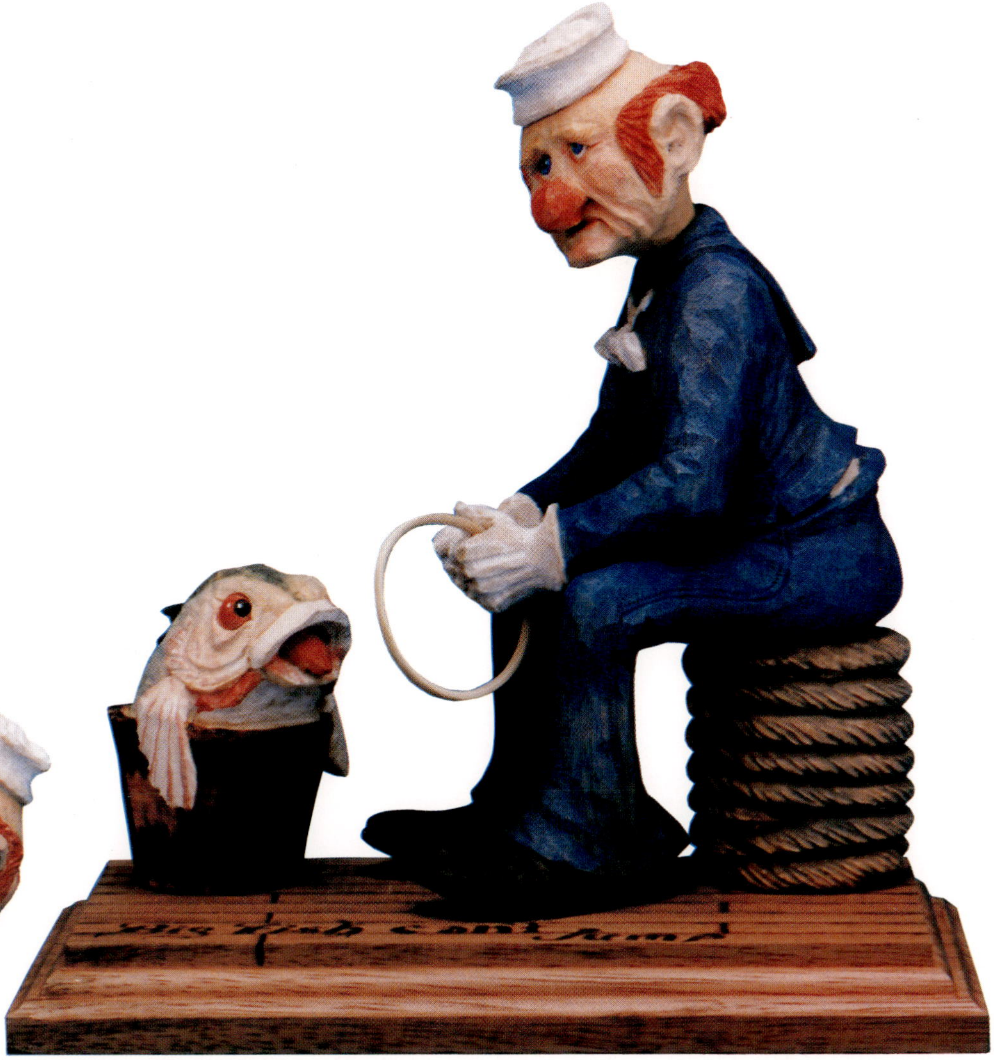

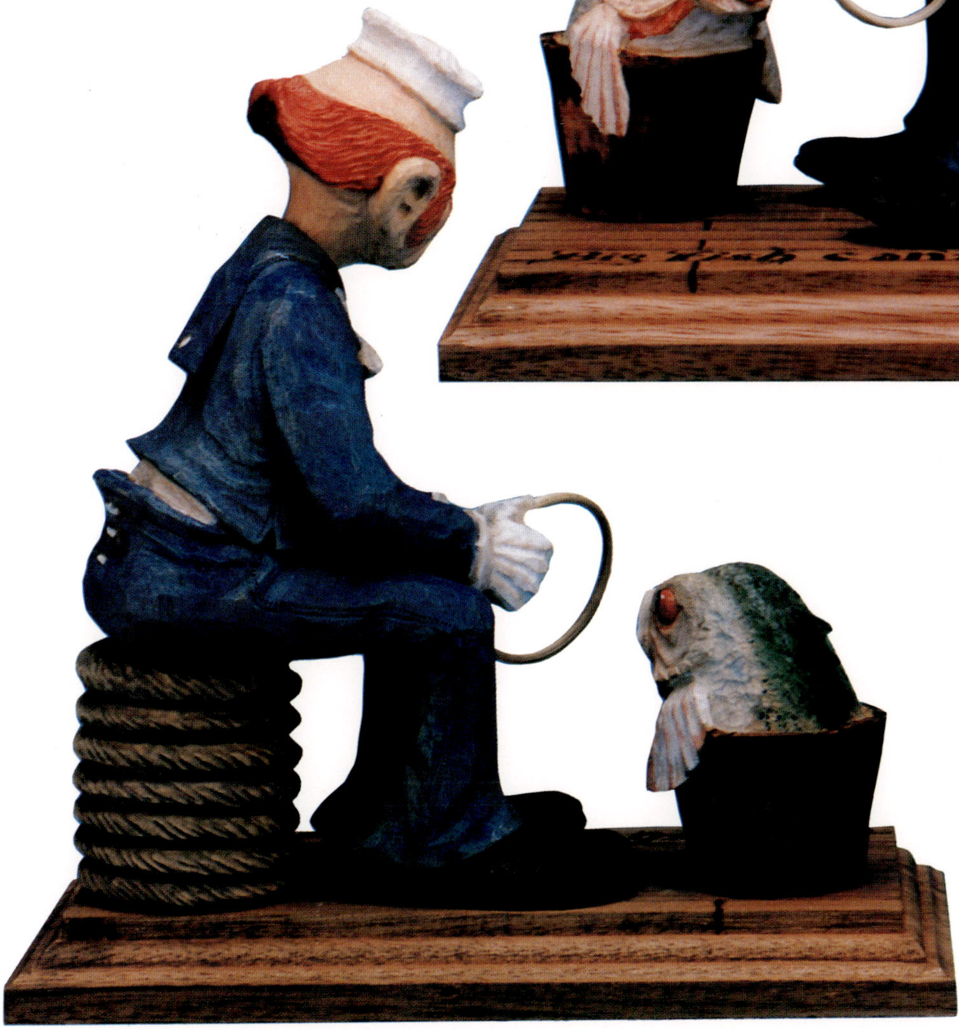

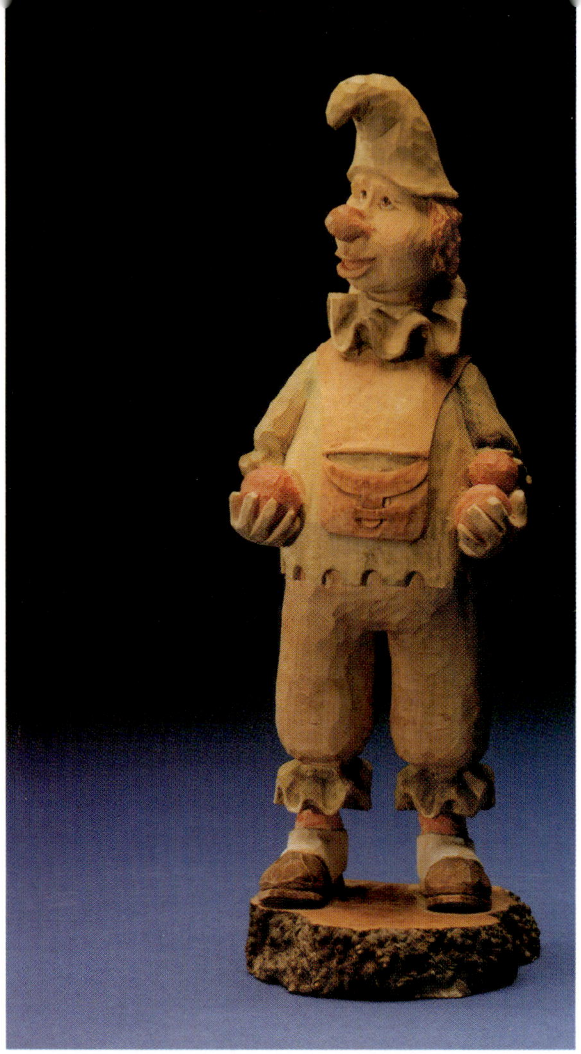
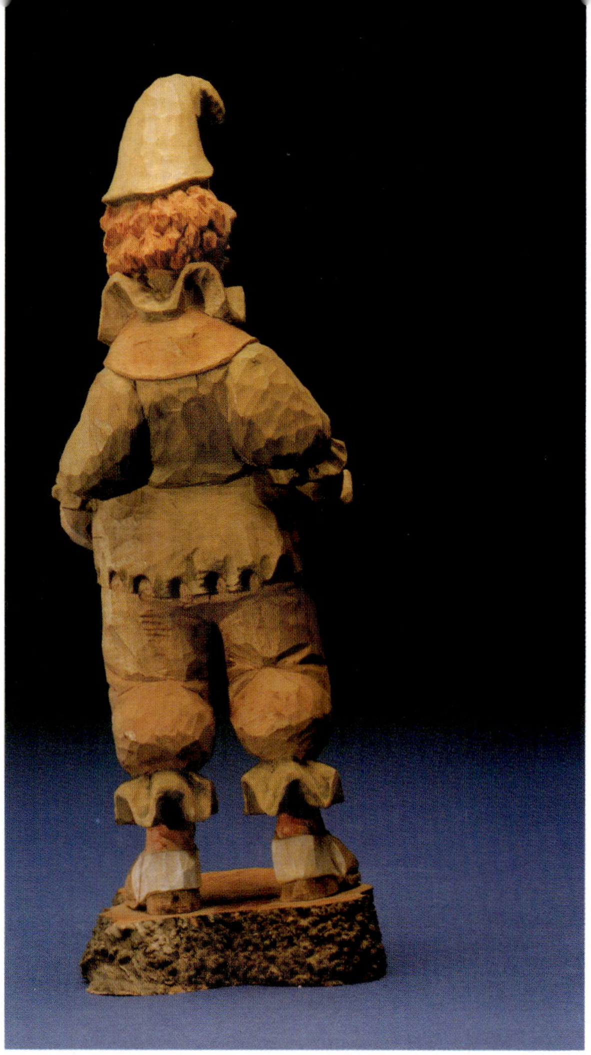
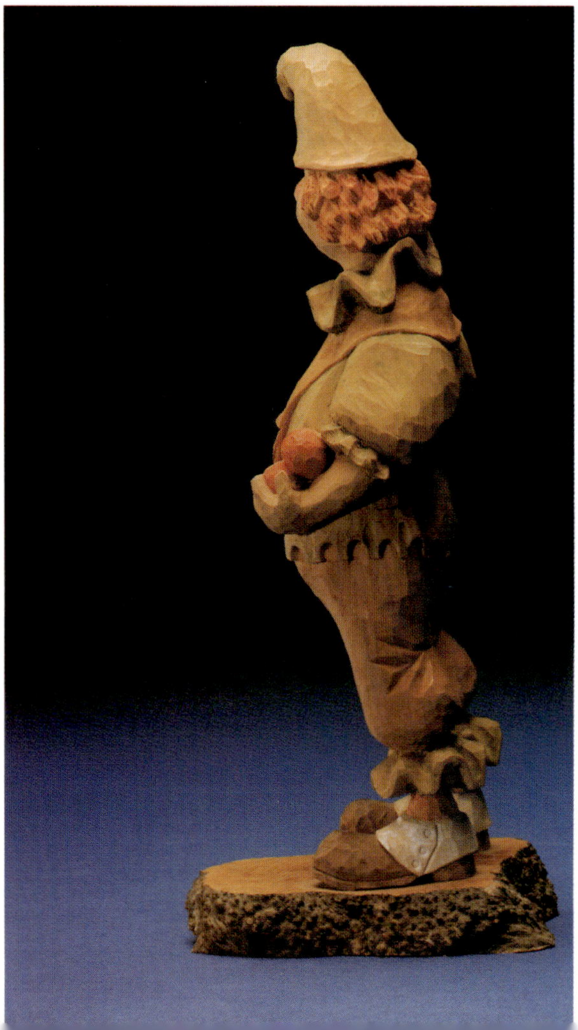
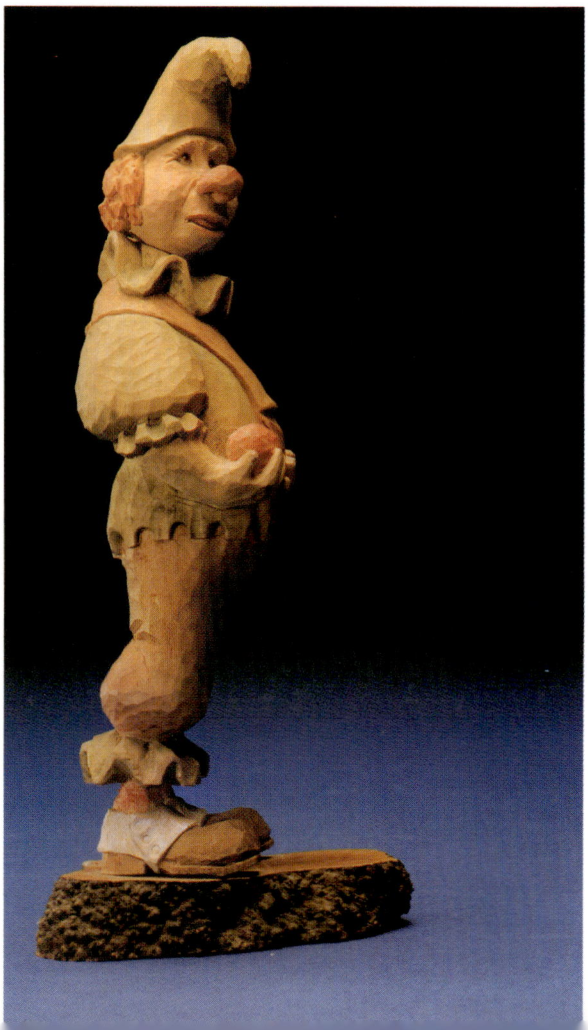

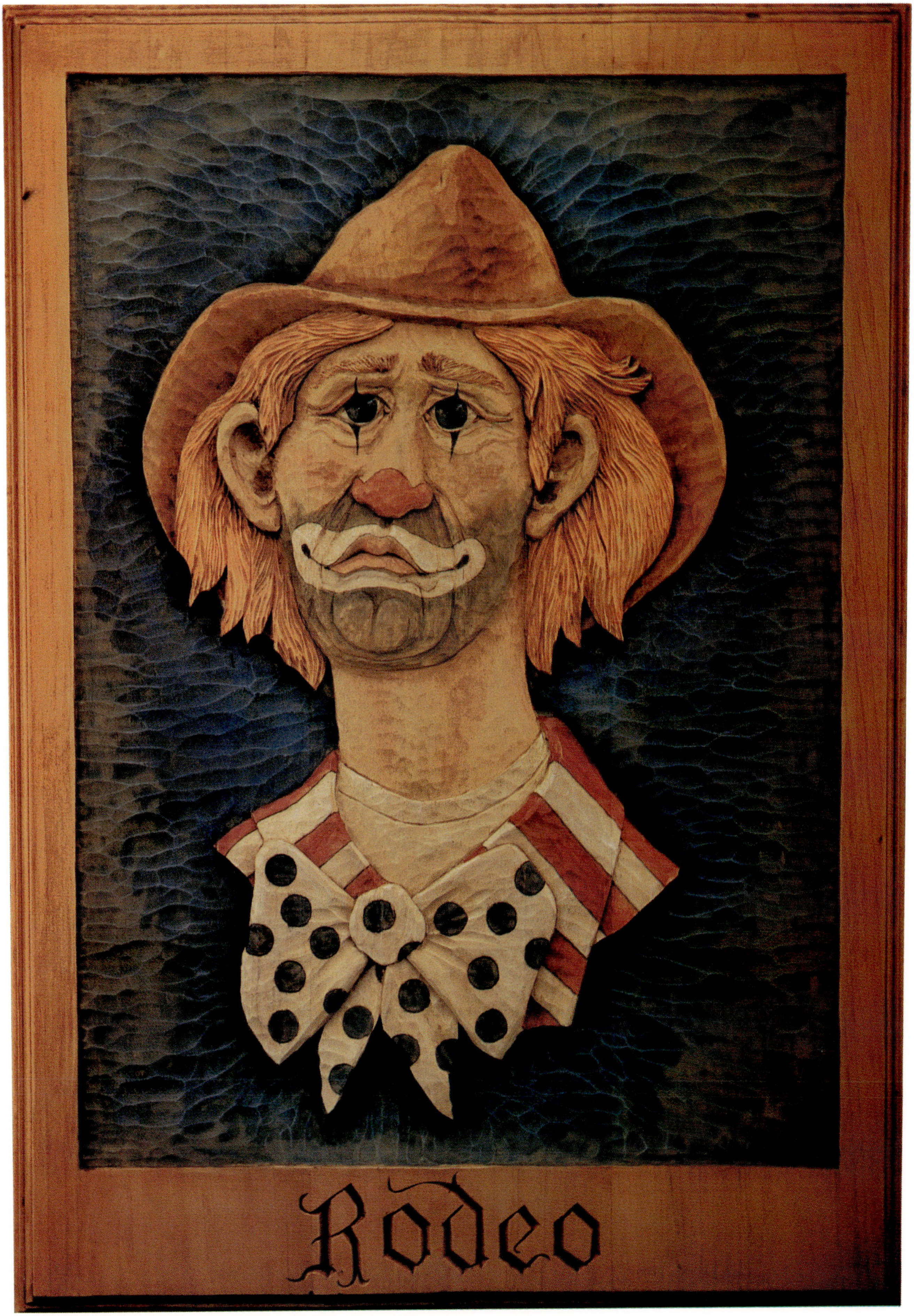
Rodeo

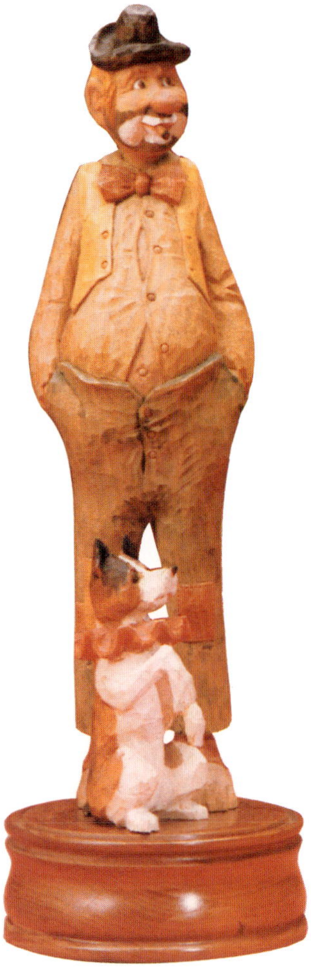

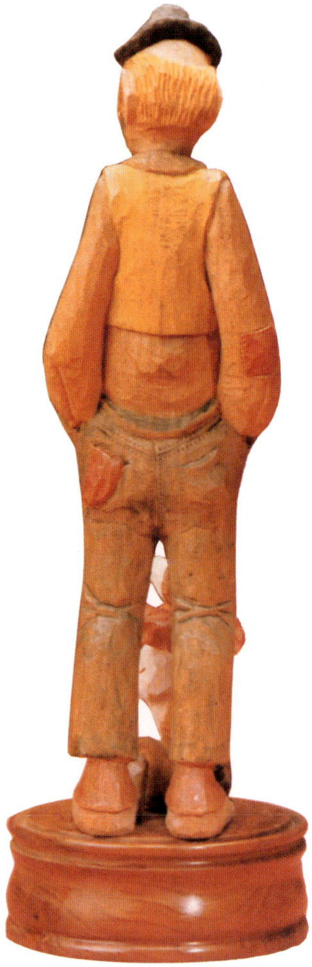

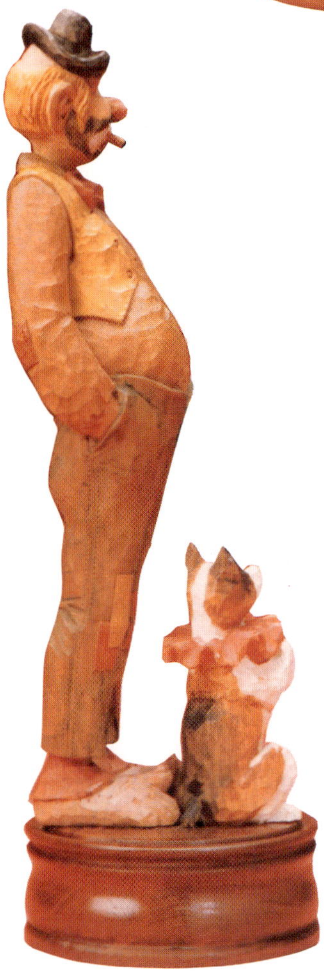

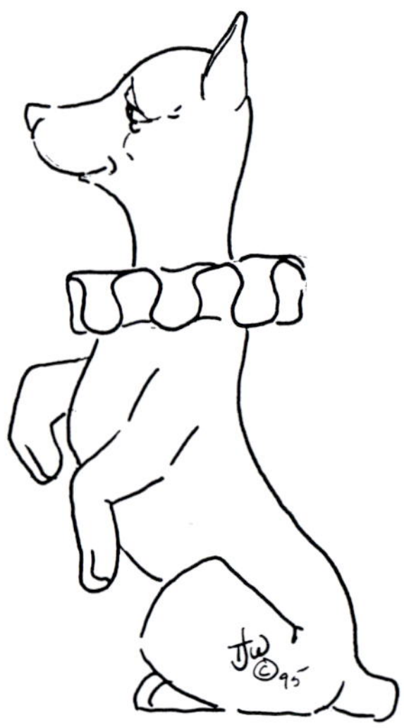

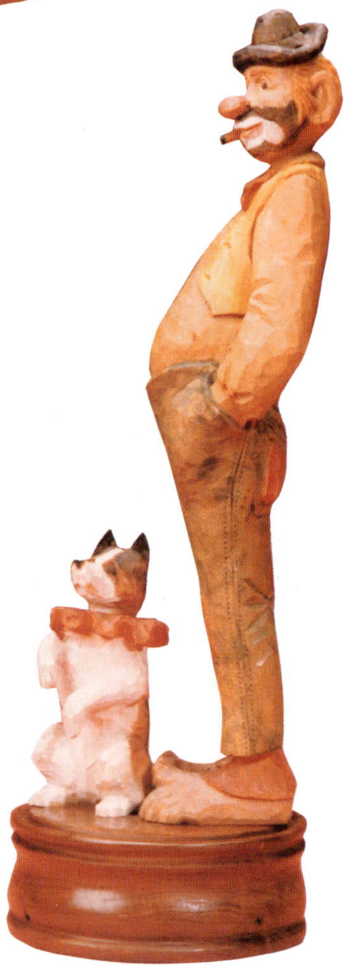

PATTERN IS 70% OF ORIGINAL SIZE.